WHAT IS A JEW?

NEW AND COMPLETELY REVISED EDITION

Rabbi Morris N. Kertzer

REVISED BY

Rabbi Lawrence A. Hoffman

A TOUCHSTONE BOOK
Published by Simon & Schuster

TOUCHSTONE
Rockefeller Center
1230 Avenue of the Americas
New York, NY 10020

First Touchstone Edition 1996

TOUCHSTONE and colophon are registered
trademarks of Simon & Schuster Inc.

A portion of this book is published by arrangement with Harry N.
Abrams, Inc. (successor to The World Publishing Company).

Manufactured in the United States of America

23 25 27 29 30 28 26 24 22

Book design by Cathryn S. Aison

Library of Congress Cataloging-in Publication Data
Kertzer, Morris Norman, 1910–1983
What is a Jew? / Morris N. Kertzer; revised by Lawrence A.
Hoffman.—New and completely rev. ed.
p.   cm.
Includes index.
ISBN-13: 978-0-684-84298-1
ISBN-10:   0-684-84298-X
1. Judaism.   2. Judaism—Customs and Practices.   I. Hoffman,
Lawrence A., 1942–   II. Title.
BM561.K45   1993   92–35518   CIP
296—dc20

CONTENTS

v

Introduction to the New Edition

Rabbi Morris N. Kertzer wrote his now classic *What Is a Jew?* for an audience who knew little or nothing about Judaism. Since its first appearance in 1953, the continued popularity of this work has necessitated thirty-eight printings and three revisions, most recently in 1978, six years before Kertzer died. It is still the most widely read introduction to Judaism—and for good reason.

Morris Kertzer was a genius: multitalented, gifted in a thousand ways, and above all, single-mindedly committed to the victory of the human spirit. He commanded several languages, loved sports, lectured everywhere, traveled the world, authored books, played the piano, and never tired of ideas, people, and events. People were attracted to this handsome, outgoing man with a smile on his face and a passion for God's truth and justice in his heart.

He was a global personality. As a World War II chaplain, he served on the Anzio Beachhead and received a Bronze Star. For his work in pioneering Jewish-Christian dialogue, the University of Rome awarded him its prestigious Pro Deo citation. In 1956, he was the first rabbi from the West to be admitted behind the Iron Curtain; it was his articles in *The New York Times* that exposed Soviet anti-Semitism in all its ugliness. When jet travel was still relatively rare, his adventurous spirit took him as far away as Japan, India, Turkey, Brazil, Thailand, and especially Israel, which he visited more than thirty times, both before and after it became an independent state.

He was above all a rabbi who loved his faith and his people in equal measure and who committed his life to bettering the lot of every human being he met, as well as the hungry and tortured masses of humanity around the world whom he did not.

I knew him well. He was my uncle. Were he alive today, he would be revising his work one more time. Since he is not, it is a labor of love for me to do it for him.

I have tried to follow Rabbi Kertzer's wonderfully engaging style. That means that this book continues to be written in the first person, regularly citing stories and anecdotes that "I" have experienced. But who is the "I" of the stories, the original author, Morris N. Kertzer, or the reviser, Lawrence A. Hoffman? Truth be told, it is sometimes one and sometimes the other. Larry Hoffman became a rabbi largely because Morris Kertzer showed him what a rabbi could be. This book is essentially Kertzer's, so most of the stories are his; but every once in a while, I (Hoffman speaking, now) slipped in an anecdote of my own. It would have been unwieldy to identify which of us wrote what on every page, and in any event, I have every belief that my uncle would smile happily at everything I added. He was most insistent on seeing Judaism as an evolving reality. This revision simply records its evolution between the 1950s, when the book was first written, and the 1990s, when its annual popularity warranted a newly revised edition.

Rabbi Kertzer introduced *What Is a Jew?* with the following anecdote:

A number of years ago, I invited a Japanese army officer, who was studying in the United States, to attend a religious service which I was conducting. At the end of the service, as we were walking home, he asked me, "What branch of Christianity does your church represent?"

"We are Jews," I answered, "members of the Jewish faith."

My Japanese friend was puzzled. He was a Shintoist, but he had read the Christian Bible. "But what are 'Jews'?"

"Do you remember the Israelites in the Bible—Abraham and Moses and Joshua?"

He recalled those stories.

"Well, we are those Israelites."

Major Nishi gasped in amazement. "What! Are those people still around?"

Now in 1992, it is hard to imagine a Major Nishi or anyone else being so surprised that Jews are "still around." The majority of men and women know that Jews still populate the globe. Tragically, it was the Holocaust, a historic aberration that threatened to eradicate all Jews, that demonstrated our continued existence. Another event still (a miracle, Jews might say), the birth of an independent Jewish State of Israel, continues to remind the world how "around" we are.

But we are less "around" than you might think. As of 1990, there were about 13 million Jews in the world. Jews are therefore only 0.025 percent of our planet's total population; that is, for every two thousand people, there are five Jews. About half of the world's Jews live in North America, so that in the United States, two out of every hundred people are Jewish—not a lot. In Canada, it is half of that: only one in every hundred. Nonetheless, news stories about Jews appear with remarkable regularity. Events in the State of Israel are followed with care. Jews leaving the Soviet Union or being airlifted out of Ethiopia make front-page stories. Most large American cities have Jewish newspapers and a network of Jewish institutions, including synagogues, community centers, and old-age homes. Every ten years or so, a survey predicts the demise of American Jews, not through persecution, but through assimilation. So far, however, we have proved the pundits wrong. The modern-day descendants of Sarah and Abraham plan on being here for a while.

We believe that long ago, standing at Mount Sinai, we promised God we would do just that. In ways both planned and unplanned, we have been doing God's work for close to four thousand years! Why stop now?

So people know we are here, here to stay. What they do not know is why Jews are still here, what we believe and do, the reason we seem sometimes so stubbornly bent on retaining our Jewish identity, and the answers to a host of other questions raised by the media or suggested by the behavior or attitudes of Jews they meet. Why do Jews care so passionately for Israel, or continually vote against their own economic self-interest in order to further the betterment of America's poor? People may wonder also about Jewish spirituality—Jews are less likely than Christians to attend public worship, or to talk about God. Then too, Jews are more likely than most Christians to go to college, support charities, and take liberal positions on issues of social conscience. Why?

Even Jews themselves have trouble keeping up with modern answers to questions like these. Old answers learned as a child pale after a while. New questions prompted just by being an adult require consideration.

Everyone—Jews and non-Jews alike—finds modern life, with its moral challenges and personal uncertainties, at times confusing, at times overwhelming. Judaism has something to say to people whose lives are so full that they want only to be responsible in their happiness, and to people whose lives are so empty that they cannot figure out how to put together the shattered fragments of their childhood dreams, or even how to go on in the face of broken marriages, addicted children, terrible illnesses, a decaying environment, crime on the streets, and the empty loneliness or grim despair that have become hallmarks of our time.

This book is an accurate photograph of Jews and Judaism as we prepare to say farewell to the twentieth century—almost fifty years after the Holocaust, nearly that long since the birth of a Jewish state, and in an age in which Jews (at least in most Western countries) have freedom and opportunities undreamed of by their immigrant ancestors. It does not shrink from the hard questions: why rabbis may not agree to perform interreligious marriages, for instance; or why Jews worry so much about the State of Israel, and what American Jews do when they sometimes disagree with the Israeli government's policies; or why, as I said before, fewer Jews than Christians attend weekly worship services, yet they may nonetheless be equally religious.

But at the same time, the book is a photograph by a photographer who is in love with the subject. As Rabbi Kertzer said in the original introduction, its portrayal of the Jewish way of looking at things conveys some of the warmth, the glow, and the serenity of Judaism; the enchantment of fine books; the mirthful spirit of scholars more than sixteen centuries ago; the abiding sense of compassion that permeates our tradition. I would add to his list the captivating color of the multifaceted Jewish experience drawn from centuries of life in countries around the globe, and the keen insights available in a tradition that includes Italian mystics, German philosophers, Polish legalists, and Spanish poets (to name but a few) whose wisdom is alive and well in a tradition that values the study of the past in the hope of a future.

This revised edition includes transliterations of key Hebrew and Yiddish words that Jews are apt to use these days. When *What Is a Jew?* was first written, Jews were busy translating their culture so that non-Jews could understand it. They would call their holidays "Booths," or "the Sabbath," for example. Nowadays, Jews prefer the original terms for such things: not "Booths," but **Sukkot** [soo-KOTE]; **Shabbat** [shah-BAHT], not "the Sabbath." A glossary (with a pronunciation guide) lists all such words, providing a practical lexicon of Jewish life. I provide a pronunciation key whenever a new term is introduced, or even (on occasion) when I think it has been a particularly long time since the term was encountered (there is nothing more frustrating for readers than to see a technical term and not even to be able to pronounce it silently as they read down the page). The capitalized syllable is always the accented one. I accent the word exactly as most Jews say it, not always the way grammarians would prefer, and where there are two accepted versions, I give you both. The most important things to remember are that 1) Hebrew words are usually accented on their last syllable, and 2) the most usual vowel is a long "a" as in "father"—which I render "ah."

About 50 percent of this book is still the original, but an equal amount has been reformulated with contemporary readers' needs in mind. The organization of the book has been revised as well. You can still pick up *What Is a Jew?* to find the answer to a particular question that disturbs you; but you can also read through the book, chapter by chapter, to find out what Jews believe, or what our sacred calendar is like, or what Jewish ethics consist of, or to find out about any other somewhat larger topic covered by not just one but many questions.

In the original version, Kertzer thanked several people for their help. The list grows, as a second generation has passed on its own advice, for which I (Hoffman) am profoundly grateful: Sherri Alper, Arlene Chernow, Mary Crigler, Nancy Gad-Harf, Ellyn Geller, Stuart Geller, Bruce Gionet, Dru Greenwood, Kathy Kahn, David Kertzer, Julia Kertzer, James Kessler, Lydia Kukoff, Baila Shargel, Nachum Shargel, Debby Stein, David Teutsch, and Bill Waller—and finally, Natalie Chapman, Nancy Cooperman, and Philip Turner at Macmillan, who insisted all along that in the 1990s no less than the 1950s *What Is a Jew?* could be a superior gateway to the soul of the Jew and the world that is Judaism, and whose professional care helped make it so.

Lawrence A. Hoffman, 1993

INTRODUCTION TO THE FIRST EDITION

A number of years ago, I invited a Japanese army officer, who was studying in the United States, to attend a religious service which I was conducting. At the end of the service, as we were walking home, he asked me, "What branch of Christianity does your church represent?"

"We are Jews," I answered, "members of the Jewish faith."

My Japanese friend was puzzled. He was a Shintoist, but he had read the Christian Bible. "But what are 'Jews'?"

"Do you remember the Israelites in the Bible—Abraham and Moses and Joshua?"

He recalled those stories.

"Well, we are those Israelites."

Major Nishi gasped in amazement. "What! Are those people still around?"

The majority of men and women in the English-speaking world are aware that the descendants of Moses are "still around." But there is, nevertheless, an amazing lack of knowledge about the Jews, their religion, and their philosophy.

On the other hand, my experience has taught me that there is an ever-growing interest and a curiosity in these matters; so, though the beliefs and practices of Judaism are to many a closed book, it is a book that they are willing, even eager, to open.

Judaism is one of the oldest religions known to man, with a tradition that reaches back to the dawn of recorded history. It is a faith that has contributed richly to civilization and has grown and developed and kept pace with the changing spiritual needs of more than a hundred generations. It has a genealogy, a ritual, and a wealth of lore and custom richer, perhaps, than any other religion on earth. It has survived in the face of relentless persecutions, despite the fact that its adherents are vastly outnumbered and are scattered over the face of the entire globe.

For all these reasons, as well as for the special impetus lent by recent history, people are curious about the Jewish faith. This interest is shown, not only by non-Jews who want to know about the creed from which the concept of one God originated and out of which Christianity and Mohammedanism were born, but also by many Jews who, despite their ancestry, are personally far removed from the traditions and rituals of their fathers.

There are, of course, many learned volumes dealing with Jewish history, law, custom and belief. But most of these are, because of their very depth of scholarship, somewhat forbidding. The average man and woman has curiosity, but, usually, neither the time nor the inclination to delve into lengthy treatises. They turn, therefore, to the mass media: newspapers, magazines, radio, television, motion pictures. Both authors and readers realize that the answers found there only skim the surface of all there is to know about Judaism. But they help, nevertheless, to erase some of the misconceptions and to substitute some of the understanding so vital to human survival.

The questions included in this book are, of course, by no means exhaustive. No attempt is made to set down a manual of Jewish law or a system of religious practice. It is not meant to be a definitive formulation of what all Jews subscribe to, or what they should believe. I asked a number of friends, Christian and Jewish, to list for me those questions about Judaism which they most frequently encountered. I compared these with a list I drew out of my own experience with students in my college classroom. In addition, numerous queries came to me in the wake of an article appearing in *Reader's Digest* under the same title as this book. The hundred-odd questions in these pages appeared on all those lists.

I have answered these questions with a minimum of theorizing and a stress on direct, factual information. I did so for two reasons: first, because it would take many thousand words for each question, rather than several hundred, to expound with justice on the deep underlying philosophy of the Jewish faith; and second, because I am convinced that there is a genuine need for this kind of brief introduction to Judaism among many who would not, at this point, read any more comprehensive dissertation.

It is my hope, of course, that some of my questions will whet the interest for those who read them—that my brief quotations from the *Talmud* will entice readers to look for more of the same; that my few examples of biblical wisdom will remind them of the great storehouse of wisdom to be found in the Old Testament, and that my occasional quips of traditional Jewish humor will awaken a curiosity about the wealth of laughter that exists in Jewish lore. But, even if I fail to accomplish that much, I will still consider these labors worthwhile if I have made some Jewish readers feel closer to, and prouder of, their heritage, and some non-Jewish readers more understanding of Judaism as a way of life.

The questions are divided into nine parts. Actually, the division is quite arbitrary, for there is a great deal of overlapping and cross-referencing that help make most of the answers more meaningful. The part headings simply indicate the broad subjects which have seemed to arouse general interest: the basic beliefs of Judaism, the specific ritual requirements of an observant Jew—and their meanings, the traditions and customs, the relationships between Jew and non-Jews, the different Holy Days, and so on. Many of the questions might just as readily have been placed under several different headings, and the one selected represents no more than an arbitrary choice among them. It should also be pointed out that, though the answers are in terms of "what Jews do" and "what Jews believe," it is impossible to speak for *all* Jews on *any* subject. And, indeed, these very differences in custom, practice and belief are an integral part of the Jewish tradition.

I have deliberately refrained from weighing down the book with original Hebrew and Aramaic quotations. Since a very limited number of readers would understand them well enough to make their own translations, such references would only tend to obscure the thought and could have no real value. I agree, too, that something is usually lost in translation. Maurice Samuel crisply observed that a translation from the Yiddish is frequently not so much a rendition as it is a pogrom. To avoid that difficulty, I have usually preferred to paraphrase rather than to translate literally. In general, this portrayal of the Jewish way of looking at things attempts to convey some of the warmth, the glow, and the serenity of Judaism: the enchantment of fine books; the captivating color of Chasidism; the keen insights of the Babylonian rabbis into human relations; the sane, level-headed wisdom of the medieval philosophers; the mirthful spirit of scholars more than sixteen centuries ago; and the abiding sense of compassion that permeates our tradition. It is in this way— and only in this way—that anyone can give a meaningful answer to the question: "What is a Jew?"

I wish to record my thanks to several colleagues whom I consulted during the course of writing this book, particularly Rabbis Bernard J. Bamberger, Mordecai Waxman, Emanuel Rackman, and Amram Prero. I am especially indebted to Dr. Moses Jung for many of his helpful suggestions. (The reader will understand that these scholars assume no responsibility for the material which the book contains.)

My grateful appreciation is extended to members of the staff of the American Jewish Committee Library of Information, headed by Mr. Harry J. Alderman; to Miss Naomi A. Grand, Mrs. Madeline C. Marina, Mr. Ralph Bass, and Mr. Herman Horowitz for their valuable assistance.

To Mrs. Sonya Kaufer, whose editorial aid and guidance helped me to make this volume possible, I offer my heartfelt gratitude.

My special thanks go to Leo Rosten, who, in a real sense, provided the original inspiration for this book, particularly in the form and method of presentation.

Morris N. Kertzer, 1953

THE SAGA OF THE JEW

This book focuses attention on Judaism through a single dimension—Jewish tradition as it is lived by Jews here and now. A second dimension is the past, the history of the Jewish people; and a third, a study of the literature that they have produced. For a thorough understanding of Judaism we really need all three. We need to know what happened to Jews through the centuries and to read the creative works of their writers. I will not presume to summarize the literature, though Part II describes the most important works, like Talmud and midrash. As background for what follows, however, I need to provide at least an outline of Jewish history.

The dates that follow are labelled either B.C.E. (not B.C.) or C.E. (instead of A.D.) The usual designations, B.C. and A.D., stand for "Before Christ," and *Anno Domini* (Latin for "The year of our Lord"). Since Jews do not believe that Jesus is the Christ, which is to say, "Our Lord," Jewish history books prefer "Before the Common Era" (B.C.E.) and "Common Era" (C.E.) to describe the same two eras of Western history.

Jewish history begins, as does all history, in misty origins. We know almost nothing for sure about the age of the patriarchs and matriarchs, Abraham and Sarah, Isaac and Rebekah, Jacob, Rachel, and Leah. Even the life of Moses and his sister and brother, Miriam and Aaron, are the subject of much controversy among historians.

2000 Years B.C.E.

Abraham and Sarah: The period of the matriarchs and patriarchs	Exodus from Egypt and settlement in Land of Israel under Moses and Joshua	King David begins First Jewish Commonwealth	Palestine divided into Northern Kingdom of Israel and Southern Kingdom of Judah	Age of the Prophets begins (see p. 122)	Northern Kingdom destroyed by Assyria	Southern Kingdom destroyed by Babylonia—end of First Jewish Commonwealth	Return from Babylonian exile. Beginning of Second Jewish Commonwealth	The Torah is edited (see pp. 42, 43)	Hasmonean (Maccabean) Revolt. Period of the Rabbis begins (see pp. 19–20)	Hillel (see p. 19)
2000 B.C.E.	c.1250 B.C.E.	c.975 B.C.E.	c.925 B.C.E.	800 B.C.E.	722 B.C.E.	586 B.C.E.	536 B.C.E.	c.400 B.C.E.	167 B.C.E.	1
A	B	C	D	E	F	G	H	I	J	K

A — B — C — D — E — F — G — H — I — J — K —

scale: 1 inch = 200 years

2000 Years C.E.

Hillel	Rome destroys Second Temple, End of Second Jewish Commonwealth	Promulgation of Mishnah (see p. 20)	Promulgation of the Talmud (see pp. 47–50)	Crusaders massacre German Jewry	Death of Rashi (see p. 56)	Church militant passes anti-Jewish laws	Jews expelled from England	The Zohar composed (see p. 57)	Jews expelled from France	Jews expelled from Spain	Shulchan Arukh first printed (see p.52)	First Jewish settlement in North America (New Amsterdam = New York)	Czarist persecution forces largest migration of Jews to America)	Dreyfus case; Theodor Herzl begins Zionism (see p. 26)	The Holocaust (Sho'ah) (see p. 159)	Birth of the State of Israel; the Third Jewish Commonwealth
1	70 C.E.	200	c.550	1096	1105	1215	1290	1295	1305	1492	1565	1654	1881	1894	1933–45	1948
K	L	M	N	O	P	Q	R	S	T	U	V	W	X	Y	Z	AA

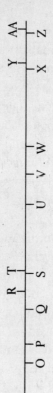

K L M N O P Q R S T U V W X Y Z AA

Traditionalists accept every detail of the biblical narrative as fact. Modernists are inclined to accept only its broad outlines as literal truth. The Exodus from Egypt and the settlement of the Hebrews in Canaan (later called Palestine, after the Philistines who lived there) took place sometime between 1300 B.C.E. and 1200 B.C.E., perhaps around a coalition of what the Bible identifies as twelve tribes. A kingdom—usually called the First Commonwealth, or the period of the First Temple—was established under David and Solomon about ten centuries before the Common Era. After Solomon's death, Palestine was divided into two separate states: Israel, in the north, and Judah in the south. Judah's capital was Jerusalem.

In 722 B.C.E., Israel (the Northern Kingdom) was destroyed by Assyria, the imperial power that controlled Mesopotamia (modern-day Iraq). The only Hebrews left now were Judeans. The word "Jew" is simply an abbreviation of Judean. From then on the people once known as the Hebrews would be called Jews.

Judah continued as a small nation leading a precarious existence in the shadow of mighty empires until 586 B.C.E., when it was laid waste by the conquering armies of the Babylonians, who had replaced the Assyrian empire in the east. Judah's capital, Jerusalem, was destroyed; its central religious institution, a temple where priests had offered daily sacrifices, was demolished; its leaders were driven into exile in Babylonia.

These critical centuries, full of bloodshed and chaos, produced the greatest spirits of ancient Israel: prophets, like Isaiah, Jeremiah, Amos, Hosea, and Micah, who railed against a society of injustice, idolatry, and war.

The Second Jewish Commonwealth was reestablished in 536 B.C.E., when Persia conquered Babylonia and allowed the exiles to return home. Not many did, but eventually, under one of them, Ezra (a priest), Jerusalem and its temple were rebuilt. The first five books of the Bible were edited then, and used as a sort of constitution for the new commonwealth. Those five books, which we call the Torah, serve still as the primary document that Jews read and study for guidance from our past.

The Second Commonwealth continued for six hundred years under many foreign powers, culminating in the Romans, who eventually ended it by destroying the Second Temple in the year 70 C.E., and even banning Jews from Jerusalem some sixty-five years later. In that whole period of time, Jews celebrated only a brief century of independence, when they were led by the Hasmonean dynasty (known popularly today as the Maccabees), native Jewish leaders who rebelled successfully against their overlords in 167 B.C.E. To this day, we keep a festival called Chanukah, which celebrates their victory.

By the year 200 C.E., many Palestinian Jews had been dispersed throughout the world, a few reaching faroff places in Central Asia, some settling in North Africa, and others founding homes in Italy and Spain. It was in Babylonia, that part of the world where the first Hebrews, Abraham and Sarah, had been born, that the most influential community was established, lasting well over a thousand years. Babylonian Jews gave us a huge literary heritage, including 1) a multivolume work of law and lore called the Talmud, on which all Jewish life has been based ever since; 2) the first known prayer book, from which all further prayer books, including our own, have been derived; and 3) the first responsa, public letters in which esteemed rabbis write answers to important questions of their day, and the means by which Jews even now address current concerns, from the morality of abortion to the ethics of investing in junk bonds.

Jews had reached Europe as early as the days of Julius Caesar, but only scattered settlements existed until the tenth century. Then Spain became a center of Jewish life. Under Moslem rule, in an era later called "The Golden Age," Judaism produced more philosophy, poetry, science, and religious literature than in any other period in its history. Simultaneously, Jews in northern Europe established communities where a wealth of biblical commentary and legal development took place.

But the late Middle Ages introduced hard times for Jews. Crusaders massacred German Jewry in 1096; the Church militant passed anti-Jewish regulations in 1215; Jews were expelled altogether from England and from France; and 1492 brought expulsion from Spain as well, after more than a century of relentless and devastating persecution.

Communities of some consequence grew up in Turkey, Holland, Germany, and medieval Palestine (Jews had never ceased living there), but it was in eastern Europe that the concentration was most marked—more than one and a quarter million men, women, and children at the dawn of the nineteenth century! Despite the hostility of czarist regimes, a flourishing community came into being, creating incomparable institutions of learning and (once again) countless tomes of Jewish scholarship.

By the end of the nineteenth century, the Russian-Polish community contained most of the Jews of the world. Germany had a vigorous group, but it was relatively small. And the United States, which saw its first Jewish settlers in 1654, had barely a million Jews at the turn of the century (937,000 in 1897). Another one and a quarter million immigrated here, primarily before 1924, when strict immigration laws were adopted, largely to stem the tide of newcomers.

Then in the 1930s and 1940s came further persecution of eastern European Jews by Stalin, and (above all) the Nazi massacres, in which almost 40 percent of the Jewish population of the world lost their lives. The deep trauma of that period spurred the drive for the reestablishment of Israel as a Jewish state and as a haven for those who miraculously survived the Holocaust.

Today, in all of Europe, and excluding the eastern European countries that were once the Soviet Union, there remains, except for Great Britain and France, only a skeleton Jewish community: for example, only 19,000 Jews in Switzerland (or 0.2 percent of the Swiss population); 26,000 in Holland (0.1 percent); and 12,000 in Spain (only 0.03 percent). Even in Great Britain, there are only 322,000 (0.5 percent); and in France, 530,000 (0.9 percent). Nearly all European Jews who remained alive in 1945 have emigrated, either to Israel or to the Western Hemisphere, where today the number of Jewish residents equals nearly the total of Jews in other parts of the world, including Israel.

It is estimated that the entire world's Jewish population is somewhere in the region of 13 million, with 6 million in the United States and Canada, 3.5 million in Israel, and (until 1990) up to 3 million in Russia and eastern Europe. Of the large Jewish community that was once behind "the Iron Curtain," there may be a million or more who still remember what Judaism is, and who want to reclaim their Jewish heritage. Many of those are in the process now of taking advantage of their newly found opportunity to move to Israel.

American Jews tend to envision the Jewish world not as a circle with one center, but as an ellipse, in which two religious and cultural centers, North America and Israel, are in the process of building a new and vibrant Jewish life that will carry Jews optimistically into the next century. But a Jewish renaissance is evident elsewhere too, particularly in England, and in some countries of Latin America as well. Jews are even moving back to Germany, and small Jewish enclaves are being established in Russia and in the other countries that once were Soviet satellites. Who knows what the twenty-first century will bring?

Despite the Holocaust, Judaism is not a religion of suffering. Our recent memory of violent persecution should not cloud our vision of the norm for Jewish life: centuries of peaceful existence in one country or another, dedicated to the continuation of the Jewish tradition that this book describes. Our age-old Jewish way of life will remain intact, and will be handed down to our children just as faithfully as it was handed down to us—a cherished heritage of thousands of years.

I

A Road Map of Jewish Community,
Past and Present

It is hard to discuss Jews, Judaism, Jewish beliefs, Jewish spirituality, or Jewish anything, without first describing Jewish community. Not that Jews are a tightly knit group united on everything. Far from it. Community does not mean unanimity of opinion, or commonality of action.

But being a Jew does mean having a profound love and respect for the ideal of community. It means seeing yourself as a sacred link between past and future, a link that is shared with all other Jews of your generation, forming a sort of mystical continuity.

It also means believing, as Jews do, that however much we may disagree on things, we have a common destiny. Hitler did not ask what kind of Jews he killed. They were all the same to him. The State of Israel does not ask what kind of Jew you are, if you try to escape persecution by moving there; any Jew can claim immediate citizenship in the Jewish state. Moreover, we believe that we shall accomplish God's task not singly, but together with other Jews. We pray in a group of at least ten people (see p. 86)—symbolic of community. We believe in redemption for all the world, brought about by communities of Jews working together to instill in every single Jew the best that God has given us.

Being Jewish also means formulating some common concerns—fighting anti-Semitism, educating the next Jewish genera-

3

tion, helping Israel, bettering society by applying the ethics of Judaism to business and to public policy, and the like. For those purposes, Jewish organizations are founded. The mystical community therefore is actualized through real community building and action.

Jewish community is positive, not negative; it is open, not closed; anyone who wishes to link his or her own personal destiny to that of the community that began with Abraham and Sarah, so many years ago, may join it.

This section describes Jewish community, past and present, and prepares us for questions about what that community believes, what its ethics are, and so forth. The first questions deal with the community of today, defining Orthodox, Reform, Conservative, Reconstructionist, and chavurah Judaism: the religious options of contemporary Judaism. Then we look briefly at several special cases taken from the community of history: the Pharisees, the Rabbis, Chasidim, Sephardim, Ashkenazim, and Zionists. Finally, we return to the present, looking at the way the Jewish community actually operates, and how it relates to the non-Jewish community in which it exists.

QUESTIONS IN PART I

1. What Is a Jew?
2. What Are Orthodox Jews?
3. What Are Reform Jews?
4. What Are Conservative Jews?
5. What are Reconstructionist Jews?
6. What Is a Chavurah?
7. Who Were the Pharisees?
8. Who Were "The Rabbis"?
9. Who Are the Chasidim?
10. What Are Ashkenazim and Sephardim?
11. What Are Zionists?
12. Who Speaks with Authority for the Jews?
13. What Is the Relationship between the Jewish Community and the Larger Community in which Jews Live?

1. What Is a Jew?

It is difficult to find a single definition of a Jew.

A Jew is one who accepts the faith of Judaism. That is the *religious definition*.

A Jew is one who seeks a spiritual base in the modern world by living the life of study, prayer, and daily routine dedicated to the proposition that Jewish wisdom through the ages will answer the big questions in life—questions like, Why do people suffer? What is life's purpose? Is there a God? That is the *spiritual definition*.

A Jew is one who, without formal religious affiliation, and possibly with little Jewish practice, regards the teachings of Judaism—its ethics, its folkways, its literature—as his or her own. That is the *cultural definition*.

Judaism has also been called "a civilization," so that Jews are a cultural group, primarily religious, but not exclusively so, linked by a self-perception of enjoying a common history, a common language of prayer, a vast literature, folkways, and above all, a sense of common destiny. In this sense, Jews would be *a people*, not in the national or racial sense—but in a feeling of oneness. Judaism is this people's way of life.

There is an *ethnic definition* too. Once, Jews were almost inevitably born as Jews. Growing up in Jewish neighborhoods, they took for granted the folkways of their parents and grandparents. They were very much an ethnic group. Increasingly nowadays, however, the Jewish community includes people who have converted to Judaism, or who were born as Jews but were raised with no ethnic identity whatever. In a sense, all Jews are Jews by choice today, since even born Jews now have to make the conscious decision that they will remain Jewish, rather than join another religion or become nothing in particular. The ethnic definition is going the way of the dinosaur.

> A Jew is therefore a member of a people, by birth or by conversion, who chooses to share a common cultural heritage, a religious perspective, and a spiritual horizon derived uniquely from Jewish experience and Jewish wisdom.

An important part of any valid definition is what a Jew is not. To begin with, the Jews are not a race. Our history reveals countless additions to our numbers through marriage and conversion. There are dark Jews and blond, tall Jews and short; there are blue-eyed, brown-eyed, and hazel-eyed Jews as well as those whose eyes are jet black. Though most Jews are of the white or Caucasian race, there are black African Jews from Ethiopia and African-American Jews in the United States; until recently, there were Chinese Jews in Kai-Fung-Fu and there still are Jewish communities in various places on the subcontinent of India.

It would be equally misleading to speak of the Jews as a nation, though in antiquity they were. Today, Jewish, Moslem, and Christian citizens of Israel do constitute a nation, with Jews the majority and Jewish culture predominant. But there are no national ties that unite all Jews throughout the world.

Jews are part and parcel of every community in which we live. But we share with Jews everywhere the distinctive traditions of Judaism and, to a historically unique degree, a sense of a common destiny. "All Jews are responsible for one another," goes a talmudic adage.

That is why Jews raise and spend enormous amounts of money to save other Jews halfway around the world, Jews of different races, Jews who speak languages we never heard of, Jews who practice

Judaism in ways that differ markedly from our own. In 1948–49, "Operation Magic Carpet" airlifted forty-four thousand persecuted Yemenite Jews into Israel; in 1991, fourteen thousand Ethiopian Jews were saved by an equally miraculous "Operation Solomon," a thirty-six-hour airlift that rescued a Jewish community on the verge of extinction. Jewish responsibility extends beyond the Jewish people, of course (more on that later). But to be a Jew is to recognize the bond of peoplehood, the tie of community that knows no geographical boundaries.

Finally, Jews are not free to believe or practice just anything they want. We shall see, for example (pp. 275, 284), that they do not keep Christmas, or believe that Jesus is the son of God. What Jews believe, the rituals they follow, and the moral code that governs their behavior are the topics of later chapters.

2. *What Are Orthodox Jews?*

Until the nineteenth century, all Jews could best be described as premodern. There were different kinds of Jews then, just as there are now, but the differences were between Ashkenazim and Sephardim (see p. 23), or Chasidim and Mitnagdim (see p. 20). There was as yet no Orthodoxy.

In the nineteenth century, some modern Jews, primarily in Germany, undertook to reform their medieval tradition so as to bring it up to date with the optimistic rationalism of their time. Those Jews who objected to such changes in age-old traditions became the first Orthodox Jews. To this day, Orthodoxy is that brand of Judaism that most resists change, on the grounds that the Torah (see p. 39) was literally given to Moses on Mount Sinai, so that no law deduced from it may be tampered with even if our modern sensitivities do not like what the law says.

There are many kinds of Orthodox Jews. Some are fundamentalists who do not even recognize the Jewish state (even though they may live there), on the grounds that it was established by human

9

beings, not by God. By contrast, modern (or centrist) Orthodoxy is a movement that tries to harmonize ancient traditions with contemporary perspectives. Nevertheless, if modern ideas (such as feminism) conflict with traditional teachings, the tradition always takes priority. Thus Orthodox women retain traditional roles in the home, and they may not become rabbis; in the synagogue they sit separately from men during prayer and are not counted in the **minyan** [MIN-y'n or min-YAHN], the quorum required for public worship (see p. 86).

The basis of belief and practice for Orthodox Jews is the traditional body of Jewish doctrine recorded in the Talmud (see p. 47) and codified over time in a series of law codes, especially the Shulchan Arukh (see p. 52). The name given to the entire legal tradition based on the Talmud and the law codes is **halachah** [hah-lah-KHAH] (see p. 53). Orthodox Jews search out the halachah in Talmud, codes, and commentaries, and then live by it, regardless of how modern thought or personal conscience may view the practice in question.

Of America's 6 million Jews, approximately 6 percent identified themselves as Orthodox in 1990, a decline of 5 percent from the 11 percent figure reported in 1970.

3. What Are Reform Jews?

Reform Jews believe that Jewish tradition has always been in a state of flux, since Judaism itself is an evolving entity. They trace their roots to nineteenth-century Europe, when Jews who had just been freed from the ghettos tried to make premodern Judaism responsive to the changing conditions of their newly found civil status.

Reform Jews are committed to the eternal validity of Jewish tradition, but they emphasize the need to interpret that tradition from the perspective of individual conscience and informed choice. They believe, therefore, that Jews must study Jewish tradition. Whenever possible, they should adapt it to modern life. They may question ancient practices or attitudes that are inconsistent with the life of a modern person, and they may reject those ancient or medieval teachings that run contrary to one's moral conscience and contemporary spirituality.

Reform Jews study the same books that Orthodox Jews do— that is, they consult halachah too. But in the end, their individual conscience is their guide to what they accept as valid for our time. For example, Reform Jews were the first to declare women equal to men. They admit women to the rabbinate, not because the halachah is egalitarian, but because modern life informs our conscience that gender inequality could not possibly be what God wants.

Reform Judaism can be described by its different stages.

Classical Reform Judaism predominated until the 1960s. It was a brave new vision of the possibility of being Jewish and modern at the same time. Recognizing that Jews no longer had to live in ghettos, Reform Jews dreamed of working together with their non-Jewish neighbors to perfect a world of justice and of peace. They reread the Bible and focused on the prophetic mandate to champion the cause of society's victims. Emphasizing also the Jewish discovery of the one true God, they defined Judaism as a religion of ethical monotheism, fully compatible with scientific truth, reason, and evolution. In their synagogues, Reform Jews introduced such modern "innovations" as decorum, a sermon, choirs, and prayer in the vernacular rather than in Hebrew alone.

Reform Judaism then turned to its past, doing away with many medieval practices and rituals on the grounds that they were just the husk of Judaism that could safely be stripped away, leaving only the kernel, the things that truly mattered: ethics, monotheism, universalism, and reason. It eliminated many antiquated customs rooted in superstitious folklore or the outmoded perspective of the Middle Ages. However, it also took steps that later Reform Jews would consider too extreme, officially opposing Zionism, for instance, and allowing universalism almost completely to negate concern for Jewish peoplehood.

By the 1960s, however, Reform Judaism had undergone considerable change, and initiated a *postclassical period*. It retained its primary commitments, like the priority of an individual's conscience, the belief that Judaism must change with the times, and the commitment to social action derived from the biblical prophetic vision of a world without such social ills as poverty, discrimination, and war. It remained committed to ethical monotheism, and reaffirmed more strongly than ever its belief that the one true God demands an absolute commitment to justice, universal harmony among peoples everywhere, and such elementary rights as human dignity and freedom. But it reacted also to claims that it had thrown out the baby with the bath water. It took another look at tradition and reclaimed things that previous generations had discarded: greater support for Jewish peoplehood, for instance. It thus recaptured much of tradition, adopted Zionism as a primary religious value, and urged support for specifically Jewish causes as well as universal ones.

Reform worship is therefore a combination of tradition and modernity. It features prayer both in Hebrew and in English (or any vernacular); its music is both ancient and modern, vocal and instrumental. There is complete gender equality in its temples. Reform Jews enjoy a greater flexibility in worship, since the Reform prayer book contains both the traditional legacy of prayers and many new readings on traditional themes. Its sacred music too encompasses both the oldest chants and melodies that Jews have used and modern music too, either with or without instrumental accompaniment. In its classical period, Reform Judaism did away with such traditional prayer garb as the **tallit** (tah-LEET—see p. 91) and **kippah** (kee-PAH—see p. 90). But in its postclassical phase, it emphasizes informed choice as a principle, so it now asks worshipers (men and women) to either wear these things or not, depending on their own spiritual needs.

Today North American Jewry is about 42 percent Reform, making Reform Judaism the largest and fastest-growing Jewish movement.

4. *What Are Conservative Jews?*

The founders of Conservative Judaism, known in Europe as Historical Judaism, were a group of German Jewish scholars who viewed
Judaism as the evolving religious culture of the Jewish people. They
embraced Jewish ethnicity and Jewish law (halachah), but understood both in the light of contemporary historical scholarship. A
second generation of scholars transmitted these ideas to America,
where Conservative Judaism was transformed into a movement.

Originally, its primary appeal here was to eastern European
immigrants who arrived in America during the first decades of this
century. They wanted to be modern, but felt uncomfortable in
Reform temples, which lacked the warmth and traditional appeal of
their hometown synagogues back in Europe. Moreover, it was clear
that Reform congregants, who by and large hailed from central
rather than eastern Europe and had already gone through a process
of Americanization, looked down on them. Furthermore, even
though these eastern European newcomers did not follow all Jewish
laws, they nonetheless respected them in principle and were not
ready to abandon publicly the dietary code, Hebrew prayer, and the
Sabbath and festival regulations. They also embraced many Jewish
folkways that their Reform coreligionists had abandoned.

Philosophically and theologically, Conservative Judaism
stands between Orthodoxy and Reform. Like the Orthodox and
unlike Reform, Conservative Jews accept Jewish law as the primary
Jewish expression for all time. For them, the halachah is a living,
growing entity that changes to meet new circumstances. Thus, the
ultimate grounds for making personal decisions for them is not
individual conscience, as it is for Reform Jews, but the consensus
of learned scholars and the accepted practice of the community.
Change, for this reason, does come about, but more slowly and
deliberately than it does in Reform Judaism.

For example, it was only in 1985 that the Conservative move-

13

ment began ordaining women as rabbis, since doing so went counter to the way Jewish law had been interpreted up to that point. As its grounds for accepting women rabbis, Reform Judaism simply affirmed our modern moral consciousness, which insists on gender equality; change thus occurred relatively rapidly, with the first Reform woman rabbi being ordained in 1972. But Conservative Judaism was able to take the same action only after sustained study of halachah by its leading legal scholars. Only after Jewish legal sources were reinterpreted to admit the possibility of women rabbis could the Conservative movement formally alter its policy of admitting men alone to the rabbinate. In due time, however, at least a majority of the rabbis assembled to study the matter provided such a reinterpretation, and women were added to the seminary rolls.

Today, Conservative Judaism defines its synagogue practices as traditional but modern. In most, but not all, Conservative synagogues, women are admitted as equal participants in the service. The service retains its traditional flavor, with men (and some women) donning traditional Jewish prayer garb (the tallit, kippah, and tefillin—see pp. 91, 90, 92). Hebrew is still the principal language of prayer.

The middle road did not please all Conservative Jews. Two groups have broken away. On the left is Reconstructionism (see below), and in 1985, a right-wing splinter group called the Union for Traditional Judaism was founded in opposition to the acceptance of women as rabbis. It is too early to know whether the latter group will last. In 1990, approximately 40 percent of North American Jews claimed to be Conservative, but the number was shrinking from what it had been ten years earlier.

5. *What Are Reconstructionist Jews?*

Reconstructionist Jews trace their origin to the philosophy of Rabbi Mordecai Kaplan, a leading American Jewish thinker during the first half of the twentieth century. Kaplan believed that Judaism is an evolving religious civilization, comprising three primal elements: God, Torah, and the People of Israel. In addition, this civilization embraces the Land of Israel, the Hebrew language, and various folkways. Though Kaplan taught at the seminary of the Conservative movement, he broke with his colleagues over theology. Wanting to make room for a broad spectrum of people who emphasized different aspects of Jewish civilization, he taught that God, Torah, and Israel were all equal elements in Judaism. Any Jews wanting to seek out God, study Torah, or even just associate with other Jews were welcomed by him, even if they were not, strictly speaking, religious.

Kaplan failed to institute his views at the Conservative seminary, so in 1935, he founded a magazine called *The Reconstructionist,* urging that Judaism be "reconstructed" for modern American Jews. He once described "reconstruction" as "more drastic than reform and less disturbing than revolution." Tradition, he maintained, "should have a vote but not a veto."

Among the innovations such a reconstruction would require would be the realization that even secular Jewish activity has a place in Judaism—some Jews, after all, would want to associate with the Jewish People, but not search out God or study Torah. Kaplan therefore advocated building not only synagogues, but Jewish centers, where worship spaces and classrooms are combined with such things as a gymnasium and a pool.

Early Reconstructionists adopted Kaplan's own theological views, some of which were (and still are) considered radical. He did not believe in a personal God. Instead, he thought of God as a force, like gravity, built into the very structure of the universe. God, he said, is the "power that makes for salvation." By salvation, however, he meant nothing otherworldly, but just the guarantee that our striving after ethical behavior and personal satisfaction is not in vain. Since the universe is constructed to enable us to gain personal happiness and communal solidarity when we act morally, it follows that there is a moral force in the universe; this force is what the Reconstructionists mean by God.

Kaplan intended his Reconstructionist Foundation merely to propagate his views, not to form a separate movement in Judaism. Indeed, he was highly successful in inculcating his philosophy into the personal views of many rabbis, in both the Reform and the Conservative camps.

Nonetheless, Reconstructionism did become its own movement, though in keeping with Kaplan's own recognition that Judaism must evolve, it has developed in ways that Kaplan could not have imagined, even adopting positions in conflict with some of Kaplan's own most strongly held beliefs. For example, while many Reconstructionists still believe in God as a natural force, others are willing to affirm the existence of a personal God once again.

Still, Reconstructionism remains true to Kaplan's vision of Judaism as a total civilization. In ritual, it remains traditional, but in ideology, it adopts many nontraditional views (it ordains women, for instance), just as its founder did. It emphasizes the decision-making role of the community, rather than the individual, and in that sense, as well as in its ritual, it resembles Conservative more than Reform Judaism.

Reconstructionism is the smallest movement in Judaism. In 1990, less than 2 percent of North American Jews said they were Reconstructionist.

6. *What Is a Chavurah?*

If you add up the numbers of all the people who *say* they belong to one of the four Jewish movements, you will discover that there are still many Jews left over—Jews, that is, who identify with Judaism, but who do not say they are any particular type of Jew. In fact, even of those Jews who *say* they belong to a movement, only about half actually attend a synagogue.

In the 1950s, synagogues (like churches) expanded their educational facilities to serve the baby-boom generation. By the 1960s and 1970s, the baby-boomers were in college, fighting the Vietnam War and joining the counterculture. When they graduated from college and looked for a synagogue to join, many of them were disappointed by what they found. Most synagogues were still oriented to children. They also faulted the synagogue for its staid suburban style. It seemed to them that their fathers and mothers who spoke for the synagogue were shallow in their knowledge of Jewish tradition and passive in their unwillingness to "own" Judaism and to direct its destiny.

So rather than join an established synagogue, some of these young men and women banded together to form alternative Jewish communities called **chavurot** [khah-voo-ROTE] (sing., **chavurah** [khah-voo-RAH]; words ending in *ot*, like words ending in *im*, are usually plural).

The word *chavurah* is ancient. Some two thousand years ago, it meant an informal "tableship" group, that is, a group of Jews who met over common meals to celebrate the sacred moments of the year or of their family's life cycle. (Jesus and his disciples were a sort of chavurah.) This original chavurah fell out of fashion by the third century of the Common Era. But for many reasons, "chavurah" proved a good title for the alternative Jewish communities of the 1970s.

The first modern chavurot prided themselves on being radically egalitarian. Rather than hire a rabbi to lead services, give sermons,

17

and teach religious school, the entire chavurah community sought to empower each of its members as a competent and knowledgeable Jew.

Today, there are all sorts of chavurot. Some are independent, holding firm to the original radical democracy of the founders. Others are small groups of independently minded Jews who, however, have a rabbi, even as they proudly retain the smallness necessary to inspire a feeling of intimacy and community. Still others are subgroups within synagogues that meet independently to enrich their synagogue experience by additional study or prayer.

In 1979, many chavurot banded together into a national association, and in 1981 that organization merged with the Reconstructionist movement.

The number of Jews who still belong to independent chavurot is minuscule, probably less than 1 percent of the entire North American Jewish population.

7. Who Were the Pharisees?

The Pharisees were a political-religious party in ancient Israel at the time when Jesus was born. Today, we would call them religious liberals, in that they believed in reinterpreting the Bible for their time. They thought this possible, because they believed that along with the unchangeable written Torah revealed at Mount Sinai, God had supplied a variable system of oral interpretation that could be used for all time. They taught also that there is life after death, in which God rewards the righteous, but they cautioned their followers to serve God without regard to reward, but merely out of love. Modern Judaism is essentially the religion of "the Rabbis," and the Pharisees were the first Rabbis.

Many of the sayings of Jesus are paralleled in the teachings of the Pharisees. He and the prominent Pharisee Hillel, who lived at the same time, both advocated the golden rule, for instance. Similarly, Jesus said, "When two are gathered together in my name, I am there, in their midst." The parallel Pharisaic teaching is, "When two sit together and the words between them are God's Torah, the divine presence is in their midst." For Christians, God is present in the body and life of Jesus. For Jews, God is present in the words of Torah; the word does not become flesh; it remains the word.

The party opposed to the Pharisees were the Sadducees. They opposed reinterpretation of the Torah, insisting instead on strict observance of the letter of the written law.

Curiously, in the English language, the word "Pharisee" came to mean the exact opposite of its original connotation. This switch stems from a misunderstanding of the New Testament, which mistakenly denounces the Pharisees as hypocrites.

Actually, far from being alien to Christianity, the teachings of the Pharisees were adopted by it and form an important link between it and Judaism. It was the Pharisees, for instance, who insisted that the most important attribute of God is God's love for us. Pharisees introduced daily worship, grace at meals, and communal charity systems for the poor.

The most famous Pharisee was Hillel, who taught:

"A name made great is a name destroyed."

"Be of the disciples of Aaron, loving and pursuing peace, loving people and drawing them near to Torah."

"If I am not for myself, who is for me? but being for my own self alone, what am I? and if not now, when?"

Hillel's chief Pharisaic colleague, Shammai, is remembered for saying, "Say little and do much; and greet everybody cheerfully."

8. Who Were "the Rabbis"?

Regularly, Jewish sermons and books cite "the Rabbis" (I use a capital "R" for them), meaning not rabbis who live today, but the original Rabbis who invented the rabbinic tradition in the first place, and who, therefore, gave us Judaism as we know it. The earliest Rabbis were the Pharisees (see p. 18), though the title "Rabbi" did not exist that early. The three most important groups of Rabbis (after the Pharisees) were known by different titles and lived at different times and places.

The first group, the **Tanna'im** [tah-nah-EEM] (sing., **Tanna** [TAH-nah]), lived in the Land of Israel from 70 C.E. to 200 C.E. They wrote the **Mishnah** [MISH-nah], the most basic and influential collection of Rabbinic teachings on which all later Judaism depended. Tanna means "teacher."

The second group, the **Amora'im** [ah-moe-rah-EEM] (sing., **Amora** [ah-MOE-rah]), lived from about 200 to 550 in the Land of Israel, but also in Babylonia (present-day Iraq). They wrote commentaries on the Mishnah, known as **Talmud** [TAL-m'd] or **Gemara** [g'MAR-ah]. Along with the Bible and the Mishnah, the Talmud is the basis for all branches of Judaism. Amora means "teacher" too, but in the sense of "an oral instructor."

The third group, the **Ge'onim** [g'oh-NEEM] (sing. **Ga'on** [gah-OAN]), lived in Babylonia from the seventh to the eleventh centuries. They canonized the Talmud for all time. Instead of adding to it, they initiated the practice of writing separate documents called *responsa*, answers to questions posed by new Jewish communities in Europe, Africa, and Asia, who wanted Jewish guidance for their lives. Jews still write Responsa to this day. Ga'on is a biblical word, with connotations similar to the honorific title given to judges in our society: "Your Honor."

9. *Who Are the Chasidim?*

The **Chasidim** [khah-see-DEEM] were a sect within Judaism that began early in the eighteenth century and flourished first in eastern Europe. They emphasized the mystical side of Jewish tradition, which they hoped would provide novel spiritual piety. Their movement appealed especially to peasant people who were unhappy with the elitist stress on the intellect rather than the heart. The Chasidim therefore glorified simple piety that was within the reach of anyone. Their opponents, who continued to emphasize formal academic learning and who objected to the mystical piety of the new sect, were called **Mitnagdim** [mit-nahg-DEEM], meaning "the opposition."

The founder of the Chasidim was the Baal Shem Tov, meaning the "Master of the Good Name," a title derived from his reputed ability to use God's name to perform miracles. He is usually referred to as "the Besht," a nickname formed by joining the initials of *Baal SHem Tov* together into one short form, and adding an "e" for pronunciation: BeSHT. He preached that God should be worshiped directly and simply: not only in fancy synagogues, but in the woods, under a tree, or while walking along a country lane.

God demands no temples, declared the Chasidim, but the temple of a sincere heart. Prayers need not be clothed in words if they are shaped by a devout spirit. A typical Chasidic story tells of a simple wagon-driver who stopped his cart at the side of the road to repeat the Hebrew alphabet, letter by letter. "God," he cries out, "I don't know the prayers, so I am sending you the alphabet. You must know the prayers. Make them up out of the letters I am sending."

The Chasidim thought of worship as a thing of joy, not heavy solemnity. Better than the spoken word was the song of prayer, especially wordless melodies called **niggunim** [nee-goo-NEEM] (sing., **niggun** [nee-GOON]), beginning slowly but then rising in tempo, carrying the singers away into a trancelike state in which they would lose themselves in the joy of being with God. And song accompanied by dance was even more expressive. "All my bones shall declare you God," the Bible says. Not only the lips, but the whole body should speak God's praise. Many Chasidim were carried away to the point where they gesticulated wildly or even did somersaults during prayer.

Imaginative Chasidim revived an old mystical tradition that somewhere on earth there are always thirty-six saints, righteous individuals who go about their daily business disguised as ordinary human beings, unaware, in fact, of who they really are. They were called **lamed vov'nicks** [lah-med VOHV-niks]—*lamed vov* means thirty-six. The coach driver traveling the road to Warsaw; the village blacksmith; the kindergarten teacher: Any of them might be one of the thirty-six. Scores of stories were woven about this tradition, all pointing to the moral that one must treat all strangers kindly—for among them might be one of the world's immortals come to test one's religious faith! In turn, the world is sustained, despite its misery, by these secret thirty-six pious people, who insist on lives of righteousness come what may.

Rabbi Zusya, one of the early Chasidic masters, had his own version of the Shakespearian line, "To thine own self be true." "When I die," he used to say, "God will not inquire of me, 'Why were you not more like Moses?' But God will ask, 'Why were you not more like Zusya?' "

A vast treasury of folktales illustrates the Chasidic concern for addressing everyday life. For example:

One Chasidic rabbi remarked, "Even modern technology teaches religious lessons. Take the telephone, for instance," he continued, as he pointed with one hand to the phone and with the other up to heaven. "From the telephone we learn that what is said here, will be heard there."

"Rabbi," one of the disciples complained, "some of the congregants are gossiping in the midst of prayer!" "How wonderful are your people, O God," The rabbi retorted. "Even in the midst of gossip, they devote a few moments to prayer!"

"Can you tell me, Rabbi, why the wicked are always looking for companions while the righteous are not?" "The answer is simple: The wicked walk in darkness, so are anxious for company. Good people walk in the light of God; they don't mind walking alone."

To be sure, Chasidism goes much deeper than these folktales. Chasidic Judaism popularized the mystical approach in Judaism called Kabbalah (see p. 57), and its leaders were enormously deep spiritual thinkers, who left behind complex treatises on such topics as the annihilation of the self and mystical union through meditation.

Chasidism has also featured some characteristics that most moderns do not find appealing. Its spiritual creativity, for instance, was aimed purely at men. Chasidic masters established "courts" where men from miles around would come for holidays and study periods, leaving their wives and families back home. Moreover, these same Chasidic leaders were often charismatic to the point of being tyrannical, telling their followers exactly how to lead their lives and demanding complete obedience.

Shortly after Chasidism began, it splintered into many competing factions, each led by a master, with leadership passing from father to son. In many cases, the movement did not sustain the lofty spiritual level of its founders, in later years becoming instead very narrow, even puritanical. Today, Chasidism is still a series of competing sects with names like Lubavitch, Satmar, and Ger—names derived from their European place of origin. These are the most fundamentalist of Jews, even dressing as their founders did in eighteenth-century Poland in an effort to protect Judaism from any change whatever.

But the spiritual insight of Chasidism transcends the movement's failures. Its insights into worship, especially its breakthrough in terms of music, are part of Jewish practice everywhere. Its mystical depth is recorded in its literary legacy. Its aphoristic wisdom has become part of the vocabulary of Judaism.

10. *What Are Ashkenazim and Sephardim?*

By the Middle Ages, Jews had settled all over Europe. Their destiny depended largely on the local conditions in which they lived. But global politics were as important then as they are today. Jews in Spain and Portugal found themselves living under Moslem dominion, while Jews in France, Germany, Northern Italy, and England were subject to Christian rule. The first group, the Jews in Spain and Portugal, were called **Sephardim** [s'far-DEEM or S'FAR-dim], and their Jewish culture is described as **Sephardic** [S'FAR-dic] or **Sephardi** [S'FAR-dee]; the other group, largely in northern Europe, were called **Ashkenazim** [ash-k'nah-ZEEM or ash-k'NAH-zim], and their culture is known as **Ashkenazic** [ash-k'NAH-zic] or **Ashkenazi** [ash-k'NAH-zee].

Jewish culture developed differently, depending on which of the two spheres of influence Jews found themselves in. Influenced by the Moslems, Sephardic Jews pioneered poetry and philosophy; Ashkenazic Jewry mastered the detailed study of Jewish law in a manner akin to the way Christian scholastics pursued theology. By now, they differ in their rituals—for example, in the foods that each community prefers or allows for Jewish holidays, or the folk melodies that people like to sing.

Eventually, both Sephardim and Ashkenazim were chased eastward. The Ashkenazic communities were expelled from England and France in the thirteenth and fourteenth centuries, so that Ashkenazic Jews tended more and more to live in Germany and then in Poland and Russia, where they developed their own folk language, **Yiddish**, a combination of Hebrew and Old German, with some Slavic words from eastern Europe thrown in. Moslem Spain was overrun by Christian forces, with the result that Sephardic Jews were finally expelled in 1492, but only after they too had cultivated a folk language, **Ladino** [la-DEE-no], a mixture of Hebrew and Old Spanish. Most Sephardic Jews ended up in Arab countries in North Africa and the Middle East.

Sephardic Jews escaping the seventeenth-century Spanish Inquisition in South America were the first Jewish settlers in the United States, but in the nineteenth century, they were joined by much larger numbers of Ashkenazic Jews from Germany; by that century's end, huge numbers of Ashkenazim fleeing czarist persecution in eastern Europe arrived here. The basis for the modern State of Israel too was laid by those same Russian Ashkenazim, but the Ashkenazim in Israel were eventually joined by Ashkenazic Holocaust survivors from Europe and by waves of Sephardic Jews on the run from Arab countries. Israel thus became a mixture of the two traditions. By the 1980s, Sephardic Jews outnumbered Ashkenazim there. In 1991, Jews from the defunct Soviet Union began arriving, thus adding once again to the Ashkenazic mix of the Israeli population. Today, therefore, North American Jewry is still mostly Ashkenazic, while Israeli Jewry is mixed.

Actually, even though we still use the words "Ashkenazic" and "Sephardic," they are becoming irrelevant. Most Jews hardly know where their ancestors came from; almost no one speaks either Yiddish or Ladino anymore, and American Jews have blended the best of Ashkenazic and Sephardic traditions to form our own unique Jewish culture, which is still in the making. American Judaism is really neither Ashkenazic nor Sephardic, but plain American by now.

11. *What Are Zionists?*

Jews have never ceased living in Israel, and as part of their faith, Jews everywhere have prayed regularly for the rebirth of their homeland. The daily liturgy, the marriage ceremony, the mourning ritual, and the Passover prayers—all include the hope for a Jewish state.

But as a political movement, Zionism began only in the nineteenth century. It sought to reestablish the Jews as a people in the land of Israel. A Zionist believes that such a homeland will secure the welfare of Jews throughout the world and serve as a source of spiritual and cultural inspiration to the Jews of all lands. In addition, classical Zionist theory maintains that a nation built on the principles of social justice as laid down in Jewish tradition will become a model of a high ethical order that will remind humanity anew of the moral teachings of the Hebrew prophets.

The political efforts that led to the creation of the new Jewish state began as a response to the terrible anti-Semitism that broke out all over Europe by the end of the nineteenth century, particularly in czarist Russia, where the foreign minister announced a plan to end the "Jewish problem" by converting one-third of the Jewish population, killing off a second third, and expelling the final third. Many Jews being crushed by the rigors of this czarist tyranny saw in Palestine the only answer to the age-old problem of homelessness.

At first the Jews of western Europe had little sympathy for Zionist ideas. But they soon discovered that emancipation had not rooted out the evil of anti-Semitism. In Vienna, an openly rabid anti-Semite was elected mayor, and in Germany, riots against Jews broke out. The most striking sign of the times occurred in France, in 1894, when Captain Alfred Dreyfus, a Jew, was falsely imprisoned for treason as part of an army coverup to protect the real culprit. Spurred on by the press, thousands of French citizens took to the streets to shout anti-Semitic slogans.

A young Viennese journalist, *Theodor Herzl*, who was covering the Dreyfus affair, found himself reluctantly led to the conclusion that Jews would never be safe except on their own land. In 1897, he founded the official Zionist movement.

Another famous Zionist ideologue went by the pen name *Ahad Ha'am* [ah-KHAHD hah-AHM], meaning "one of the people." He emphasized *cultural* rather than *political* Zionism, in that he looked to a revived Jewish homeland to bring about a rebirth of Jewish culture and the Hebrew language. There were religious Zionists too, especially a revered modern mystic and rabbi, Abraham Isaac Kook, who saw the establishment of the state as the beginning of redemption, the end of human history, and the dawn of a messianic age. *A. D. Gordon* taught the spiritual doctrine that working the land with one's hands constitutes religious labor—planting trees or caring for vegetables is God's work! Orthodox Zionists believed that in a homeland of their own they could adhere to the rituals of their faith more fully; still others saw in Zionism a safeguard against assimilation.

Today, there are many shades of opinion among Jews regarding Zionism. At one extreme, there are those who interpret it to mean the "ingathering of the exiles"—the return of all Jews to Israel.

Quite naturally, this view has its strongest adherents in those lands where life is intolerable for Jews. In the United States, on the other hand, even the leaders of Zionism reject Zionism's extreme claim that to be a good Jew, you must move to Israel.

Almost all Jews in North America are Zionists, in the sense that we all support the right of Jews to have a Jewish state, even though we continue to consider ourselves an integral part of the lands in which we live. We support the State of Israel spiritually and financially, making trips that are like religious pilgrimages to see the miracle of a homeland that was built out of malarial swamps on one hand, and bleak barren desert on the other. We consider Jerusalem our spiritual capital, and we pray, just as Jews have prayed forever, "for the peace and welfare" of that sacred space where we began our religious odyssey some three thousand years ago.

We look upon Israel as a haven for the persecuted, the only place that would accept refugees from Hitler half a century ago, and the only place that would take Jewish refugees from Ethiopia in 1991. Jews have not exercised power over their own destiny since the Romans conquered Jerusalem nineteen centuries ago; and the exercise of power once again has proved as difficult for Israel as it has for other nations, including the United States. In practice, it is very difficult to decide when military might in pursuit of self-defense is called for. Sometimes, official government policy in Israel falls short of what most Jews take to be ethical expectations, at which time Jews may object to the Israeli government, much as Americans protested during the Vietnam War.

All Jews would agree that the government of the State of Israel should exercise power in ways that are compatible with the highest values of the Jewish people. Increasingly also, most Jews support the right of all people in the region to have a similar land they can call home, providing the Jewish state is recognized by its neighbors and Israeli citizens are protected from harm.

In general, Jews take great pride in Israel's many accomplishments. Culturally, it has revived Hebrew and made the ancient language of our people into a living tongue. Its literacy rate is probably the highest of any country in the world. It is a leading developer of technological and medical breakthroughs. Politically, it is the sole democracy in the Middle East.

12. Who Speaks with Authority for the Jews?

Is there any authoritative body or person who speaks for the Jewish community? Not really. There are many groups who speak for parts of the community, but Jews have no one comparable to the pope, and no single authoritative body to which all Jews owe allegiance. An old expression is, "Where you find two Jews, you find three opinions."

Reform, Reconstructionist, Conservative, and Orthodox Jews all have their own synagogues and rabbinic organizations, which pass resolutions and set standards, but in the end, each congregation does what it thinks best. Orthodox Jews generally care more about the opinions of individual rabbis known for their learning of Talmud than they do for official pronouncements of synagogue bodies. Reform Jews especially stress personal autonomy; individuals follow their own conscience on every issue. Some Conservative and Reconstructionist Jews are closer to Reform; others are more similar to Orthodoxy. They practice congregational, not individual, autonomy, some congregations accepting the ruling of the national body and some not.

There is therefore wide diversity within all synagogue groups, for there is no element of compulsion in the American synagogue.

In the Middle Ages, it was possible to excommunicate recalcitrant Jews by banning them from the community until they agreed to conform to Jewish standards. Nowadays, except among the very Orthodox, that is impossible and not even considered desirable. Even highly secular Jews, Jews who deny every aspect of Judaism as a religion, may claim great loyalty to the Jewish people and may insist on providing their children with Jewish education and identity.

There are also nonsynagogue bodies that sometimes speak for Jews—but again, never for all of them. The *B'nai B'rith*, for instance, is a service organization that began in the nineteenth century as a German Jewish men's club. It is best known for its *Anti-Defamation League*, which monitors anti-Semitism. Another organization concerned with civil rights in general is the *American Jewish Committee*. The largest and best-known women's group is *Hadassah*, an international organization with some 385,000 members, mainly in the United States, dedicated to Zionism and the welfare of the State of Israel. The list of organizations is actually endless, but most of the best-known Jewish organizations can be found listed in *The Encyclopedia of Jewish Organizations*.

Three national bodies stand out as especially important.

All the religious groups in America belong to the *Synagogue Council of America*, the only forum in which representatives of all branches of Judaism talk through issues of common concern, and increasingly establish task forces to accomplish goals that all religious Jews share.

The most important link among Jewish organizations both religious and secular is the *Conference of Presidents of Major Jewish Organizations*. If anyone speaks for the Jews, it is probably the Conference of Presidents, since it claims to have under its umbrella organizations representatives of two-thirds of America's Jews.

But the organization that affects Jews most is the *United Jewish Appeal–Federation of Jewish Philanthropies*. United Jewish Appeal began as a fundraising mechanism for the State of Israel. Federation of Jewish Philanthropies collected money for charitable work in America. Today the two institutions have merged. Since charity is such an important part of Jewish life, *UJA-Federation* (as it is known) has become the single most influential Jewish organization in almost every American city. It supports hospitals, Jewish educational initiatives, Jewish newspapers, hospices, social work agencies, homes for the aged, studies of Jewish life, and so forth.

13. What Is the Relationship between the Jewish Community and the Larger Community in which Jews Live?

Whenever Jews have been allowed to participate in public affairs, they have done so. This is because Jews are urged to put their religion into action. "Talking is not the main thing; action is," goes a talmudic maxim, and action includes not just activity within the confines of the Jewish world, but working for the welfare of the larger society in which we live. We call this **tikkun olam** [tee-KOON oh-LAHM], meaning the "reparation of world." Jews tend to vote in higher numbers than the norm, and to support such liberalizing movements as civil rights, clean air acts, and higher education budgets.

The core of Judaism is found in the Jewish formula for treating our neighbors fairly and respecting their rights, their property, and above all their person. One of our talmudic Rabbis declared that the world rests on three foundations—justice, truth, and peace. Out of the first, the other two emerge. If we deal justly with other people, truth will triumph and peace will reign.

This passion for just human relations dominated the ethical teachings of Judaism down through the centuries. Whenever the biblical prophets saw an act of injustice they appealed to the conscience of the community. When King Ahab confiscated the vineyard of one of his citizens, the prophet Elijah issued a scathing denunciation of the heartless king and his queen, Jezebel. Amos and Isaiah were equally excoriating in their denunciation of all kinds of exploitation. "Favor no one in matters of justice," the law of Moses declared. And to the prophets the most grievous sin in God's eyes was to remain silent in the face of oppression, especially when the victim was the underprivileged.

"If God does not build a house," the Bible tells us, "the builders toil in vain." An unjust society has within it the seeds of its own destruction. The Rabbis used telling parables to illustrate this point. Why did the Tower of Babel crumble? Because the leaders of the project were more interested in the work than in the workers. When a brick fell to earth, they would pause to bewail its loss; when a worker fell they would urge the others to keep on building. The brick was more important than the human being. So God destroyed the imposing edifice.

The law of acting fairly toward one's neighbor is the starting point for all Jewish teachings. Judaism has no elaborate philosophy of justice. Unlike that of Plato and Aristotle, Jewish teaching made little attempt to develop a systematic democratic philosophy. In point of fact, there is no Hebrew word for democracy, except that which is borrowed from the Greeks. But the social creed by which the Jews have lived for centuries is in democracy's highest traditions.

Basic to Judaism are these fundamental principles, which are also basic to democracy: 1) God recognizes no distinction among us on the basis of creed, color, gender, or class; all of us are equal in God's sight. 2) We are all our brother's and sister's keepers; we bear responsibility for our neighbors' failings as well as for their needs. 3) All of us, being made in God's image, have infinite capacity for doing good; therefore the job of society is to evoke the best that is in each of us. 4) Freedom is to be prized above all things; the very first words of the Ten Commandments depict God as the Great Liberator: "I am the Eternal your God who brought you out of the land of Egypt."

The theme of freedom and equality runs constantly throughout our three-thousand-year history. The frequent taste of injustice meted out against Jews reinforced a tradition already rooted in our faith. Thus, Jews responded readily to the thrilling challenge of the American Declaration of Independence and the Bill of Rights. And the French Revolution also found Jews sympathetic to the cries of Liberty, Equality, and Fraternity. It is no accident that the words found on the American Liberty Bell, "Proclaim liberty throughout the land to all the inhabitants thereof," stem from Hebrew scriptures. The love of liberty is woven into the fabric of Judaism.

The democratic ideal inherent in Judaism is naturally incompatible with totalitarianism of any kind—not only political totalitarianism, but coerced conformity of all sorts. Dictators always found their Jewish citizens indigestible. Fascists and Communists alike have not tolerated the maintenance of the Jewish tradition because it represents a denial of the repression for which they stand.

The prophet Jeremiah exhorted his followers to seek the welfare of the country in which they live. And Jews have always felt the obligation to participate fully in the life of the community.

The voice of the synagogue will therefore be heard in all the issues that would have aroused the ancient prophets of Israel: integrity in public office; civil rights and civil liberties; equality of economic opportunity; decent education, housing, and health standards for all citizens; peace among the nations of the world.

The Talmud says: "If people of learning participate in public affairs, they give stability to the land. But if they sit at home and say to themselves: 'What have the affairs of society to do with me? . . . Let my soul dwell in peace,' they bring about the destruction of the world."

II

The Way to God:

A Life of Torah

As we saw in Part I, there are many kinds of Jews. Unifying us all, even when we disagree with each other on important matters, is our commitment to live a life of Torah, by which we mean that the totality of Jewish wisdom, which we refer to generally as "Torah," forms the basis for what we do.

We have been called "The people of the Book," and indeed, we are that. Torah is therefore primarily a series of books, beginning with the Bible, and then constituting rabbinic writings thereafter: the Mishnah, the Talmud, midrash, law codes, commentaries, and commentaries on commentaries. Jewish literature encompasses legal texts, philosophical inquiry, mysticism, poetry, prayer books, history, satire, autobiography, and even ethical wills—wills that record how parents lived their lives and advise their children who survive them how best to continue the values for which the parents stood.

In this section, we turn to the life of Torah, first the most important books that motivate Jewish lives, and then the nonliterary sources of Jewish culture, our music and our art.

QUESTIONS IN PART II

1. What Is Torah?
2. What Is the Jewish Bible?
3. Do Jews Believe Literally in the Bible?
4. Do Jews Still Follow All the Biblical Laws, Even the Harsh
   Ones Like "An Eye for an Eye"?
5. What Is the Talmud?
6. What Is Midrash?
7. Is There a Single Book of Jewish Law?
8. What Is Halachah?
9. How Do Jews Read the Bible?
10. What Is Kabbalah?
11. Is There Such a Thing as Jewish Music?
12. Is There Such a Thing as Jewish Art?

1. *What Is Torah?*

The word *Torah* has two usages in Jewish tradition. Broadly speaking, Torah is our way of life, all the vastness and variety of the Jewish tradition, as someone once called it. It is the very essence of Jewish spirituality. It is synonymous with learning, wisdom, and love of God. Without it, life has neither meaning nor value. When we want to speak of Torah in this broad sense, we say just "Torah," not "the Torah." When someone offers a homily or an interpretation of a Jewish text, we say that person has given a **d'var torah** [d'VAHR TOE-rah], "a word of Torah."

More narrowly, when we speak of *The* Torah, we mean the first five books of the Bible. So central to Judaism are these five books that a section of them is read publicly in worship services every week, from a specially handwritten scroll. Thus, "Torah" has yet a third meaning: It may be a **sefer torah** [SAY-fer TOE-rah], the name given to the scroll in which the five books of Moses are written and from which they are ritually read.

The Torah scroll is made of parchment wrapped around two wooden poles or rollers. It is then covered with an embroidered cloth. Silver ornaments rest on the poles, and a silver breastplate adorns the covering. The text of a Torah must be letter-perfect. The scribes who prepare it belong to a sacred profession going back more than a thousand years. They learn how to handwrite every single letter in its own unique way, using a Hebrew style unchanged through countless generations. Even the size of the spaces between the sentences is determined by age-old tradition. Every Torah text is thus prepared with painstaking veneration. As if technology had ceased a thousand years ago, the scribe literally pens the scroll, letter by letter, using an old-fashioned quill and specially produced indelible black ink. A Torah containing scribal errors may not be used in worship.

A portion of the Torah is read aloud every Sabbath during worship, beginning right after the autumn High Holy Days and continuing each week thereafter. We begin in the first week with the first few chapters of the book of Genesis, and then read consecutive chapters week after week until the entire Torah has been read by the end of the Jewish year. In order to read the entire Torah in one year, the weekly portions have to be long. Since the reading is in the original Hebrew, which few people understand, it can become tedious after a while. In some synagogues, therefore, only a part of the weekly portion is read.

Each weekly section is called the **sedra** [SED-rah] or the **parashah** [pah-rah-SHAH], and is given a name drawn from the first significant word within it. Thus, for instance, the first parashah in the Torah, the beginning of the book of Genesis, starts with the Hebrew word *bereshit* [b'ray-SHEET], meaning "in the beginning," so the name of that parashah is Bereshit. Rabbis will customarily tell a congregation, "We read this week from parashah Bereshit" (or whichever one it is); the reading will take place, often chanted in an age-old system of sounds, and then after the reading is over, the rabbi will discuss the parashah by giving a d'var torah.

The central focus of the synagogue sanctuary is the ark, a recessed cabinet in the front wall, where the Torah scrolls are kept when not in use. Worshipers stand whenever the ark is opened so that a Torah scroll can be removed to be read aloud to the congregation. Before the reading begins, many congregations have someone carry the Torah around the room in sacred procession. Worshipers follow the path of the Torah with their eyes, and as it passes, they may move out of their seats to the aisles so as to touch it with the *tsitsit* (fringes on the *tallit*—see p. 92) or with their prayer book, and then kiss the tsitsit or the book, as a sign of respect.

In Jewish folklore, the Torah is said to antedate the time of creation. It was at the Creator's side when the world came into being. To the observant Jew, the Torah is the very breath of life. It is referred to as a "tree of life." "Turn it and turn it," goes an old rabbinic expression, "for everything is in it."

Jews have bled and died to save this sacred scroll from desecration. If forced to flee their homes in the face of tyranny and persecution, Jews abandoned all their worldly goods but carried the Torah with them into the unknown. The Nazis made a point of destroying Torah scrolls, or of saving them in what was to become a museum of Judaism celebrating the end of the Jews. After the war, Jews recovered these scrolls and pieced together whole ones from the shreds and fragments found in Nazi warehouses. These "Holocaust scrolls," as they are called, now sit in synagogues around the world on permanent loan as a reminder of the great European Jewish communities that once used them in prayer. Someday, perhaps, those communities may be rebuilt, at which time they can reclaim their scrolls, and with them, the very essence of Jewish life.

2. What Is the Jewish Bible?

No one really knows who wrote or edited the Bible. Those who preserved the Holy Scripture and gave it to the world in its present form were writers with a passion for anonymity. As a matter of fact, when the Rabbis debated which books to include in the third and final section of the present Bible, anonymity was one of the tests they used. Except for the prophets, none of the authors were known. This modesty was not just a matter of individual temperament. Pride of authorship was alien to ancient Hebrew tradition. Writers who had something worthwhile to contribute preferred to attach their ideas to names already revered, such as David, Solomon, or Isaiah.

This explains why the Prophecies of Isaiah are not all his, nor all the Psalms of David and the Proverbs of Solomon the creation of those two monarchs.

The final "editing" of the Bible as a whole, like the original compilation of the Torah, was also the product of group effort. Centuries of study and discussion on the part of our wisest scholars went into this task.

The Jewish Bible differs from the Christian Bible in two ways. First, it contains only what people sometimes call the "Old Testament." Jews (and many Christians now, too) do not call it "Old Testament" anymore, because the term might imply that the Jewish witness to God is outdated. Instead of Old Testament, then, it is sometimes called the Hebrew scriptures. There is a second difference also. We organize our Bible around different principles from the ones used by Christians, so that even though Christians too consider the Hebrew scriptures holy, they arrange the books in a different order.

The Jewish Bible is made up of three distinct parts, which were edited (or canonized) at different times.

The first five books of the Bible (Genesis, Exodus, Leviticus, Numbers, and Deuteronomy)—sometimes known as the Five Books of Moses, or the Pentateuch—are considered the most sacred. As we saw above, they are recorded separately in a scroll and known as the Torah. Jews read the Torah publicly during worship services. We begin each Jewish year with the first few chapters of Genesis, and then week after week, Sabbath after Sabbath, we read a bit more, until we end the year with the last few lines of Deuteronomy.

Orthodox Jews believe God literally gave the Torah to Moses. But Abraham Ibn Ezra, one of our greatest medieval Bible commentators, concluded in the eleventh century that Moses could not have written all of the Torah, since, among other things, the last book contains the account of how he died, and the statement, "No prophet of Moses' stature has arisen unto this very day." Afraid to argue his case publicly, however, Ibn Ezra merely suggested his "heretical" conclusion, saying that "discerning people will understand my point." Today, most Jews no longer find Ibn Ezra's position heretical. We accept the scientific finding that the Torah is composed of several documents recorded at different times, and eventually edited sometime in the fifth century B.C.E.

The historical books of Joshua, Judges, I and II Samuel, and I and II Kings, along with the books that bear names of prophets (such as Isaiah or Micah), constitute the second section, and are known as *The Prophets*—in Hebrew, **Nevi'im** [n'vee-EEM]. These biblical books begin with the entry of the Israelites into Canaan, and take the reader all the way through the reigns of the famous kings, David and Solomon, as well as their less renowned successors. Finally, we read of the moral evil spawned during the era of later monarchs, the prophetic call for justice, and the destruction of the First Jewish Commonwealth at the hands of Assyria and Babylonia. The whole section of the Nevi'im was probably organized in its final form somewhere in the late first or early second century C.E.

What we call the **Ketuvim** [k'too-VEEM], the "writings," make up the third part of the Bible. Its compilation evoked many controversies around the issue of which books to canonize and which to eliminate. There was no question about Psalms, Proverbs, and Job. But a number of the Rabbis wondered whether the Song of Songs, a poetic account of a very sensuous love affair, belonged in the sacred scripture. Nonetheless, it too was admitted. Other books that existed at the time were rejected, for reasons we can only guess at. I and II Maccabees, for instance, provide accounts of the Hasmonean victory for freedom in the second century B.C.E. They explain the holiday of Chanukah. But they were omitted. Some of the books left out of the Hebrew Bible were later adopted by the Catholic church as part of its scripture. These books (including Maccabees) are called the Apocrypha, but are not part of Jewish sacred writ.

When the last section of the Hebrew Bible—the Writings or Ketuvim—was finally concluded, it contained, and contains to this day, Psalms, Proverbs, and Job; Daniel, Ezra, Nehemiah, and the two Books of Chronicles; and what we call the five **Megillot** [m'gee-LOTE], or scrolls, because of our custom of writing them also on separate scrolls, which we read publicly at particular times of the year. The Megillot are the Song of Songs, Ruth, Lamentations, Ecclesiastes, and Esther. The Ketuvim were canonized in the middle of the second century, and nothing was added to the Bible after that.

Jews use a Hebrew word to refer to the Bible. Taking the first letters of the three sections (*Torah*, *Nevi'im*, and *Ketuvim*) and adding vowels for pronunciation, we get *TaNaK*. For reasons of Hebrew grammar, the final *K* is pronounced *KH*, so that Jews refer to the Bible as **Tanakh** [tah-NAHKH].

3. *Do Jews Believe Literally in the Bible?*

Our forebears regarded the miracles of the Bible as literally true. They made no distinction between the natural and the supernatural, since the same all-powerful God who set the course of nature could alter it at will. The dividing Red Sea, the crumbling walls of Jericho, the sun's hesitation at Gideon's command were all accepted as normal historical events, no different from the fall of Jerusalem or the writing of the Talmud. In the Bible itself, no reference is made to the miraculous nature of these happenings; in God's world all things are possible. History was not so much the recording of events as the interpretation of them. So the descriptions of the Exodus from Egypt, the Babylonian exile, or the victory of Judah Maccabee were entrusted to the religious teacher rather than the matter-of-fact historian. But interpretation was felt to presuppose historical truth.

There are some Orthodox Jews today who still maintain that position. They believe in the miracles as literal historical events, and they accept interpretations of their significance from later Jewish books, especially the Talmud.

But most Jews look upon the accounts of miracles as inspiring literature, rather than as actual historical events. That is to say, we do not necessarily accept older interpretations of their significance, since an important lesson for the fifth century may be unimportant in the face of today's spiritual questions; but we do use these tales as sources of inspiration ourselves, trying to draw religious lessons from the text, even the text of an event that may not be literally true. God did not create the world in precisely six days, just as the biblical text insists, but we can learn lessons for our lives from such stories as the Garden of Eden or the Tower of Babel.

This broader view is fully in keeping with that of many of our greatest minds even in the Middle Ages, who often doubted the literal veracity of the Tanakh. A number of outstanding Jewish scholars, including Moses Maimonides (twelfth century), suggested that the authors of the Bible deliberately used parables, allegory, and hyperbole, not expecting them to be taken literally. Their purpose was to convey great spiritual truths in a way that would be understood and appreciated by the general public.

Some people have devoted considerable energy to finding natural explanations for the miracles recounted in the Bible. They argue that the events that our ancestors considered miraculous were really an unusual combination of natural phenomena. The dividing of the Red Sea developed as a result of low tides and sudden high winds; the walls of Jericho tumbled because of an earthquake; and so on. Such explanations, while interesting, are unproven, and in fact, superfluous. Those who insist on the "scientific" approach to the Bible must still find answers to explain why these "natural" phenomena all took place at such highly propitious moments. The eternal truths of the Bible, clothed frequently in phrases of poetic imagination, do not depend in the slightest on archaeological confirmation.

4. Do Jews Still Follow All the Biblical Laws, Even the Harsh Ones Like "An Eye for an Eye"?

No. In fact, many of the laws laid down in the Bible were never kept, even in biblical times. Frequently the last writers of the Torah (living in the fifth century B.C.E) wrote accounts of events that had occurred years or even centuries earlier, in which they imagined stories of people keeping laws and customs that could not have existed at that time.

Still, the Rabbis of talmudic times took the Bible literally, and could not have known that. Moreover they had to deal with the fact that some biblical laws seemed outdated to them, even cruel. How would they follow the law of "an eye for an eye," for example? In such cases, the Rabbis simply interpreted the law in such a way that it need not be kept. In the case of "an eye for an eye," they reasoned that in an ideal world, we would never allow someone who maims another person to get away with a monetary payment alone, or even jail. Rather, we would insist that we punish such a person with perfect justice—an eye for an eye. In the actual world, however, who is to say that the use of an eye is identical for each person? Thus, they exchanged the ideal solution for a real one: The guilty person had to pay an indemnity, much as American law prescribes for accident cases. At the same time, we can learn a moral lesson from the Torah's *ideal* statement of the case: Though we *allow* indemnity as the punishment, we should never be so callous as to let the mere monetary payment blind us to the sacred uniqueness of a human body.

It was the Pharisees' insistence on liberalizing biblical law that outfitted Judaism for survival through the centuries. Later rabbis frequently referred to the need to readjust Jewish law in general so that people would enhance their life with it, rather than see it as a burden. "Never pass a law that the people cannot bear," became a Jewish legal principle. If the people are generally disobeying a law, it may be because the law is unrealistic; in such cases, Jewish judges were warned not to tell the people what the law is, since "it is better that they sin unknowingly than that they sin knowingly." Unenforceable laws would thus cease functioning of their own accord, except in the minds of the scholars and theorists.

Perhaps the greatest challenge to Jews today is to continue the Pharisaic practice of endlessly reexamining Jewish laws. Probably nothing receives more Jewish attention than those areas where Jewish law seems incompatible with our modern sensitivities.

5. *What Is the Talmud?*

The **Talmud** [TAL-m'd] consists of sixty-three books of legal, ethical, spiritual, theological, ritual, and historical insight. It was edited by the Rabbis over a period of time, from the fifth to the seventh century. It is the primary record of rabbinic discussion and decision during those centuries.

Each book is called a *tractate*. Another word for Talmud is **Gemara** [g'MAHR-ah].

There are actually two Talmuds: a Palestinian Talmud, reflecting rabbinic deliberations in Palestine (and edited by the end of the fourth century), and a Babylonian Talmud (edited about two hundred years later). It is the Babylonian Talmud that people refer to when they say *The* Talmud, without specifying which one they mean.

As a giant compendium of law and lore, the Talmud has been the major textbook of Jewish schools for centuries. Study of its contents constitutes, even today, the largest block of time in the training of Orthodox and Conservative rabbis. Orthodox Jewish law is based largely on the decisions already found in the Talmud.

The Talmud is enormously difficult to read, since it is written in ancient Aramaic, without vowels and punctuation marks, thus forcing the reader to interpret the flow of what is usually a highly technical and logically dense argument that goes on for pages. The final editors arranged it as if all the Rabbis were alive at one time, sitting in a single room debating points of law and theology with each other. Coming to the end of even one page of the Talmud is therefore the source of great satisfaction. Finishing an entire tractate—if you ever get there!—is the occasion for a spectacular celebration called a **siyyum** [see-YOOM]!

Most Jews never get to study Talmud in the original, but it is available in translation, and synagogues are increasingly offering courses in it. On the other hand, there exists an old custom called **daf yomi** [DAHF YOH-mee or DAHF yoh-MEE], meaning "a daily page," whereby Jews put aside time each day to study one page of the Talmud. Many people still observe this practice. Eventually, the pages add up to a whole tractate.

People enjoy the Talmud for its content and for the mere fun of figuring out the rabbinic argument, a sort of Jewish puzzle in logic. The Talmud is interlaced with thousands of parables, anecdotes, and epigrams that provide an intimate glimpse into Jewish life and lore. More important, it is a storehouse of spiritual wisdom as valid today as it was when it was composed. There is nothing quite like it.

Many of the maxims of the Talmud have become household phrases:

"Give everyone the benefit of the doubt."

"Look not at the bottle, but what it contains."

"One good deed leads to another; but an evil deed brings another in its wake."

Talmudic wisdom extends to every aspect of life. Regarding education, for example, we read:

"A classroom should never have more than twenty-five pupils."

"When you encounter a child whose head is as solid as iron, you may be sure that the child's teacher did not have a pleasant way of explaining things."

"Always begin a lesson with a humorous illustration."

One Rabbi classified students into four categories: "the sponge: one who absorbs and retains everything; the funnel: everything that goes in comes out; the sifter: one who remembers the trivial and forgets the significant; the sieve: one who retains the important and sifts out the incidental."

Another scholar proclaimed, "I have learned much from my teachers; even more from my classmates; but most of all, from my students!"

The Talmud is filled with pithy sayings:

"Bad neighbors count your income but not your expenses."

"Judge people not according to the words of their mother [we might add, father] but according to the comments of their neighbors."

Talmudic parables include the story of a traveling Rabbi who met a very old man busily planting a carob tree.

"When will you be able to eat the fruit of the tree?" he asked.

"In seventy years," the old man replied.

"Do you expect to live that long?" the traveler queried.

"I did not find the world desolate when I entered it," came the reply. "So I plant for those who come after me."

A particular talmudic favorite of mine is this: "Why is it that we are born into the world with clenched fists and leave it with outstretched fingers? To remind us that we take nothing with us."

But Talmud is not just page after page of sayings and stories. It is a spiritual well that Jews are urged to study daily. More than the ideal daf yomi—one page per day—is almost impossible. Discussions roam from topic to topic, comparing, classifying, contrasting, and endlessly considering both sides of the issue. Talmudic style is so dense that as you wend your way through the complexities of the debate, you can very easily forget what the issue was in the first place. Someone once said that the problem with studying Talmud is that every page presupposes you already know every other page—except the one you are on. The lines you are reading may refer you to ten other passages, as if you have read them in advance.

Over the years the greatest talmudists have supplied commentaries, and commentaries on commentaries—whole libraries of them. To study a page of the Talmud is therefore to study great masses of interpretations that preceded us. It is to cut through history and capture the wisdom of every time everywhere.

There is a special convention for printing the Talmud. The talmudic text itself is displayed in the middle of the page, with commentaries from throughout the centuries that expound upon it around the margins. Any single page is thus a slice of Jewish history. You read the words of the talmudic text, consider two diverse answers to a question raised by medieval commentators, move back to the words of the Talmud with these solutions in mind, and maybe discover yet a third solution of your own. Finally, you close the book, perhaps having "mastered" only a line or two.

6. *What Is Midrash?*

The same Rabbis who gave us the Talmud also compiled the **midrash** [mid-RAHSH or MID-rahsh], a collection of rabbinical commentary on the Bible. Midrash is often cited in sermons and Jewish literature. Midrash is like filling in the gaps in the biblical narrative. By reading the Bible very closely, the Rabbis would ask questions of it:

Why does the Bible begin with the second letter of the Hebrew alphabet, not the first?

Why did God appear to Moses in a little burning thorn bush, rather than a grand tree more befitting the Divine One?

How could Abraham have told the two lads who accompanied Isaac and him up the mountain, "We shall return"? He was already planning on sacrificing Isaac; surely he knew that if his plan succeeded Isaac would definitely *not* return! Would saintly Abraham have lied?

To each such question, the Rabbis suggested solutions, recognizing that more than one answer may be right. The complexity of life itself is thus revealed in the abundance of midrashic answers, each one revealing a possible truth about human nature, our relationship to God, social justice, human institutions, or the world of nature.

The aphorisms of the midrash, like those of the Talmud, have become part of the language not only of Israel, but of all humanity. Many of the "sayings of the Rabbis" quoted in these pages are taken from that source.

"All is well that ends well" is at least as old as the midrash; or, "Offer not pearls to those who deal in vegetables and onions."

"When in a city, follow its customs," is the Jewish expression for "When in Rome . . ."

But these brief insights into life and people are only a small portion of the wisdom of the midrash. Another telling example is the answer given the students of the Torah when they asked why God handed down the Law in the wilderness, rather than in some important city. "So that no nation could lay exclusive claim to its teachings," decided the Rabbis. "So that all people who follow its precepts may share equal possession of the Torah."

Inventing new midrash virtually ceased in the late Middle Ages, as people contented themselves with studying the opinions of the Rabbis of old. Lately, however, modern men and women have reclaimed their right as Jews to make modern midrash. Rather than simply study the midrash already collected in ancient and medieval literature, we are encouraged to come up with our own. This is especially important for women, since the Rabbis were all male, and were thus unable to bring women's experience to bear on the biblical text.

Modern midrash, for instance, may ask, "What did Sarah think when her husband took her son away to sacrifice him, especially given the fact that nowhere in the biblical text does Abraham ever discuss his plans with her?" Questions like this one give women a voice in Jewish tradition. In a thousand years, we will have a great second collection of midrash, the opinions of both men and women over the course of time, including our own.

7. Is There a Single Book of Jewish Law?

No single book embodies all the religious laws binding upon Jews.

The closest anyone has come to compiling a single legal code is the **Shulchan Arukh** [shool-KHAHN ah-ROOKH or SHOOL-khahn AH-rookh], a sixteenth-century work by a man who was simultaneously a great legalist and an intense mystic: Joseph Caro. This book contains the basic law that today guides most Orthodox Jews in the Western world. But though Orthodox Jews accept most of the Shulchan Arukh, they still do not consider it the full body of Jewish law, which goes beyond Caro's work to include volumes and volumes of codes, commentaries, amendments, and responsa (rabbinic answers to problems arising from actual experience—see p. 54) that are to be found throughout the library of Jewish learning.

Reform Jews, however, do not accept the Shulchan Arukh as binding, and Conservative and Reconstructionist Jews also no longer abide by many of its regulations, since all of these movements understand Jewish law to be in a state of continuing change. Each in its own way takes the Shulchan Arukh and its many commentaries very seriously, but does not observe its laws literally and rigidly.

In recent years, some Reform Jews have expressed the need for a standard code of Reform practice. But there are many who fear that any form of standardization would defeat the very liberation for which Reform Judaism stands. For the same reason, Conservative Judaism also has not created a single book of law, which many Conservative Jews believe would stunt the natural growth and evolution in Judaism. On the other hand, both of these movements do provide written guidelines that explain their stand on issues of importance.

Even the Bible cannot be considered the unchanging standard for religious practice. The biblical laws concerning polygamy, interest, tithing, slavery, and a score of other subjects have been reinterpreted out of existence, ever since the Pharisees. In this sense, rabbinical law and the Bible are not identical. In biblical times, for instance, a childless widow was required to marry her husband's brother. This was known as levirate marriage. Release from this obligation entailed a special ceremony akin to divorce. This law was gradually modified until several centuries ago, when it was ended altogether by a rabbinic ban on this sort of marriage. Orthodox Jews preserve a vestige of the old law by continuing to require the ceremony of release. Thus, a Jew who followed the biblical command of levirate marriage would be violating the rabbinical law that forbids that practice.

8. *What Is Halachah?*

Halachah [hah-lah-KHAH or hah-LAH-khah] comes from a root meaning "walking," or "the way." It is one's path through the world, the way one should proceed. From this literal meaning, the word has come to mean "Jewish law."

All branches of Judaism use halachah, but they do so differently. Suppose you want to know whether it is moral to perform experiments on fetal tissue; whether smoking cigarettes is permissible; whether working in your garden violates Sabbath work regulations; or whether a synagogue can accept a donation from someone who has just been convicted of insider trading, so that there is reason to suspect that the donation comes from illegally gained income. These are all questions that have arisen in recent years. For a Jew, they are all *halachic* [hah-LAH-khic] questions, since they are about the way we should live our lives.

Halachic rulings usually proceed by the method known as case law, as in the American system: Until someone asks about something, rabbis do not rule on it. In Jewish law too, the first step is for someone to write a letter stating a problem and asking for guidance. Orthodox Jews usually write such letters to well-known halachic experts, rabbis renowned for their knowledge of the many

Jewish sources and for their intellect in dealing with them all. Other movements have official law committees to which questions are directed. Sending such a letter begins the process that will eventually result in an answer known as a *responsum* (pl., *responsa*).

The rabbi or committee goes patiently through the Bible, the Talmud, the medieval law codes, the mountains of commentary on all these books, and the volumes of precedent that exist in prior responsa. Also considered are relevant scientific and technological discoveries that earlier generations of Jews could not have known about.

Orthodox Jews work with less personal leeway in interpreting their sources than the non-Orthodox movements do, though all would agree that the history of Judaism demonstrates that Jewish law was consistently in flux. Biblical men were polygamous, for example, so a medieval rabbi issued an ordinance officially preventing a man from having more than one wife at a time. Earlier still, by the second century B.C.E., the Rabbis were disturbed by the ease with which a man could divorce his wife, or retain her in the marriage relationship even if he beat her. So they invented a marriage document that was a conditional promissory note; a woman who was unfairly treated by her husband could present it to the rabbinic court and demand payment for damages (in the first instance) and divorce as well (in the second). Using these and other such cases as their examples, liberal Jews make a point of claiming that what was binding or permissible in earlier times may not be desirable or even acceptable now; and similarly, that humanity may have developed to the point where we now consider something proper, even though our forebears many centuries ago did not— rabbis who are women, for example.

Conservative and Reconstructionist Jews emphasize the will of the community more than Reform Jews do, and Conservatives feel bound by what their sources tell them even as they struggle with the dictates of the times in which they live. Change is therefore slow and often difficult for Conservative Jews. Reform Judaism emphasizes the individual conscience, and in cases where one's conscience

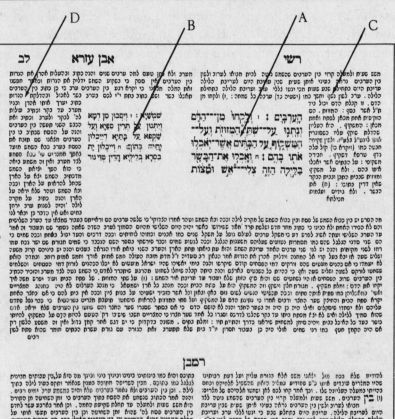

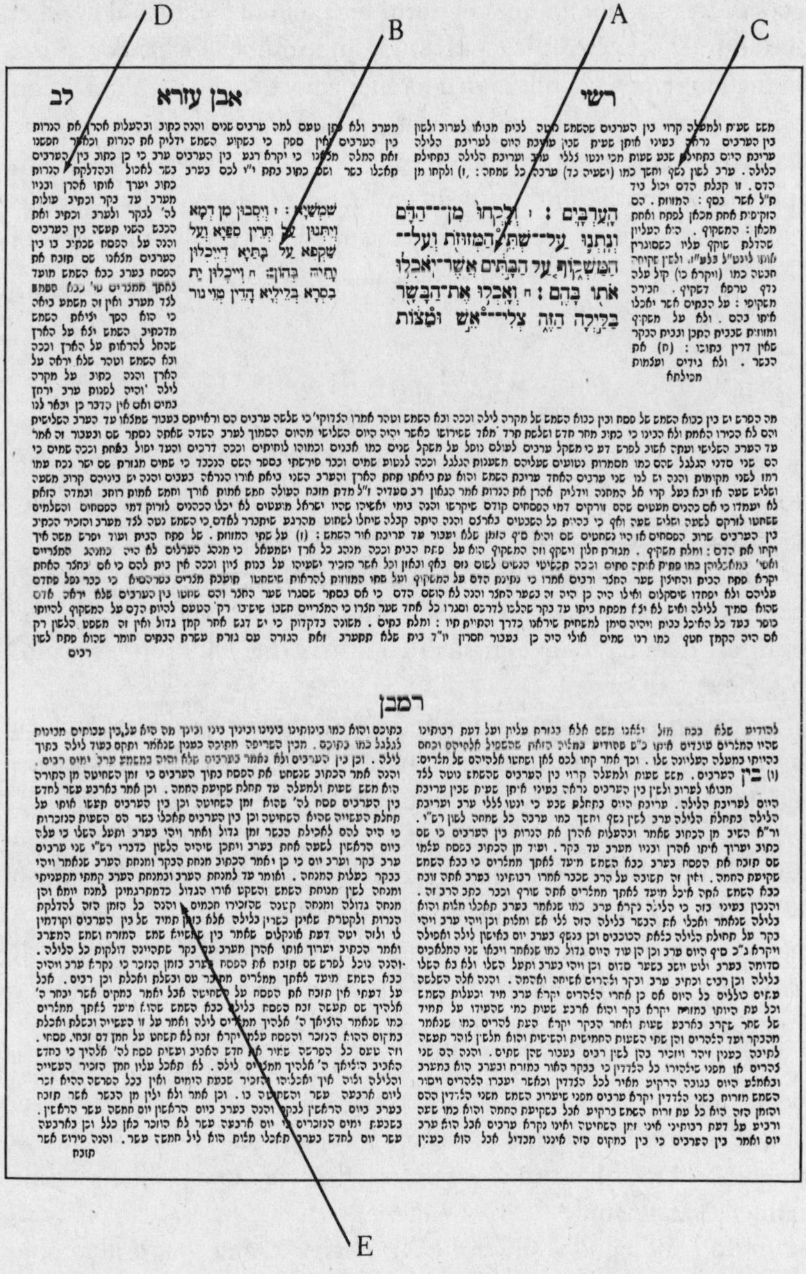

לב   אבן עזרא   רש"י

Center Torah text (Exodus 12:7–9):

וְלָקְחוּ מִן־הַדָּם וְנָתְנוּ עַל־שְׁתֵּי הַמְּזוּזֹת וְעַל־הַמַּשְׁקוֹף עַל הַבָּתִּים אֲשֶׁר־יֹאכְלוּ אֹתוֹ בָּהֶם: ח וְאָכְלוּ אֶת־הַבָּשָׂר בַּלַּיְלָה הַזֶּה צְלִי־אֵשׁ וּמַצּוֹת

רמב"ן

55

goes contrary to the sources, Reform Jews do not feel bound by what the sources say. Reform rabbis study the sources for guidance but in the long run feel empowered to offer advice that is a combination of many factors: traditional sources, individual conscience, and the standards of the age in which they live. All modern Jews take Jewish tradition seriously, but relatively few adhere to it slavishly. It is our guide from out of the past, to be consulted as we solve problems of the present.

9. *How Do Jews Read the Bible?*

Traditional Jewish books arrest your attention just by the way in which they are printed. The Bible, for example, is traditionally printed so that the biblical text appears only in the very center of the page (see illustration). Around the outside are a series of commentaries on the text, taken from many different eras. The example here has only four such commentaries, but some versions have many more.

The parallel columns in the middle (A and B) are the biblical text itself (A) and an Aramaic translation (B), which often contains variations that stretch back to antiquity.

C is the most famous commentary of all, a line-by-line explanation of the Bible prepared by Rabbi Shlomo ben (*ben* means "son of") Isaac of eleventh-century France. He is known as *Rashi*, a name formed by combining the Hebrew initials of his name: R (from *R*abbi), SH from the first Hebrew letter of *Sh*lomo), and the I of *I*saac. The "a" is added just to make pronunciation possible.

D is a medieval Spanish commentator, Ibn Ezra, who had been influenced by Islam and was especially interested in Hebrew grammar and the scientific meaning of unusual Hebrew words in the biblical text. E is from Spain too, the work of a brilliant mystic named Nachmanides.

So Jews spend a long time on a page. We do not read rapidly through the biblical text, so much as we read a single verse or two, and then let our eyes meander through the various commentaries on the page, playing with the various ways Jews in times past have read the passage before us. Rashi, especially, often cites the Talmud and midrash collections as well, so any given page of the book in our hands is like a guided tour through the inner landscape of the collective Jewish soul: all the way from an ancient Aramaic alternative version of the biblical text itself, to medieval mystics and rationalists, with stop-off points in classical rabbinic sources along the way.

Modern versions of such books exist in English too, with the commentaries selected and summarized judiciously by the editor, and updated with contemporary commentators as well. Most synagogues have such volumes and use them for discussions of the Torah reading during services.

10. *What Is Kabbalah?*

Kabbalah [kah-bah-LAH or kah-BAH-lah] (sometimes spelled Cabala) is the most important mystical tradition in Judaism. There was a time when European Christians too studied Kabbalah, believing that it contained secret knowledge about spirituality. Catherine the Great of Russia, for example, wanted to learn Hebrew, not as the tongue of the Bible, but in order to read Kabbalah.

At the end of the thirteenth century, a Spanish Jew named Moses de Leon produced a book called the **Zohar** [ZOE-hahr]. It was, he professed, a long-lost work, handed down from ancient days. People believed him. By the sixteenth century, the Zohar had become a virtual handbook of mystical lore for Kabbalists.

The new doctrine maintained that every word, even every letter, of Torah has not only an obvious interpretation, but an esoteric one as well. The secrets of creation were said to be available by reading between the lines of the biblical text. Every detail of scripture was carefully weighed to discover its secret meaning.

By calculating the hidden message, the Kabbalists described a universe in which the fate of humanity and even of God are inter-twined. God's primeval act of creation was said to have gone wrong, so that unintended evil had entered the cosmos. It is the human lot to suffer until the defect is repaired. For Kabbalists, therefore, repairing the universe is Judaism's supreme ethical goal. Every time a Jew does a *mitzvah* (see p. 71), every time a sacred act is performed, every time a good deed is done, the world moves inexorably forward to its ultimate destiny of complete repair: a state of being in which evil will have vanished and war and sickness be unknown. Repara-tion of the world is called **tikkun olam** [tee-KOON oh-LAHM]; and to this day, many Jews explain their purpose in life by saying that they are put on earth to play their own personal role in tikkun olam.

God may have started the process of creation eons ago; but it is up to us, God's partners in creation, to finish it.

Some Kabbalists thought they could even predict such things as the expected date of the messiah's arrival. Indeed several so-called "messiahs" eventually appeared, using the authority of Kabbalah to establish their legitimacy. The most famous was the seventeenth-century Shabbetai Zevi [SHAB-tye TZVEE]; he eventually con-verted to Islam rather than be executed by the sultan, who consid-ered his successful religious movement potentially revolutionary and therefore dangerous.

But Kabbalah should not be judged by the false messiahs it has produced. For centuries it has elevated Jewish spirituality to heights undreamed of by pure rationalism. Jews who were exiled from Spain in 1492, for instance, faced understandable despair as they were forced to establish new communities in strange lands on the other side of the Mediterranean. It was Kabbalah that sustained them in their time of anguish. Kabbalah assured them that the fragmented world where dreams are shattered is not the ultimate state of exis-tence, and not even the only possibility for human experience. It taught them to surmount the drudgery of the everyday with spiritual exercises that would grant them actual mystical union with God. Momentarily, at least, God would be as close as breathing; pain and anxiety would be replaced by the surety and radiance of God's love.

Moreover, every Sabbath could exemplify that ultimate world with its closeness to God. Shabbat was thus "a taste of the world to come," twenty-four hours of sheer bliss. Using Kabbalistic insight as their basis, these mystics revised the Friday evening liturgy, inventing a ritual for greeting the Sabbath, and celebrating their meal of Sabbath eve with hour after hour of singing.

Kabbalistic adepts developed their personal spirituality by using music and meditation to achieve a spiritual trance. One famous Kabbalist, for instance, Eleazar Azikri, composed a well-known poem entitled *Yedid Nefesh* [y'DEED NEH-fesh], which is sung as a popular Shabbat song now. Each of its four stanzas begins with one of the four Hebrew letters that constitute the ineffable name of God. In his diary, the author explains that he would recite his poem while staring at the four letters until he perceived them as four leaping flames coming together in divine fire.

Yet the mystics followed Jewish law to the letter. One of them was Joseph Caro, who wrote the Shulchan Arukh, the best-known Jewish law code of all (see p. 52). He maintained that at night, a divine messenger communicated with him, directing his efforts.

The insights of the Zohar and later Kabbalistic works are usually elusive, requiring the prior mastery of the entire mystical system. But sometimes, one comes across a bit of immediate wisdom that proves memorable. Consider this view of the day we die: "On the day of death, it seems that we have lived but a single day."

Nineteenth-century rationalists saw Kabbalah as too mystical to be worthy of study, so for a long time it was ignored. But Kabbalah has received a new lease on life. Popular books about it abound, and it is a favorite subject on university campuses. Its metaphoric descriptions of the universe and God address such grand human themes as loneliness and alienation, and its emphasis on repairing a universe where evil still abounds challenges us to retain our steadfastness of purpose, come what may.

11. *Is There Such a Thing as Jewish Music?*

Though we are the people of the book, we have never been blind to spiritual art nor deaf to religious music. Jewish music, especially, has a rich history in Judaism. In ancient times, when sacrifices were offered, Temple worship was accompanied by a veritable orchestra, even though we have no record of what those instruments sounded like or what music they played. The Psalms speak of lyres, harps, trumpets, and drums as they urge us, "Sing a joyful song" to God.

The oldest Jewish music known to us is the system of traditional chants associated with synagogue worship, going back (in part) to the twelfth to the fifteenth centuries, if not earlier. But Jewish music has always been central to our prayers. Its sound varies with the host culture in which Jews have lived. The melodies heard in a Moroccan synagogue bear no resemblance to those sung by an eastern European cantor. In the former case, the sounds are distinctly Oriental; the latter has overtones of northern European and Slavic musical forms.

The late Rabbi Abba Hillel Silver once referred satirically to a custom that had been "hallowed by twenty years of tradition." Much music that Jews think must go back to antiquity is actually relatively modern—even, perhaps, less than a generation old. American composers this century have added the newest chapter to Jewish music. Modern worship features not only the traditional chanting, but also classical art music, songs from Israel, sophisticated contemporary compositions, and even folk music composed (in some cases) by teenagers in summer camps.

On the grounds that they are mourning the destruction of the Temple in Jerusalem, and also because they conscientiously try not to model their worship after that of non-Jews, Orthodox congregations do not allow musical instruments on the Sabbath, so music there is limited to cantorial vocal performance, chants, and traditional tunes that everyone sings. On the other side of the spectrum, Reform congregations may have an organ, a piano, or even flute and cello accompaniment on special occasions, and often a guitar for the folk idiom.

Music written by Jews, however, is not necessarily on that account Jewish. George Gershwin's "It Ain't Necessarily So" is modeled directly upon the traditional music for the blessing its Jewish composer had sung when he was called to the Torah for his bar mitzvah! But the use of a Jewish melody does not make that familiar song Jewish. On the other hand, composers such as Leonard Bernstein and Ernest Bloch have written music that is Jewish— Bloch wrote a sacred service, equivalent in scope to the great masses composed by classical Christian composers, and Bernstein wrote a composition called *Kaddish*, exploring the theme of martyrdom and death after the Holocaust.

12. *Is There Such a Thing as Jewish Art?*

What has been said about music applies equally to art. A Jewish artist depicting a scene from the life of Jesus would not be producing Jewish art. Does that mean that the work of a non-Jewish artist portraying a character from the Hebrew Bible, Michelangelo's David, for instance, is Jewish art? Jews may admire, even love, the statue in Florence, but we can hardly claim it as "Jewish." Since the personalities of the Hebrew Bible have been embraced by both Jews and Christians, it would be inaccurate to claim the Sistine Chapel scenes of the Garden of Eden and the Flood as Jewish. But other artists—Marc Chagall, for instance—have left us a great deal of Jewish art, such as his pictorial re-creations of eastern European Jewish life.

So there is Jewish art. Contrary to popular opinion, the prohibition in the Ten Commandments against making a graven image was not interpreted by Jews as banning art in general. One ancient synagogue is surrounded with wall paintings of biblical and midrashic scenes. Others have beautiful mosaic floors. Medieval prayer books were often illustrated with ritual or biblical scenes in living color, and even embossed with gold leaf. Then too for both synagogue and home, artists have created many ceremonial accoutrements that add beauty to objects used in Jewish ritual: the covers and crowns that sit on the Torah scroll, for instance, or the wine cups and spice boxes for home ritual.

Jewish art has had a fine renaissance in the last few decades. Most synagogues have Judaica shops that display newly created artistic ritual objects. Many new prayer books are illustrated by contemporary artists. In Israel, the old center where Jewish mysticism once flourished—a northern mountain town called Safed [pronounced tsfaht]—is now practically one large art colony. And here in North America, Jewish artists are everywhere at work expressing the Jewish experience in today's art media so as to express Jewish visions in ways that surpass the expressive capacity of mere words.

III

Rituals and Customs:

The Warmth of Tradition

One of the most distinctive features of Judaism is its great variety of rituals covering every aspect of life. Elsewhere (Part VIII), we talk about the rituals of a life cycle. Here we survey some of the Jewish rituals for home and synagogue.

Every human relation, every human aspiration, means more to us if it is clothed in some symbolic act. From the food we eat to the very passing of time—the birth of a child, say, or the death of a parent—our lives are a mixture of the ordinary and the profound, reminding us that human existence can be beautiful or painful, but above all, inexplicable. Why should we have food or time at all? Why do people live and die? In the end, a power greater than ourselves controls our destiny. There are moments when our thoughts transcend the ordinary and we feel ourselves propelled toward the sacred source that lies behind life's mysteries. To celebrate the sacred, we develop rituals.

In a ritual, ordinary things become symbols of something greater than themselves. An engagement ring, for example, is more than a metal band that goes around a finger. It is a symbol of love. I recall a couple soon to be married who had no money but insisted on buying an engagement ring from Woolworth's for seventy-five cents. It was the symbol that mattered. Or consider the flag, which is not just a decorated patch of fabric flapping in the wind. A few years ago when some people threatened to burn the flag in angry protest, the president went on the air to suggest jail terms for the protesters, and Congress considered a special constitutional amendment to make burning the flag unconstitutional.

Jewish rituals are similar, in that they invest "ordinary" acts and things with symbolic meaning, thus moving us beyond the ordinary to the holy. They relate ourselves and what we do to the Source of our being.

To say such ceremonies are superfluous is to say that words can get along without music, or that having prose, we need no poetry. But words alone become "wordy," and prose is "prosaic." Music and poetry, on the other hand, raise the casual to the important and the humdrum to the exalted. Rituals lend symbolic poetry to life; they are the music of our souls; they provide the inner passion without which life becomes hardly worth continuing.

The Hebrew word for holy is **kadosh** [kah-DOSH], from the Hebrew root K-D-SH. In its various forms, that root and its concept of sanctifying the ordinary appear throughout Jewish ritual. On the Sabbath and festivals the Jew recites **Kiddush** [kee-DOOSH or KID-ish], the "Sanctification" prayer that celebrates the arrival of sacred time. Reciting the prayer as we sit down to eat dinner on the eve of a sacred day is a simple act, yet it evokes the beauty and serenity that the Sabbath promises.

The prayer called the **Tefillah** [t'fee-LAH], a central piece of liturgy recited at every service, contains a section called the **Kedushah** [k'doo-SHAH or k'DOO-shah], in which the worshiper repeats the words of the prophet Isaiah, declaring God to be "Holy, holy, holy."

Marriage too is sacred, so a wedding is called **Kiddushin** [kee-doo-SHEEN], thus indicating the sanctity of the relationship between bride and groom; when someone dies, mourners say the **Kaddish** [KAH-dish] prayer, an affirmation that despite the most profound grief, life is sacred, filled with the promise of the ultimate reign of God, of which the narrow window of our lives is but the tiniest reflection.

The late Rabbi Milton Steinberg often spoke of the consolation that the Kaddish afforded him. "It is easier for me to let go of life with all its treasures, because these things are not and never have been mine. They belong to the Universe and the God who stands behind it. True, I have been privileged to enjoy them for an hour but they were always a loan to be recalled.

"And I let go of them the more easily because I know that as parts of the divine economy they will not be lost. The sunset, the bird's song, the baby's smile, the thunder of music, the surge of great poetry, the dreams of the heart, and my own being—all these I can well trust to the God who made them. There is a poignancy and regret about giving them up, but no anxiety. When they slip from my hands they will pass to hands better, stronger, and wiser than mine. . . .

"Life is dear; let us then hold it tight while yet we may. But we must hold it loosely also! It is at once infinitely precious and yet a thing lightly to be surrendered. Because of God, we clasp the world, but with relaxed hands; we embrace it, but with open arms."

I have talked so far about the rituals called for by Jewish law, the obligations mandated by the many rabbinic legal works (mostly the Talmud) that constitute the way of Torah. These legal requirements are the ritual side of what we have called **halachah** [hah-lah-KHAH or hah-LAH-khah] (see p. 53), literally, the Jewish way of walking in the world. But Jewish life also contains a variety of customs that have grown up over the years, some of which may not be technically necessitated by the Bible or the Talmud, but which are followed carefully by many Jews nonetheless. Such a custom is called a **minhag** [min-HAHG or MIN-hahg]. (The plural is **minhagim** [min-hah-GEEM].)

It is therefore hard to draw any rigid line separating law from custom. A Jewish saying actually holds that a strongly held custom becomes law. Another ancient source holds, "Custom takes precedence over law." Jews used to praying one way but who find themselves in a place where people worship another way are counseled to follow "the custom of the place" (**minhag hamakom** [min-HAHG hah-mah-KOME]). We have respect for each other's way of doing things.

The history of Judaism reveals many religious laws that originated in long-accepted folk practices. Solomon Schechter, an early leader of Conservative Judaism, described this phenomenon with the curious phrase "catholic Israel" (catholic in the sense of universal). When the vast majority of Jews adopt a certain ritual, it ultimately becomes law. In any standard manual of Jewish law, we often find such introductory comments as: "This is the practice among Italian Jews; the French follow another custom," or, "Among the Spanish Jews, there is a tendency to be lenient in this matter; German Jews are far more stringent." No authority suggests that there is a single unalterable form of practice, or, for that matter, even a single prayer book to be followed by all Jews.

The pliability of Judaism has always permitted a great range of traditions. Compared to Protestantism, for instance, Judaism has known relatively little sectarianism, and Jews who consider themselves Reform or Conservative, for instance, by and large see each other as exercising free choice along the gamut of options available to contemporary Jewish men and women. This one likes lots of Hebrew in services, that one does not, and so forth. But we will readily join each other in worship, since more than we are a particular denomination of Jew, we are just Jews.

QUESTIONS IN PART III

1. *What Is a Mitzvah?*
2. *How Do Jews Decide What Rules to Keep?*
3. *Are Some Jewish Customs Just Superstition?*
4. *What Are Rabbis and What Do They Do?*
5. *What Is a Cantor (a Chazzan)?*
6. *Is There a Priesthood in Judaism?*
7. *What Are the Most Important Prayers that Jews Recite?*
8. *What Is a Minyan? Are Some Prayers Said Only if Ten or More People Are Present?*
9. *What Is "Keeping Kosher"?*
10. *What Special Clothes Do Jews Wear?*
11. *Are There Special Jewish Foods?*
12. *Do Jews Have Their Own Language?*
13. *What Jewish Meal Rituals Are There?*

1. *What Is a Mitzvah?*

If one were to look for a single word to catch the spirit of Judaism it would be **mitzvah** [MITS-vuh or meets-VAH]. Technically, a mitzvah is "a divine command," what God requires of you.

Judaism has few accounts of finding God in a momentary flash of discovery. The essence of Judaism is a day-to-day, hour-by-hour practicing of **mitzvot** [mits-VOTE or meets-VOTE] (plural of mitzvah), deeds that are pleasing in the sight of God. Authentic religious experience for the Jew is the joyous feeling that we have performed a mitzvah. The word is used nontechnically to mean any good deed, an act of kindness, of compassion, or of justice, for the benefit of another human being.

In the technical sense, a mitzvah may be of various sorts. Many are ritualistic acts: eating unleavened bread (matzah—see p. 225) on Passover, dwelling in a sukkah on the feast of Sukkot (see p. 219), or kindling the Sabbath candles. They may equally well be ethical: giving to charity, working in a soup kitchen, honoring the dead as a funeral procession passes by. A child who becomes sufficiently adult to be expected to take the mitzvot seriously and to be held accountable for practicing them is called a bar mitzvah (for boys) or a bat mitzvah (for girls), literally, a member of the class of people who live by and for the responsibility of doing a mitzvah.

The Rabbis were particularly passionate about the proper way to do mitzvot. They must not be performed merely out of a sense of duty; one does them for their own sake, not to gain anything thereby; we hurry to do them, knowing that one mitzvah tends to lead to another. Some mitzvot have limitations—for example, you give to charity, but you may not give away everything you have, since you yourself are obliged to enjoy God's bounty. Others have no limitations: study of Torah, for instance, since one can never learn too much, and because it is said that Torah study is equal to all the other mitzvot combined, in that study of God's word leads to the will to do God's mitzvot. In a joyous acceptance of mitzvot, sincere Jews live up to the demands of our faith. The ideal life is a string of mitzvot performed every day.

2. How Do Jews Decide What Rules to Keep?

Rabbinic tradition has provided us with a vast repertoire of rules covering every aspect of life. Some are laws, in the sense that the Talmud or the law codes mandate them, and others are just customs, but so overlaid with tradition that they might as well be laws. It is difficult deciding which ones apply to our day and how they make life more meaningful for those who keep them.

Some Jews make the primary commitment to be Orthodox. This elemental decision makes many further decisions unnecessary. Of course Orthodox Jews still must study to discover what the rules are and then must think through how best to apply them, but the option of choosing *not* to keep a rule is no longer open to them. As you move to the other end of the spectrum, you find first Conservative and Reconstructionist Jews and then Reform Jews, all of whom take the rules seriously but have made the primary decision that not all the rules are intended for our time. They therefore have the additional burden of determining which ones are outdated, which ones run counter to modern Jewish ethical stands (such as rules favoring men in ritual matters, a position that is not in keeping with modern egalitarianism), and by contrast, which ones God surely intends for us in our own day and age. Conservative and Reconstructionist Judaism tend to decide these matters as a group. Law committees pass regulations, and then local communities decide whether to enforce them. Reform Jews operate with the principle of individual autonomy. Not the communities, but the individual men and women themselves determine the extent to which they consider traditional rules binding upon them.

Many Jews on the liberal end of the spectrum advocate trying out particular practices in the hope that they will prove meaningful in their lives. They will want to keep Shabbat, but may not know in advance how to go about doing that. So they take on the various Sabbath mitzvot, keeping those that seem to bring about the spirit of Sabbath peace and sanctity that they seek. They will decide to have a Jewish home, but once again, only after experiencing the various home ceremonies will they know which ones really speak to them and best express or embody their Jewish values.

Being Jewish is not a static thing. Human nature is in flux; we constantly grow in life, and as we do, the rituals that we follow are likely to change. What we find meaningful without children is not necessarily what we crave if there are children in our homes. What provides spiritual comfort is different for a couple newly married and a single elderly retiree. The rituals of Judaism are actually symbolic ways to shape our lives around a single set of values and the feeling that we belong to a history greater than the scope of our own existence. They point toward the life of the spirit, and remind us of the covenant we have with God. They provide visible reminders of Jewish commitment, especially at home. But precisely which rituals we keep is a matter of choice, which may change as we do.

3. *Are Some Jewish Customs Just Superstition?*

Many people object to religious rituals or customs on the grounds that they are rooted in superstition. It is true that especially in antiquity and the Middle Ages many common superstitions were adopted by Jews, but in general, the practices that lasted were imbued with religious meaning that transcended their superstitious origins. People who follow such customs today do so because they know that how things begin is not as important as what they end up being.

On the other hand, some people find no higher meaning in these customs. They may, therefore, simply decide not to keep them. Ritual is not an "all or nothing" proposition. Wanting the richness that a life of ritual provides, most Jews elect to follow even those customs that have superstitious origins, as long as their extra spiritual significance warrants their continued observance; but they feel free also to dispense with customs that previous generations may have considered "necessary" but that people today find meaningless.

A good example is the Jewish practice of covering the mirrors in a house of mourning. In all probability, that custom is rooted in the superstitious notion that the spirit of the dead hovers menacingly in the mourners' home; confused by its own image, it may decide to take up permanent residence there. Many modern Jews therefore find no purpose in covering the mirrors. On the other hand, other Jews still do so, not because they are afraid of confusing the spirits, but because they interpret the covering of mirrors as an attempt to banish needless vanity in our moments of grief. Primping in front of a mirror hardly befits a house of mourning, where those who enter should be considering the inner spiritual and moral dimensions of life, the values for which the deceased stood, and the need for those who are still alive to come to terms with God before their own death arrives.

Rabbis therefore vary in their advice about such customs. Some will simply inform people of the "rules" and assume that the higher meaning implicit in them will become apparent as they are followed. Others will tell people the entire gamut of customs and then leave it to them to determine which ones they want to keep and which ones not.

Sometimes, people follow old customs just because they are traditional. They may be unaware of their roots in popular superstition, and they may not even care. Only the most confirmed rationalist would advocate doing away with the automatic "Gesundheit" (or the Hebrew equivalent, **Labriyut** [lah-bree-YOOT], "to your health") evoked by someone who sneezes—a custom widely practiced by almost every faith and nationality; or such common expressions as **Mazal tov**! [MAH-z'l tuff or mah-ZAHL TOVE], which originally meant "May you enjoy an auspicious constellation" but which nowadays is the Jewish equivalent of "Congratulations!" So too, most Ashkenazic Jews observe the taboo against naming children after living relatives, not because they really believe that doing so will cause an early death to the person whose name the child has acquired, but because there is a certain warmth about following tradition for its own sake.

On the other hand, some superstitious traditions may have negative consequences. In Orthodox synagogues, children with living parents are sent out of the sanctuary during the memorial service for fear that if they mistakenly recite memorial prayers, their parents will die before their time. Obviously the Orthodox Jews who follow this custom find it meaningful, and do not necessarily believe in the superstitious reason that once motivated it. Most Reform Jews, however, find the custom undesirable because the memorial service in Reform liturgy has been expanded to include victims of the Holocaust, and they believe children should be present to say a prayer for the six million who lost their lives and who may have no family members left to cherish their memory.

In the long run, then, it is not the superstitious origin of customs that matters. It is what we make of them. Just the fact that they are time-honored components of Jewish tradition may be sufficient for us to follow them; or they may have secondary meanings that the religious imagination has invested in them over the years. But they may also be needless accretions to Judaism, folk customs from eastern Europe, perhaps, that simply get in the way of our attempt to live full religious lives. If they are not matters central to Judaism, they may then be abandoned without fear or guilt.

4. *What Are Rabbis and What Do They Do?*

Literally, rabbis are teachers, who transmit the Jewish heritage to young and old alike. Their authority is based not on their position but on their learning. Rabbis lay claim to no special privileges, human or divine. They are not in any sense intermediaries between their congregants and God. In Orthodox practice, rabbis do not usually even lead worship services. Any well-informed worshiper may do so.

The same theory of radical democracy is held by liberal Jews too, although it is more likely that the rabbi will lead services and give a sermon as well.

There is no religious hierarchy in the Jewish faith. The influence of the individual rabbi is determined solely by his or her ability to gain and to keep the respect of laypeople and colleagues as an interpreter of Jewish law and tradition.

The title *rabbi* was first used roughly nineteen hundred years ago. Before that time, scholars even of the stature of Hillel bore no title. The Gospels refer to Jesus as "Rabbi," but in so doing the Gospel writers are incorrectly reading back their own practice to an earlier time. Jesus, like Hillel, would have gone only by his name.

Modern American rabbis are graduates of seminaries that offer a course of religious studies on a graduate level. Four or five years of graduate studies are generally required. Unlike the clergy of the Christian church, rabbis are ordained by the seminary, not by their denomination or synagogue body; and some seminaries do not even use the word *ordination,* because they honor an old tradition that true ordination may occur only in the Holy Land. Liberal seminaries, on the other hand, do use the word *ordination* and award an ordination certificate called a **semichah** [s'mee-KHAH or SMEE-khah].

In addition to traditional religious training, which emphasizes mastery of biblical and rabbinic literature, modern rabbinical students equip themselves in the human sciences, particularly those that are required for counseling skills, educational expertise, and management tasks. They are expected also to demonstrate leadership, compassion, and sound judgment; to acquire the discipline and depth required for a lifetime of studying Torah; and to personify those ethical character traits that are the model of human behavior and the Jewish ideal.

Orthodox seminaries are less exacting in their demands for secular education, but more demanding in their emphasis on mastery of Jewish sources. Their graduates will function as interpreters of Jewish law, and must demonstrate absolute competence at handling even the most detailed issues that their congregants (unlike congregants in the other movements) might want to know about.

Rabbis are hired the way any manager is. They interview for positions and negotiate contracts with the boards of the institution for which they work. However, they see themselves as only partly answerable to the board, since they have duties that they owe the larger community (serving on a communal advisory group for a hospital, for instance). They have particular responsibility for matters Jewish, whether within their institution or not. The rabbi of the local synagogue, for example, will feel obliged to give a Jewish burial even to Jews who do not belong to the synagogue in question. Most of all, rabbis believe they are ultimately answerable to God, and must act out of a Jewish conscience informed by the study of sacred texts.

Within the limits of their contracts, rabbis may leave or may be asked to leave their positions and seek another one. David Einhorn, for instance, was a rabbi in Baltimore when the Civil War broke out. Rather than serve the cause of the Confederacy, he left his position to go to a northern state where he would not have to defend slavery. During the Vietnam conflict, some rabbis who preached against the war found that their contracts were not renewed. Rabbis struggle every day with things their congregants want them to do (and that they would often like to do as well), on one hand, and the limitations imposed upon them by their reading of Jewish tradition, on the other. Probably the greatest conflict nowadays centers on interfaith marriages. Many rabbis would like to satisfy their congregants by performing such weddings for them, but they feel that the Jewish tradition does not license them for such a role.

Rabbis lead personal lives as well as public ones. Marriage is not only permitted, it is held to be desirable. Most rabbis thus yearn for the same sort of home life that any busy professional does, balancing the multiple tasks of their rabbinic calling with the demands of homemaking and parenthood.

The modern rabbis' duties parallel those of the American clergy generally. If they go into congregational life, and about 60 percent of all rabbis do, they are responsible for religious education, synagogue worship, preaching, presiding over life-cycle ceremonial, and pastoral guidance. More and more, they function also as managers of busy synagogues and large staffs, work with multiple committees formulating synagogue policy, and execute that policy in creative programs.

Other rabbis enter the world of academia; become chaplains in colleges, prisons, and hospitals; or hold administrative positions in Jewish institutions. Many Orthodox rabbis do not work as rabbis at all. They study to become rabbis simply because it is a mitzvah for every Jew to study. If they can afford it, they might even study all their lives and do nothing else. Most have to earn a living eventually, however, and only then do they leave the seminary and get a job.

Rabbis are expected to fulfill three roles. 1) They have a ritualistic function, in that they are to invoke God's presence through involving other Jews in worship and the study of Torah. 2) They are pastors, bringing religious wisdom and compassion to bear on the lives of the sick, the lonely, and the confused. 3) As inheritors of the ancient prophetic role, they must remain the conscience of their community, calling others to the highest standard of ethical activity. Their success is measured by their ability to do all three things, and by the trust and affection they enjoy among their followers.

5. *What Is a Cantor (a Chazzan)?*

The role of the cantor—**chazzan** [khah-ZAHN or KHAH-z'n] in Hebrew—as synagogue functionary actually goes back farther than that of the rabbi. The chazzan was originally the person who was generally in charge of whatever happened in the synagogue. In the first two centuries C.E., **chazzanim** [khah-zah-NEEM] (the plural of chazzan) did everything from clean the synagogue buildings to engage in debate with non-Jews over the validity of Judaism vis-à-vis the rival faiths of the late Roman Empire. Among the chazzan's many tasks was the leading of worship.

But the details of worship grew. Both the worship text and the chant to which it was sung became increasingly complex, so that eventually, chazzanim became specialists in leading worship, at the expense of the other tasks they once had performed.

Today, the chazzan is an expert in the multifaceted art of Jewish music; the person, therefore, charged with leading the sung sections of our liturgy, and of transmitting to the congregation the musical heritage of the Jewish people. The chazzan's role varies with the way the liturgy is conducted in the various movements.

To understand the duties of a traditionalist cantor one must recognize the idiosyncratic way in which traditionalist Jewish worship is conducted. Prayers are not read by the congregants; they are chanted. But they are not chanted neatly in unison; the cantor intones the end of a paragraph, which serves as a cue for the congregation to begin the next one. A sort of murmur fills the room as congregants read the paragraph out loud, each at his or her own speed and in his or her own way (I say "his or her" because even though traditionalist worship is primarily for men, modern Orthodoxy has attempted to empower women as well). At the end of the congregational chant, the cantor concludes the prayer and the whole process begins again. This traditional form of prayer is called a **davening** [DAH-v'ning]. Jews will say of their worship, "It is time to **daven**."

But the cantor is above all a musical expert who knows what chant to use for what occasion. Cantors master the oral art of centuries. They know that the same prayer echoes with a different melody depending on the occasion. Discriminating listeners recognize the time of year by the tune cantors use.

Cantors in the liberal branches of Judaism master the same musical standards, but the worship at which they officiate is very different from that of Orthodoxy. Influenced by modern Western worship, Reform worship is egalitarian regarding men and women, and it features many worship styles, not just the responsive chanting of a Hebrew text. In line with Western aesthetics, it has discouraged people from chanting each prayer out loud at their own speed and in their own way. Cantors thus play a more complex role here. They chant some of the prayers in the age-old manner, using the distinctive chanting pattern of the day or season; but they also lead congregational singing and introduce melodies that are not hundreds of years old but have been written by modern Jewish composers and thus reflect alternative musical renditions of a given prayer. They are masters of ancient and modern music simultaneously.

Modern Reform cantors consider themselves clergy. They train in more than music. Like rabbis, they are prepared for a variety of congregational duties beyond their primary musical role. They too may make pastoral hospital calls, arrange synagogue programming, teach bar mitzvah and bat mitzvah children, and so on.

Modern Conservative cantors vary in the way they see their task. Some are more like their Orthodox colleagues, while others work in synagogues where the worship and the conception of a cantor's broader role come closer to Reform.

Theoretically, any knowledgeable and musically able member of the congregation may serve as cantor. But, as with rabbis, the increasing complexity of the synagogue and its worship has transformed the cantorate into a profession requiring specialized learning. In addition, ancient rabbinic teaching insisted that only people of the highest moral standards conduct our worship. Thus chazzanim should be held accountable for the same uniformity of purpose as rabbis. In an ideal temple, rabbi and cantor are a team, combining their joint commitment to Jewish continuity and their service to humanity with their individual specialized training, thus reinforcing each other's calling. Rabbis are expert in interpreting Jewish texts; cantors interpret Jewish music.

6. *Is There a Priesthood in Judaism?*

There is no priesthood in Judaism that parallels that of the Roman Catholic, Episcopal, and Eastern churches. However, Orthodox and Conservative Jews still regard as priests those men who claim to be the descendants of Aaron, brother of Moses and first high priest of the tabernacle in the wilderness. They are called **Kohanim** [koe-hah-NEEM] (sing., **Kohen** [koe-HAYN or KOE-hayn]), and are awarded a variety of honorary functions in religious ritual. The same is true of people who claim to be descendants of the ancient tribe of Levi. As Levites, they too are given unique ritual status, just as they were in the Temple of old. Most Jews are neither priests nor Levites (**Levi** [lay-VEE or LAY-vee], in Hebrew). They are called just **yisra'el** [yis-rah-AYL], a regular Israelite.

In keeping with its egalitarian philosophy, Reform Judaism

does not recognize the priestly or Levitical descent, and insists instead that all Jews are the same: just Jews.

Of course, it is almost impossible to know for sure that one is a Kohen or a Levite. A Jew bearing the name of Cohen, Kohn, Kahn or even Katz may claim priestly descent, and people named Levy, Levine, Levinson, and so on may say that they are Levites. Also people with altogether different names may have family traditions that they are Kohanim or Levites. Descent of this kind is passed on through the male line, not the female.

A Kohen is in no sense clergy. But in the Orthodox synagogue, he enjoys certain ritual privileges and has several specific liturgical tasks, by virtue of his presumed illustrious heredity. During the reading of the Torah in synagogue services, for example, it is customary to call people to stand beside the Torah and recite blessings that thank God for giving the Torah to Israel. A Kohen is the first person given that honor, and a Levite is the second. Also, on certain occasions, in traditional synagogues, the Kohanim all together bless the congregation, in the formula taken from the Book of Numbers. The blessing is intoned with much solemnity, the Kohen raising his two hands over the heads of the congregants with thumbs and forefingers touching and the forefingers of each hand divided to form the letter "V." It is customary for the congregation not to gaze at the Kohanim during the moments of blessing.

In most American Orthodox congregations the blessing by priests takes place only on the three major festivals, but in Israel it occurs every Sabbath.

The Kohen also participates in the ceremony of Pidyon Haben (see p. 245).

A vestige of the original sanctity of the Temple priesthood remains in two restrictions observed by the religious Kohen to this day: The Kohen may not enter a cemetery except for the burial of his closest relatives; and he may not marry a divorcée.

Levites may recall their ancient ancestors who were responsible (among other things) for the physical care of the sanctuary, and who constituted a sacred choir at the Temple. Modern-day Levites retain the privilege of being called to the reading of the Torah immediately following the Kohen, but have no formal synagogue duties anymore.

7. What Are the Most Important Prayers that Jews Recite?

Traditionally, Jews have prayed twice each day, morning and evening. The latter service is actually two services combined, one for the afternoon just ending, and one for the evening just starting. Most services have a common structure. After some warmup time in which worshipers recite psalms and other material, there is a formal call to prayer, followed by the central affirmation of Jewish faith, the **Shema** [sh'MAH]: "Hear O Israel, the Eternal is our God, the Eternal is One" (Deut. 6:4). The Shema is surrounded by blessings praising God for creation, revelation, and redemption. At the same time, the worshiper recites from the Bible: "You shall love the Eternal, your God, with all your heart, with all your soul, and with all your might" (Deut. 6:5).

A second core prayer is the **Tefillah** [t'fee-LAH], also called the **Amidah** [ah-mee-DAH or ah-MEE-dah]. It is a string of blessings, many of them petitionary, asking God for such things as wisdom, health, and peace. Traditionally, the entire prayer is recited while standing, in semisilent devotion, as worshipers read through the benedictions at their own speed.

Concluding every worship service is the **Alenu** [ah-LAY-noo], which thanks God for the particular destiny of the Jewish people and looks ahead with hope to the day when everyone in the world will be united under the reign of God.

Another well-known prayer is the **Kaddish** [KAH-dish], yet one more instance of asserting our faith in the ultimate dominion of God. It is actually very similar to the Lord's Prayer in Christianity, and was probably composed by an unknown Rabbi at about the same time and in much the same way as Jesus did when he told his followers how to pray. Oddly enough, even though it has nothing to do with death, it eventually came to be seen largely as a prayer that mourners say. It is customary, therefore, for people who have lost a loved one during the past year and for people marking the anniversary of a death in the family to rise in the midst of the worshiping congregation and recite the Kaddish as a demonstration of their faith in God despite their loss, their insistence on hope rather than despair, and their determination to pass on a loving memory of their deceased from generation to generation.

Judaism's distinctive spirituality emphasizes praise and trust: praise of a God who created this beautiful universe that we all enjoy, and who made a covenant with us, giving us the wisdom of Torah; and trust that our lives are not in vain, that any single one of us can make a difference in the lives of others. Praise and trust coalesce in a unique form of Jewish prayer that individuals may say silently as they find the world opening up to them in all its brilliance and design. This prayer is the blessing: in Hebrew, a **berachah** [b'rah-KHAH or B'ROH-khah], or the plural, **berachot** [b'rah-KHOTE]. Jews talk all the time about "saying a berachah," and have several of them memorized for specific occasions.

Blessings are often just single sentences, beginning **Baruch atah adonai** . . . [bah-ROOKH ah-TAH ah-doe-NYE], "Praised are You, God. . . ." There then follows a reference to whatever we are in the midst of praising God for doing.

Judaism provides blessings for almost every moment of the waking day. On rising from sleep, for instance, we thank God for having "returned our soul to us"; and at bedtime, we ask God to give us peace in our sleep: "Shelter us . . . and let us not sleep the sleep of death." Traditional bedtime worship for children emphasizes trust in God. While lying in bed, and just before closing their eyes for sleep, the child prays the Shema (see p. 83) and adds, "Let me lie down in peace and rise again in peace. . . . Into Your hand I place my spirit. . . ."

If we have come through a dangerous situation safely—a hospital operation, perhaps, or a car accident—we praise God for rewarding us with goodness.

Before a trip, we recite **Tefillat Haderech** [t'fee-LAHT hah-DEH-rekh], a "prayer for the journey," in the hope of God's protection along the way.

Because of its innate trust in both God and God's world, Judaism affirms the value of life and life's pleasures. It is therefore a religion that urges us to pay attention to the wonderful universe about us. To help us do so, it provides blessings for all of life's bounties: seeing a rainbow; experiencing a thunderstorm; observing the first blossoms of springtime; putting on new clothes; even eating our first garden produce, as each crop ripens year after year.

The Israeli writer S. Y. Agnon traveled to Sweden to receive a Nobel prize. He and the other recipients of the famous award were coached in the etiquette of appearing before the Swedish king whose job it was to hand out the honors. Contrary to proper procedure, however, Agnon was seen muttering something to the king. Later people asked him what he was saying.

"I have made it a point to say blessings in every possible circumstance," he explained. "Among the many blessings of Jewish tradition, is an ancient one that you say upon seeing a king or queen: 'Praised are You, Eternal our God, for sharing Your glory with mortals.' But who sees kings and queens these days? So I am grateful for the Nobel prize but grateful also for the opportunity to say one more blessing from my tradition."

8. *What Is a Minyan? Are Some Prayers Said Only if Ten or More People Are Present?*

Personal prayer between the individual and God may take place anywhere, any time, and with no one present but God and the individual worshiper. Public services, however, have traditionally required what is known as a **minyan** [min-YAHN or MIN-y'n], that is, the presence of at least ten adult worshipers.

The number ten apparently held particular fascination for the Jews of antiquity. The Commandments were ten in number; Pharaoh was visited with ten plagues; the High Holy Day season includes ten Days of Repentance between Rosh Hashanah and Yom Kippur; ten generations are recorded between Adam and Noah and then again between Noah and Abraham; God destroys the evil city of Sodom because it does not contain ten good people, the minimum necessary to merit its survival. As with the ten good people required at Sodom, ten worshipers are required for a full service of public worship.

Behind the idea of a minimum number is the notion that Jewish spirituality is in some sense communal. We all received the Torah together on Mount Sinai. We are all part of the people Israel.

Actually, not all public prayers require a minyan; but those prayers especially associated with the concept of God's sanctity do: the Kaddish (memorial prayer), for example, which begins, "Glorified and *sanctified* be God's name!" or the Kedushah prayer, which celebrates God's sanctity with the words, "Holy, holy, holy."

In the Middle Ages, it was considered unlucky to point at people as you counted them. To avoid doing so, Jewish communities adopted prayers with ten words in them, or psalms with ten verses. People would go around the room with one person saying a word or verse, then another and another, until the last word or verse was recited. Then people knew they had a minyan.

Orthodox Judaism still requires a minyan, and true to traditional law, counts only men, not women, in the number. Conservative and Reconstructionist Jews require a minyan also, but generally include women as well as men in the count. Reform Jews usually do not observe the requirement of the minyan. Any group of worshipers, few or many, male or female, may constitute a congregation in most Reform synagogues.

9. *What Is "Keeping Kosher"?*

The Bible itself sets down dietary restrictions, upon which the Rabbis of the Talmud elaborate. The rules are quite complex, but in general, the most important regulations are the following:

1. Jews may eat meat, but only the meat of animals that chew their cud and have a cloven hoof. Thus Jews may not eat such animals as the pig and horse.
2. Jews may eat fish, but only fish with fins and scales; they may not, therefore, eat shellfish such as shrimp, lobster, crab, and oyster.
3. Jews may eat fowl, but not birds of prey, since the meat of animals that cause pain to other animals is forbidden; no carnivorous animals are kosher.
4. Animals must be slaughtered by a trained specialist, who uses a specially sharpened knife, slitting the two jugular veins and carotid arteries of the animal's throat in one swift action to guarantee a painless death. The slaughterer is to be a God-fearing person who has compassion for all God's creatures, and who destroys life only with the greatest reluctance. Jews may therefore not hunt or eat meat that has been killed by hunters.

WHAT IS A JEW?

5. The Bible (Exodus 23:19) instructs us, "You shall not boil a kid in its mother's milk." The Rabbis took this to mean that meat products and dairy products may not be eaten together, and generally may not be cooked or even served in the same pots or on the same dishes.

Food that is forbidden is called **treyfah** [tray-FAH] or just **treyf** [TRAYF]. Originally, the word treyfah meant that the meat was procured by causing suffering to an animal, but nowadays, it has the wider meaning of being unfit in general. The opposite designation, **kosher** [KOE-sh'r], means acceptable. Though used mostly for food, the word *kosher* may also be employed to describe any other object that meets ritual requirements. People who follow the rules say that they "keep kosher."

The whole set of rules are called the laws of **kashrut** [kahsh-ROOT]. All branches of Judaism except Reform advocate keeping kosher. Reform Judaism leaves the decision about following the dietary laws up to the individual. Some Reform Jews have chosen to keep kosher, and some have chosen not to.

In actual fact, except among the Orthodox, relatively few people keep kosher nowadays, and those who do may keep some of the rules but not others. People who invite Jews to their home can always ask in advance what rules, if any, they observe, so as to avoid serving a dish that their guest cannot in good conscience eat. The most common taboo food is pork, and it should always be avoided.

Jews vary in the degree to which they apply the laws of kashrut in their lives. Some Jews, for example, keep "biblically kosher." They elect to follow the rules that are actually laid down explicitly in the Bible, but not the rabbinic elaboration upon them. They thus avoid pork and shellfish, for instance, and they do not mix milk and meat, since these are prohibitions that you can find in the Bible itself. But they eat meat that has not been ritually slaughtered, and they do not keep separate sets of dishes for meat and milk, because these rules cannot be found in the Bible, but instead were first promulgated by the Rabbis in their attempt to enlarge upon the biblical legislation.

Other Jews, considering home a particularly holy place, keep kosher there but not outside. Still others observe the rules in some limited way, avoiding pork products alone, for example. In other words, every Jew decides for him- or herself the extent to which the laws of kashrut should apply. There is no way of knowing in advance what Jewish friends or relatives have decided, and it is always a good idea to ask before serving a meal that they may not be able to eat.

Those Jews who accept the laws of kashrut do not feel impelled to find "logical" explanations for observing them, even though many serious-minded Jews have tried for centuries to discover some rationale behind the regulations. Our distinguished medieval philosopher Moses Maimonides thought they were a health measure. He also saw important moral value in restraining our appetite, believing that discipline in our eating habits helps us generally to develop self-control.

Jewish ethics taught that keeping kosher with the proper attitude would develop moral character. One Rabbi advised, "Do not say, 'I dislike pork and therefore I reject it.' Say instead, 'I like it, but I do not eat it since the Torah forbids it to me.' "

Some Jews reject the laws of kashrut but accept what they see as the moral reasoning behind some of them, namely, the injunction to avoid inflicting pain on animals. Noting the pain that inevitably comes to animals as a consequence of the standard operating procedures of the food industry, these Jews have adopted vegetarianism as a Jewishly mandated moral position.

Jews who follow the dietary laws today may do so for a variety of reasons. Some keep kosher just because Jewish law says you must. Others who do not keep all of Jewish law anyway, but who pick and choose from the vast gamut of rabbinic ordinance, taking upon themselves that which is meaningful, may cite other motives behind their eating habits. They may want to keep a kosher home so other

Jews who do keep kosher can eat there. They may regard kosher practices as a symbol of their distinctive heritage, a daily lesson in self-discipline, or just a constant reminder that a human being must feel pity for all living things.

10. *What Special Clothes Do Jews Wear?*

The practice of wearing special clothes, especially during worship, is common to most faiths, Judaism included. Since originally—and still today, among the Orthodox—the obligation to pray publicly applied only to men, the special clothes tend to be clothes for men alone. On the other hand, liberal Jewish women, and modern Orthodox women as well, now frequently wear these clothes in their effort to assert their right to a full Jewish identity alongside men.

This act of recapturing the trappings of Jewish identity is taking place not only among women. Reform Jews too have reclaimed the right to wear ritual attire. Previous generations of Reform Jews divested themselves of traditional prayer garb, preferring instead to make their worship look very much like that of the Protestant mainstream around them. Their descendants in Reform synagogues today have begun wearing the special clothing once again in an effort to enhance their worship with the visual and tactile symbols of centuries past.

The most usual piece of clothing that Jews use in prayer is a headcovering called a **kippah** [kee-PAH] (Hebrew) or a **yarmulke** [YAHR-m'l-kuh] (Yiddish). The latter name used to be preferred, but nowadays the Hebrew "kippah" is more usual. Once, only a plain black skullcap was available, but now knitted and decorated **kippot** [kee-POTE] (the plural) are a booming industry.

A famous study of the kippah notes, "The custom of praying bareheaded or with covered head is not at all a question of law. It is merely a matter of social propriety and decorum." Nonetheless, people feel very strongly about the issue. A generation ago, in most

Orthodox synagogues a man had to cover his head, while in the Reform temple across the street he was not allowed to. Here and there, the return of kippot to Reform worship is still a matter of great controversy, even though in most places the right to cover your head is once again taken for granted.

Most Orthodox Jewish men wear their kippah at all times, not only during prayer. They may also wear a hat over the kippah for aesthetic purposes. It is their view that they show respect to God by covering their head, and since God is everywhere, their head should never be uncovered.

Many married Orthodox women also wear headcovers at all times, not for purposes of public prayer but as a sign of what they believe to be appropriate feminine modesty. They may wear a hat or scarf, or they may wear a wig over their natural hair. The wig industry too is a booming business among modern Orthodox women who will not allow their own hair to be seen in public but who want to enhance their appearance using the means allowed them by Jewish law.

Conservative and Reconstructionist Jewish men usually cover their head only while worshiping, and often prefer a small knitted kippah affixed to their hair by a bobby pin. Many Conservative women still use a headcovering in synagogue—often a veil or a hat—but it is more fashionable now for them to prefer a kippah like the men, or not to cover their head at all.

As already indicated, Reform Jews once dispensed altogether with the kippah, believing it to be an Old World custom out of keeping with modern Western aesthetics. They pointed out that we show respect in the Western world by taking our hat off, not by putting it on. But since the 1960s a retrieval of traditional customs has brought the kippah back into style in some Reform synagogues, both for men and women, in keeping with Reform egalitarianism.

In addition to the kippah, tradition prescribes a prayer shawl known as a **tallit** [tah-LEET]. It too was once worn only by men, and originally it was worn all day, like the kippah. Orthodox men still wear it all day, but in order to avoid looking too different on the street they wear a small tallit under their shirt, and put on the large tallit only when they pray.

In all probability, large shawls were once the normal clothing of free men and thus entered worship as a symbol of freedom. The important thing about the tallit is its specially woven fringes (called **tsitsit** [tsee-TSEET]) on each of its four corners. The Bible (Numbers 15:37–41) instructs us to look at them and be reminded that we who were freed from Egyptian bondage need to dedicate ourselves to a life of holiness.

During those portions of worship which call for complete concentration, people may lift the tallit so that it covers their heads to eliminate distraction. Also, when the Torah is carried around the room, or if they are called to say the blessing as the Torah is being read, they touch the Torah with the fringes and then kiss the fringes.

Once upon a time, every tallit was the same color: white with a blue or black stripe across it. Nowadays, Jews in search of tradition have made the tallit business soar. The tallit comes in many colors and sizes these days. Reform Judaism once eliminated the tallit along with the kippah, but both are now making a comeback in modern Reform synagogues.

Unlike the kippah, which always accompanies worship, the tallit is mandated only for morning services. An exception is the eve of Yom Kippur, what many consider the most sacred moment of the Jewish year.

A tallit is usually given to the boy or girl as a sign of adulthood on the occasion of the bar or bat mitzvah. Some Orthodox congregations withhold the right to wear one until marriage. People take their tallit very personally. They may pass it on to their children, or alternatively, when people die, their next of kin may bury them wrapped in this lifelong symbol of Jewish piety.

In addition, Orthodox (and some Conservative and Reconstructionist) Jews wear **tefillin** [T'FIL-lin or t'fee-LEEN]. A very small percentage of Reform Jews wear them too. Tefillin, or phylacteries, consist of two small black boxes, one to two inches square, with leather straps attached. They contain pieces of parchment inscribed with verses from the Books of Exodus and Deuteronomy proclaiming God's unity, God's providential care, and Israel's deliverance from bondage.

One box is fastened to the left arm, and the other is placed on the forehead, following an intricate ritual procedure in which the straps are arranged in such a way as to spell out the Hebrew letters of God's name. As a rule, tefillin are worn only in morning worship, and only on weekdays.

Chasidic men also wear long black coats, and their leaders wear specially prepared fur hats. These are remnants of everyday attire in Poland two centuries ago. The Chasidim retain them as part of their general conservative style. Actually, an exceptionally complex code determines who gets to wear what among the Chasidim. From the style of hat and coat, you can often tell what particular sect the man belongs to and his place in the pecking order in the Chasidic religious hierarchy.

Finally, in Reform synagogues, it is still common to find rabbis and cantors leading worship while dressed in black robes worn over their street clothes. These are simply common clerical garb from the turn of the century, worn to enhance worship with signs of dignity. In Europe, the vestments tend to be more formal. Many English rabbis wear a clerical collar akin to that of the Anglican clergy. In France the garb of the rabbi bears a striking similarity to that of Catholic priests. There are rabbis in Athens whose robes remind one of the Greek church. But clerical garb borrowed from the surrounding culture is by no means religiously mandated, and the trend nowadays is not to wear it but instead to adopt the traditional kippah and tallit.

11. *Are There Special Jewish Foods?*

Over time, every group develops its own favorite foods, especially associated with holidays that its members celebrate together. So Jews too tend to cook certain favored dishes for this festival or that. On the other hand, we cannot point to any universal Jewish food, simply because Jews have lived in so many different countries, adopting the cooking habits and tastes of the environment where they lived and then adapting those tastes to the Jewish calendar. Jews from Yemen or Algeria, for instance, are unfamiliar with the folk dishes of Jews from Poland or Russia. Ethnic foods borrowed from their Slavic neighbors may be regarded as Jewish by American Jews who hail from Warsaw, but a member of New York's Spanish-Portuguese synagogue feels no sense of kinship with them.

Ethnic foods associated in the popular mind with various cultures are often just the product of economic deprivation. Italian pasta was born out of poverty; Irish dishes with cabbage and potatoes arose out of the needs of the Irish poor, who couldn't afford much more than that; Jewish *gefilte* [g'FILL-tuh] fish, that is, "stuffed fish," was the imaginative creation of the impoverished ghettoes of the Old World. Adding inexpensive bread or flour made it possible for a poor Jewish family to make a single fish serve a large number at the dinner table.

Two categories of food might be considered authentically Jewish. The first is that which is dictated by Jewish ritual law: **matzah** [MAHT-sah], the unleavened bread eaten on Passover, for instance; or wine (or grape juice) prescribed for the Sabbath and festivals. But there are not many examples of such "must-eat" foods, although the dietary regulations produced lots of "must-not-eat" things for Jews who keep kosher (see p. 87).

A second category of Jewish food is a variety of dishes that grew out of Sabbath regulations. In general, following the Bible, work is prohibited on the Sabbath. The definition of "work," however, is very complicated. For example, lighting a fire is considered work—as indeed it must have been for our ancestors two thousand years ago. But by extension, among Orthodox Jews even turning on an oven counts as a form of work today. Traditional Jews would thus make sure that the oven was already on before the Sabbath began. They developed a variety of puddings and stews that could be put up to cook before nightfall Friday night and left on a low flame until Saturday noon, when they were served as a hot midday meal. Different groups of Jews invented different examples of such things, but it is mostly the Orthodox who worry about them now. Most Jews do turn on their ovens on the Sabbath, if not to cook entire meals—that might be work indeed—at least to warm up something special to enhance the joy of Shabbat. Nonetheless, you may come across the old recipes anyway.

Some Jewish homes feature festival foods called **kugel** [KUH-g'l], a sort of noodle pudding that I recommend warmly, or a Shabbat **cholent** [TCHO-lent], an all-night stew that I do not.

Beyond the requirements of Jewish law, there are certain foods that are linked to Jewish law but that developed differently in different countries. Passover, for instance, calls for a sweet, pasty mixture called **charoset** [khah-ROE-set], but Jews all over the world make it differently: usually with wine, nuts, and apples, if you lived in northern Europe, but pears and Middle Eastern spices in some places along the Mediterranean. Similarly, the Passover ritual requires food that grows in the ground. In the warm climate of Israel, people use green vegetables, a sign of spring. In northern Poland, the snows had barely left the ground when Passover arrived. Without green vegetables yet, Polish Jews used potatoes.

North American Jews come from all over, so have their own favorites. In most Jewish homes, however, you are likely to see twisted loaves of egg bread called **challah** [KHAH-lah] served on the eve of Sabbaths and festivals. The wine served then will likely still be sweet kosher wine made from red grapes.

A Passover seder has its own list of requirements: parsley to represent the springtime of the year, but dipped in salt water, reminiscent of the tears of the Hebrew slaves in Egypt; the charoset (mentioned above) made specially thick to recollect the mortar manufactured by the slaves in order to produce bricks for Pharaoh's building campaigns; bitter herbs (usually horseradish) in memory of the bitterness of servitude; and hardboiled eggs (for the same reason Christianity originally adopted Easter eggs)—a reminder of life that transcends death, just as surely as springtime follows winter and redemption from Egypt followed slavery there.

Other festive days have their own traditional tastes: an apple dipped in honey, on the Jewish new year, for instance, to symbolize a sweet year; and potato pancakes (**latkes** [LAHT-kahs]) or doughnuts on Chanukah—both being foods that are cooked in oil, an appropriate culinary reminder of the miracle of oil that Chanukah recalls (see pp. 222–224).

As Jews have acculturated to American life, they have gradually abandoned most ethnic foods that depended on Old World tastes. What any given family serves or expects as "Jewish" varies widely. Whatever it is, it can usually be purchased in specialty shops, or even ordinary bakeries, these days. And modern Jewish cookbooks for people who keep kosher abound.

12. *Do Jews Have Their Own Language?*

If an international conference of Jews were to be called, no single language would be understood by all. Like everybody else, Jews tend to be at home only in the national language of the country where they live.

Hebrew is thus a Jewish language in the same sense that Israel is a Jewish homeland. Most of the early immigrants there did not even speak the language, which, truth be told, was a dead tongue. It had not been spoken for centuries.

But Hebrew is the primary language of the Jewish people. It was the language of the Bible and of rabbis throughout history. The medieval commentator Rashi, who lived outside of Paris, spoke

French, but he wrote his biblical commentary in Hebrew. Maimonides must have spoken to his Egyptian neighbors in Arabic, but he composed his monumental fourteen-book code of Jewish law in Hebrew. So Hebrew is the language of the Jewish spirit.

There was no necessity to make Hebrew the official language of Israel. But even before statehood was achieved the early settlers went to great lengths to revive it as a spoken tongue. Eliezer ben Yehudah, the man usually credited with the task, is said never to have uttered a sentence in anything but Hebrew from the time of his arrival in the Holy Land. He even addressed his wife and children in nothing but Hebrew, whether they understood or not! Others were less zealous, I hope, but the end result was a country in which immigrants from Russia, Yemen, Syria, Algeria, Poland—all over the globe—returned to a modern-day update of the language of the Bible.

It is common for Jews all over the world to study some form of Hebrew. At the very least, they want to be able to read traditional prayers. For years, when Russian Jews were unable to practice their religion without risking the punishment of losing their job, they studied Hebrew privately, using Hebrew books smuggled in by Jewish travelers. In North America, synagogues feature religious-school curricula that supplement the secular public school education by providing classes where children can learn some Hebrew, at least. Some Jews send their children to private Jewish schools (referred to as day schools) where the normal secular curriculum is supplemented by more intensive Hebrew studies. Another common practice is sending teenagers or college students to Israel for a year of study, from which they can return fluent in this age-old but very new Jewish language.

Yiddish [YID-ish], a mixture of German and Hebrew, was once spoken by a majority of Jews in North America. It had been their folk language in the Ashkenazic ghettoes of northern and eastern Europe. Yiddish encompasses great works of poetry and fiction, including those of such world-renowned authors as Shalom Aleichem, who gave us, among others, the character of Tevye from

Fiddler on the Roof. Some people still speak Yiddish, but not many. However, Chasidic Jews retain it among themselves, in preference to the modern secular English that they hear on the streets around them. Just as they do not give up the clothes of eighteenth-century Poland, so too they hold fast to the language they once spoke there.

The parallel for Yiddish in the Sephardic world is **Ladino** [la-DEE-noe], a folk tongue of Spanish-Portuguese Jewry. It too was once the vehicle of a great literary culture, but is rarely used nowadays.

The nearest thing to a universal Jewish language since the destruction of the ancient state was *Aramaic.* It was the spoken language of Babylonian Jewry, the largest single Jewish settlement at the time. Much of the Talmud was written in Aramaic. Kol Nidre and the Kaddish, two of the best-known Jewish prayers, are in Aramaic. By the Middle Ages, a particular dialect of Aramaic mixed with Hebrew became the language of scholars, so that to this day, traditional rabbinic writing uses Aramaic as the language of record.

13. *What Jewish Meal Rituals Are There?*

Whenever observant Jews sit down to eat, they "break bread" with a blessing reminding them of their dependence on God. They call that prayer **Hamotzi** [hah-MOE-tsee], a word borrowed from the blessing in question. The Rabbis saw the blessing as more than thanks for the food we eat; it was also a prayer for the coming of the day when every human being would have enough to eat, no less, in fact, than Adam and Eve had enjoyed in the Garden of Eden.

A second prayer is the Grace after Meals, called **Birkat Hamazon** [beer-KAHT hah-mah-ZONE], which is usually chanted, at least in part, to a traditional melody. Sometimes Jews speak of saying the Grace after Meals as **benching,** from the Yiddish word *benschen*

[BEN-sh'n]—possibly derived from the same Latin root as the English word *benediction*.

Eating together has traditionally been more than merely a way to satisfy hunger. The Talmud speaks critically of those who sit through an entire dinner without exchanging "words of Torah," a practice considered akin to idolatry. But when words of Torah pass across the table, God's spirit dwells in the house. To be sure, few Jewish homes deliberately transform dining time into lessons of Torah! But the ideal of a meal shared with friends and family and dedicated to deepening relationships and expressing thanks to God before and after remains.

The Grace after Meals expresses hope that God will someday provide food for all, that the Land of Israel will become fertile once again, and that Jerusalem will be redeemed in all its glory. Finally, it praises God "who is good and who does good," a formula evocative of Jewish hope for a world redeemed, at the end of time. Worshipers express hope also that they may be worthy "in the sight of God and other people," and conclude with a prayer for peace.

On Sabbaths and festivals, when meals are eaten in a more leisurely manner, other prayers are added. As the family sits down for dinner, candles are lit and a blessing is said; that is followed by what Jews call "making **Kiddush** [kee-DOOSH or KID-ish], a combination of two blessings, one over wine (or grape juice), and another that proclaims the sanctity of the special day just beginning. Many families sing special songs as well, and use the occasion of the Sabbath or festival to invoke God's blessing on their children.

IV

Basic Jewish Beliefs:
"God, Torah, Israel"

Unlike Christianity, Judaism is primarily concerned with what God wants us to do, not what God wants us to believe. Jews talk more about behavior than about doctrine. An old rabbinic saying goes, "The teaching is not essential; the action is." Another story has it that God says, "It matters less that they believe in me than that they keep my Torah." From its very inception, Christianity was beset with dogmatic disputes, and from the time of the Reformation onward, it has splintered into various churches on the basis of what each believes: different doctrines of the Trinity, perhaps, or beliefs about what occurs in the Eucharist. As we saw in our discussion of Jewish community, Judaism too exists in several branches, but they came about largely through differences of opinion regarding the mitzvot, that is, what Jews are supposed to do. When the Chasidim wanted to emphasize their differences from their opponents, they said little about doctrine; but they charged their opposition with eating nonkosher meat, because of a technicality involving the kind of slaughtering knife that was used. In return the Mitnagdim [mit-nahg-DEEM], their opponents, announced that the prayer book used by Chasidic Jews was defective, in that it did not use the standard Ashkenazic prayers but included instead some mystical alterations and additions.

This does not mean that belief is unimportant, however; Jews do have distinctive beliefs about God and the universe that make us the unique people we are. This section answers the most common questions people have about Jewish belief.

QUESTIONS IN PART IV

1. *What in General Do Jews Believe?*
2. *What Are the Principal Tenets of Judaism?*
3. *What Do Jews Believe about God?*
4. *Do Jews Believe that Judaism Is the Only True Religion?*
5. *Do Jews Consider Themselves the Chosen People?*
6. *What Is the Jewish Concept of Sin?*
7. *Do Jews Believe in Life after Death?*
8. *Do Jews Believe in the Coming of the Messiah?*
9. *Do Jews Believe Literally in Satan?*
10. *Do Jews Believe in Fate?*
11. *Do Jews Believe in Prophecy?*
12. *Do Jews Believe in Being Saved?*
13. *Do Jews Believe in God's Grace?*
14. *Is Judaism a Spiritual Religion or an Ethnic Identity?*

1. What in General Do Jews Believe?

Students of religion who enjoy arranging the dogma of the various creeds into neat, clearly defined categories are inevitably frustrated by Judaism, for Judaism eludes a simple definition. There are things most Jews believe, but these things are organized undogmatically. There is no single official creed or formal catechism that all believing Jews—or even all Orthodox Jews—would accept. A number of years ago a Christian friend asked me what vows I had taken when I was ordained as a rabbi. The question surprised me—but my answer was even more startling to my friend. I had made no verbal commitments. I had not pronounced a single word of affirmation. Though it was assumed that of course I had Jewish faith, I had made no declaration of what it was!

To understand Judaism one must abandon the search for absolutes in dogma and examine instead the broad *philosophy* that underlies our faith. What we believe about the Bible, about miracles, about a life after death, is secondary to what we believe about the support we receive from God as we pursue our human potential, and our basic moral responsibilities toward all humanity. The changes we have made through the years in ritual and custom are of little consequence compared to the eternal values that have buttressed our faith through countless generations and kept Judaism alive in the face of every adversity.

Judaism has always been a living faith—constantly growing and changing as does everything that lives. We are a people whose roots have been replanted too often, whose associations with different cultures have been too intense for our religious traditions and thinking to remain completely unchanged. In succession, Jews have been part of the civilizations of the Assyrians, the Babylonians, the Persians, the Greeks, the Romans, and finally, the Moslems (on one hand) and the Christians (on the other). Throughout it all, ghetto walls were the exception of history rather than the rule. Inevitably these different experiences brought with them certain modifications and reinterpretations.

Our experience with diverse cultures has enriched our religion in many ways. Above all, perhaps, has been our hospitality to differences. Every question of Jewish law contains both an austere interpretation and a liberal one, and the Rabbis ruled that "both opinions are the word of the living God."

Our religion has had its dogmatists, those who thought it preferable to establish an inflexible set of beliefs, thinking that God would prove a severe judge who demands rigid adherence to them all. But we have also had our prophets who put belief distinctly second to action, and held that an uncompromising attitude is necessary only in matters of ethical responsibility, not theological precision. Demanding greater faith in human potential, they refused to compromise in matters of justice, and went so far as to insist that preoccupation with rituals and ceremonies at the expense of righteousness and compassion was deadening to true religion.

Rabbis and philosophers too tried to formulate Jewish creeds, but always in vain. One famous rabbinic aphorism pictures God as saying, in effect, "As long as Jews do My will, they need not believe in Me." That is an exaggeration, of course. Judaism does teach some beliefs, among them the firm conviction that God is real: a real presence in the lives of men and women, children and adults. We can know that reality as surely as we know the beauty of love, the satisfaction of faithfulness, or the buoyancy of hope.

We believe, then, in God: a personal God whose ways may be beyond our comprehension, but whose reality makes the difference between a world that has purpose and one that is meaningless.

We believe all human beings are made in God's image; our role in the universe is thus uniquely important, and despite the failings that spring from our mortality, we are endowed with infinite potential for goodness and greatness.

We believe too that human beings actualize their potential as part of a community. The people Israel is such a community, harking back to Sinai, existing despite all odds from then until now, and still the source of satisfaction for Jews who wish to pursue a life of purpose grounded in the age-old wisdom we call Torah.

And we believe in Torah, therefore, as a continuing source of revelation.

It has been said that you can sum up Jewish belief in these three words, *God, Torah, Israel.* As the mystics used to say, "God, Torah, and Israel are all one." If we lose our faith in any one of them, the others quickly perish.

The reality of God, the goodness and potential of every person, the eternal covenant that the People of Israel made with God, and the guidance, solace, and wisdom of Torah—these are our basic religious beliefs.

In antiquity, it was common for scholars to distill the essence of religion in a simple formula. Thus, Hillel, the great Rabbi and scholar of the first century B.C.E., was asked to sum up Judaism while the questioner stood on one foot! Hillel replied: "Certainly! What is hateful to you, do not do to your neighbor. That is all there is in the Torah. All the rest is mere commentary. I suggest you study the commentary."

A century later, Rabbi Yochanan asked five of his most distinguished pupils to offer their own pet formulas. When all had been heard, Yochanan said: "Rabbi Elazar's answer is still the best—a good heart."

Still others searched the Bible for a single verse that would distill the essence of the Jewish faith. They found it in the words of the prophet Micah, who reminds us what God wants from us: "Do justice, love goodness, and walk humbly with your God."

The other questions touched upon in this chapter may be considered, in the words of Hillel, "only commentary."

2. What Are the Principal Tenets of Judaism?

Jews believes in the existence of a God who cannot be accurately conceived, described, or pictured. But God is a real presence in the universe at large; and the lives of each of us in particular. We believe also that we most genuinely show God honor when we imitate the qualities that are godly: As God is merciful, so we must be compassionate; as God is just, so we must deal justly with our neighbor; as God is slow to anger, so we must be tolerant in our judgment.

Some eighteen hundred years ago one of our sages taught: They whom others love, are loved by God as well.

A very popular rabbinic aphorism cautions us that the very continued existence of the world depends on three things: Torah, that is, the study of God's word; worship; and the performance of good and charitable deeds.

Because of our emphasis on Torah, the love of learning dominates our faith. As long ago as the first century of the Common Era, Jews had a system of compulsory education. Education of the poor or orphans was the responsibility of the community as well as the parents! Nor were the Rabbis unmindful of the psychology of learning. On the first day at school, youngsters in medieval times were fed honey cakes shaped in the letters of the alphabet, so they would associate learning with sweetness!

Along with Torah, you find an accent on worship. From their earliest childhood, Jews are taught that God is to be worshiped out of love. The most familiar prayer, our **Shema** (see p. 83), reads:

"You shall love the Eternal, your God, with all your heart, with all your soul, and with all your might."

The third tenet of Judaism is charitable deeds—the genuine charity that stems from the heart. The Hebrew word for charity is **tzedakah** [ts'dah-KAH or ts'DAH-Kah], which means "just or righteous giving." Philanthropy is born out of the belief that all we possess is really God's, merely passing through our hands during the brief window on time we call our lives.

Philanthropy, for the pious Jew, knows no racial or religious boundaries. According to the Rabbis: "We are required to feed the non-Jewish poor as well as our own." No one is exempt from the practice of charity. The Talmud informs us, "Even one who is on relief must give to the poor!" No matter how poor you are, you can always find someone poorer than yourself, to whom you are obligated to share something of what you own.

True charity is anonymous, growing out of a genuine sense of compassion and a will to act justly, not a desire for power or self-aggrandizement. And the highest form of charity, we believe, is helping other people help themselves, raising them to a point at which they become independent and no longer need charity. But not all of us are able to live up to the highest standards of philanthropic giving, and Judaism is intensely practical. We encourage people to give regardless of their motive, arguing, "Though people may do something good for the wrong reason at first, the joy of doing it may lead them to do it for the right reason eventually."

3. What Do Jews Believe about God?

Belief in one and only one God is central to Judaism as a religion. Judaism teaches also that God has done or will do three things.

First, God created the universe. Modern Jews believe that science best explains *how* the universe was born, but nonetheless see the hand of God in that process, in some way. Moreover, creation is a continuing process. The universe is even now still coming into being, and we human beings are charged with being partners with God in bringing about creative evolution.

Second, God revealed the Torah to Israel. Revelation is primarily associated with standing at Mount Sinai, but we believe also in continuing revelation thereafter. By accepting the Torah as God's legislation that would ever after guide us, we gained also the insight to search the text of Torah for wisdom for all time.

Third, we believe in redemption. Our God is not an impersonal force that began the world but does not care about it. We therefore believe that God intervened in history once to rescue the Israelites from Egypt, and that God will in some way redeem us all at the end of time.

Our God is thus a God of *creation, revelation, and redemption.*

But Jews are divided on what exactly each of these terms means. Maimonides, for instance, did not take the Bible's creation narrative literally. Instead, he interpreted God's act of creation not as something that happened once upon a time, but as a state of being, as if to say that God creates the world every second of every day. Everything except God depends on something else for its existence; but if God did not exist, nothing else would exist either. God, therefore, is by definition that single being in the universe who would be here even if everything else were suddenly to disappear. As long as God exists, however, so does the universe. So creation of the universe is actually God's maintenance of the universe, the fact that the universe does not disappear but goes on eternally in time.

Jews differ also on what exactly happened at Mount Sinai. Very few Jews still believe that the Torah as we have it was handed down directly to Moses there, or that the events as described in the book of Exodus should be taken literally. But most would agree that the story of the Jews as a people begins with the Exodus and the molding of our religious character on the way to the promised land. Somehow, we became aware of God's presence among us, and we adopted as our purpose the furthering of God's plans in history. Beyond a historic and historical event, Mount Sinai is the symbol of becoming aware of what God's plans are. It is our commitment ever after to live a life of Torah, bringing ever nearer the dawn of God's reign on earth.

Redemption is the word Jews prefer for "salvation." It is the name we give to the dawn of that age, variously described as a messianic age, the reparation of the universe, or a world redeemed.

4. *Do Jews Believe that Judaism Is the Only True Religion?*

Jews regard Judaism as the only religion for Jews—both those born Jewish and those who choose to become Jews through conversion. But we respect the honest, devout worshiper of any faith. The Rabbis held, "The righteous of all nations have a share in the world to come."

The rabbinic metaphor is a covenant, by which we mean an agreement freely entered into between God and various religious communities. The Jewish covenant is the one made at Sinai, when Jews agreed to observe the Torah. But God makes covenants with other peoples also. The Rabbis called them *Noahide* covenants, meaning the kind of covenant God made with Noah, who was not Jewish. According to the terms of the Noahide covenants, non-Jewish religions are held responsible for recognizing the one true God and turning away from idolatry, for establishing systems of justice in their midst, and for maintaining basic moral virtues.

It is the recognition of the reality of God, and the basic moral virtues, such as kindliness, justice, and integrity, that we regard as eternal verities. But we claim no monopoly on these verities, for we recognize that every great religious faith has discovered them. That is what Rabbi Meir meant some eighteen centuries ago, when he said that a non-Jew who follows the Torah is as good as our high priest.

There are many paths to the one God.

5. Do Jews Consider Themselves the Chosen People?

Following the Bible, traditional Judaism has maintained that God selected Abraham and Sarah and their heirs for special service in the world. Israel was thus chosen to honor and perpetuate God's laws and to transmit God's heritage.

But Jews do not believe they are endowed with any special traits, talents, or capacities, or that they enjoy any special privileges in the eyes of God. Responsible Jews reject any degeneration of their sense of destiny into arrogant and hollow chauvinism or a confusion of responsibility with privilege.

Modern Judaism has reinterpreted the doctrine of the chosen people in many different ways. For many, the traditional belief is sufficient: We are chosen to serve God in distinctive ways. Reform Jews, particularly, have tended to look proudly at Jewish history, seeing in it Israel's constant witness to God's truths through Greek and Roman civilizations, then during the medieval period when Jews were often persecuted for their faith, and finally, into modern times. Using language from the prophets, they declared their faith in what they called the Mission of Israel whereby Jews were to be "a light to the nations."

A particularly popular image is the mystical doctrine of **tikkun olam** [tee-KOON oh-LAHM], literally, "the reparation of the universe." This medieval doctrine held that when the universe was created, moral flaws were inadvertently introduced into it. Thus evil, sickness, and suffering became part of what was intended as a perfectly good universe. But these flaws are reversible. Jews are nothing less than partners with God, in that they have been charged with the task of uprooting evil and perfecting the cosmos. By living the life of Torah, Jews can thus finish the work God began when, eons ago, God first said, "Let there be light."

Other modern interpreters, however, among them Mordecai Kaplan, the founder of Reconstructionist Judaism, have found the concept of chosenness difficult to accept. Many people today prefer emphasizing the other side of the coin—Israel's continuing act of choosing to act for God. Having willingly chosen our mission, we accept "the burden of the Torah," as it is sometimes called, and the responsibility for perpetuating its moral and spiritual truths.

6. *What Is the Jewish Concept of Sin?*

A postscript to every Jew's life, uttered at the time of burial, are the words: "For there lives no human being on earth who is so righteous as never to have sinned." Jews do indeed believe in sin, as we believe in the grand promise of atonement and forgiveness. We do not believe, however, in a doctrine of "original sin," and we do not hold that human beings are *basically* sinners. Rather, we speak of our being composed of two inclinations, called the **yetser hara** [YAY-tser hah-RAH] and the **yetser hatov** [YAY-tser hah-TOVE], literally, the "bad inclination" and the "good inclination," respectively. We are given free will to choose to follow either of these rival character endowments. An ancient midrash pictures Cain on trial before God for killing his brother. "Don't punish me," he shouts. "It's your fault that I committed the murder. After all, you made me this way." But God rejects Cain's argument. Cain had the free will necessary to follow his good inclination had he wanted to.

The Jewish concept of sin has changed through the centuries. To the ancient Hebrews, sin was the violation of a taboo, an offense against God, for which a sin offering had to be made. For most Jews today, sin has come to mean any shortcoming in our attempt to live up to our full moral potential—our failure to meet our responsibilities as Jews.

These "great expectations" are born out of our knowledge that we have been created in God's image and out of our loyalty to history as well. As we believe that God is a God of love and that the mandates of Torah are not impossibilities, it follows that imperfect creatures that we are, we will necessarily sin, but we will also know moments when we do precisely what God wants, and do it well, even beyond our wildest imagination.

Jewish tradition differentiates between sins against other people and sins against God. The first, transgressions against our neighbors, are forgiven by God only if we first seek out forgiveness by the people we have wronged. Neither prayers nor piety can expiate such sins. Sins against God, on the other hand, may be expiated by true penitence, known in Hebrew as **teshuvah** [t'shoo-VAH or TSHOO-vah], meaning "return," that is, a return to God and a reconciliation with our Maker. Reconciliation is achieved by an honest searching of our soul, a candid admission of our shortcomings, and a firm resolution to bridge the gap between what we are and what we know we should be.

We have confessions too, both as part of the public liturgy when the whole congregation together recites a prayer to God, admitting that human beings are collectively guilty; and as a private confession that any individual may make at any time in any language, silently or aloud, but in any case directly to God, with no human intermediary.

Jews do not expect to pass their lives entirely without sin—for no one is perfect. We have even known periods when Jews were weighted down with a sense of their sinful behavior—in twelfth-century Germany, for instance, when Christian doctrine and European piety in general infiltrated Jewish circles. But in general, Jewish tradition cautions us against brooding over our own sinfulness. "Be not evil in your own esteem," the Talmud tells us.

7. Do Jews Believe in Life after Death?

Jews have traditionally believed in some kind of life after death. Our Hebrew Bible alludes to some sort of final place where we go when we die called Sheol, and during the period of Persian domination over Israel some of the teachings of Zoroaster, among them the notion of a heaven or hell to come, became popular among the Jews. The Rabbis of the Talmud firmly believed in a life after death, as they believed in the bodily resurrection of the righteous when the messiah arrives.

But Jewish tradition rarely pictures heaven and hell in physical terms. A soul delighting in a life well lived was in heaven; a soul tormented by remorse for misdeeds was in hell. Occasionally, there was some speculation about the nature of paradise: the reward stored up for the righteous. "May her (or his) soul be bound up in the bond of eternal life"; "May he (or she) dwell in the bright Garden of Eden"; "The memory of the righteous is a blessing"—these are common ways to speak of a person who has died.

Interestingly enough, inherent Jewish optimism refers regularly to the heavenly alternative, but almost never to the opposite, hell. There is almost no speculation about the nature of hell. Jewish literature knows no equivalent to Dante's *Inferno*. The form of punishment to be meted out to the wicked never exercised Jewish imagination or folklore.

Perhaps pain and anguish were too much a part of this life; there seemed little point to dwelling on the possibilities of everlasting torture. In fact, such words as "damned" and "hell" have never been part of the speaking vocabulary of Hebrew or of Yiddish. Yiddish is a very colorful language, mind you, and there are plenty of folk curses carried in the popular imagination through the years, but they have nothing to do with damnation, a concept Judaism has rejected.

Some Jews still believe in resurrection of the body, and some even in reincarnation of the soul, a mystical idea from the Middle Ages. Most liberally minded Jews, however, reject both of these concepts. They prefer to speak of the immortality of the soul, an immortality whose nature is known only to God. And they do not accept any literal concept of heaven or hell.

Jews have always been more concerned with this world than the next and have concentrated their religious efforts on building an ideal world for the living. Thus, for instance, the twelfth-century philosopher Maimonides maintained that only the immature are motivated by hopes of reward and fear of punishment. The reward for virtuous living, he said, was the good life itself. Rather than speculate on matters of the afterlife, he urged, we should attend to our duties before God.

There is a parable often told about a visitor who came to paradise and found it entirely populated by groups of scholars, all firmly engrossed in the study of the Talmud. Surprised, the observer questioned the heavenly guide, who explained, "You have the mistaken idea that these scholars are in heaven. Actually, heaven is in the scholars."

8. Do Jews Believe in the Coming of the Messiah?

Belief in the coming of the messiah—a descendant of the House of David who will redeem humanity and establish the reign of God on earth—has been part of the Jewish tradition since the days of the prophet Isaiah. The term "messiah" is from a Hebrew word meaning "anointed," referring to the ceremony by which biblical monarchs were selected. The messiah for us is thus an extension of such biblical characters: a ruler who ushers in the righteous reign of God.

Legend depicts the messiah as a human being of very special gifts: strong leadership, great wisdom, and deep integrity. These will be used to inaugurate a social revolution that will usher in an era of perfect peace. The messiah was sometimes envisioned as a leader and warrior who would fight the final battle against evil, rebuild the Temple that had been destroyed, and establish an ideal, just world. But the Talmud also portrays a messiah who resides in a leper colony, constantly bandaging the patients there, waiting only for Israel to keep all the commandments and thus make it possible for the messiah's appearance in history. Whatever the character traits, the messiah of Jewish tradition is a human being, not divine.

For generations the promise of the messiah was a literal truth to every Jew. Especially on Passover, the time when God once redeemed Israel from Egypt, the messiah was expected to arrive. In the Middle Ages, Passover Haggadahs (the prayer book used for the Passover eve seder ritual) were outfitted with the first instance I know of "before and after." The "before" scene pictures a home seder; the householder is opening the door and watching the messiah off in the distance, about to arrive. He is riding a donkey, and the prophet Elijah is heralding his coming. The "after" scene pictures the home empty. The messiah is riding off now, carrying the family to Jerusalem. Solomon Maimon, noted philosopher of the eighteenth century, wrote in his autobiography that when he was a boy he always slept under a heavy quilt with the covers well over his head. But before falling asleep he always made certain that one ear was exposed, so that if the messiah chose that night to come down his street, he would not miss the joyous footsteps.

Jews have known many false messiahs, leaders who have initiated wars or otherwise led their followers to a bitter end, so that even as the Rabbis proclaimed that a messiah would arrive, they urged extreme caution in accepting anyone's claim actually to be the messiah. One first-century Rabbi is credited with saying, "If you are on your way to plant a tree, and someone tells you the messiah has arrived, finish planting your tree, and only then go out to greet the messiah."

Today, it is primarily the Orthodox who still cling to the literal belief in the coming of a personal messiah. Most Jews, however, have reinterpreted the age-old belief in a messiah, not as an individual Redeemer, but as humanity collectively, who by their own acts can usher in the realm of God. They thus speak not of a messiah so much as a messianic age. When humanity has reached a level of true enlightenment, kindliness, and justice, that will be the day of the messiah. There are Jews, however, who accept this general reinterpretation but insist that human efforts alone are insufficient, so that in some way the agency of God will be required. God, then, may not send a personal messiah but will in some way work with us to bring about a messianic age.

9. *Do Jews Believe Literally in Satan?*

There are a number of references to Satan in the Hebrew scriptures. But except for the brief period just before the Christian era, it is unlikely that Jews ever took these references literally to imply an actual devil at work in human efforts.

In the Jewish tradition, Satan was the mythical symbol of all the evil forces in the world. At times he was identified with the Tempter, the evil impulse that prompts us to comply with the worst side of our nature—our yetser hara (see p. 115), or "evil inclination," that is. But even this notion never took deep root. For Judaism is so strictly monotheistic that it resisted the temptation to enthrone any being other than God with authority for a whole metaphysical realm, even the realm of evil. Thus the Rabbis insisted that God is the Creator of both good and (in some way that we do not understand) evil, and that all that exists had its origin in God, no one else. There can be no Satanic dominion, for all that is falls under God's control, no one else's. God's dominion alone is real.

In the Book of Job (a very late biblical account, influenced by Greek thought), Satan does appear as an adversary who begrudges human contentment and well-being and who directly brings about Job's misery. But some of the Rabbis of the Talmud frankly suggest that the story of Job is fiction, not fact: a valuable parable or allegory, perhaps.

The Persians, under whose domination the Jews lived following the destruction of the First Temple in the sixth century B.C.E., believed that there were two great forces in the world, the God of Light and the God of Darkness. Under their influence some Jews for a time sought to equate Satan with the God of Darkness and to blame him and other "fallen angels" for all suffering, calamity, and wickedness. But gradually Judaism rejected these ideas as alien to the deeper Jewish tradition.

Thus, while references to Satan still remain in the Orthodox and Conservative prayer books, they are generally considered nothing more than figures of speech.

10. *Do Jews Believe in Fate?*

Students of religion have always been perplexed by the question of whether our destinies, known to the mind of God, are entirely beyond our control. From this stems a second question: If our future is already established by divine Providence, what difference does our will make?

Generally speaking, Judaism is not a fatalistic religion. Jewish teaching stresses repeatedly that we are, to a large degree, masters of our own destiny. Much of life is, of course, beyond our control. We cannot choose the family into which we are born, or our gender, race, color, or native nationality. But the quality of our life—our human relationships, our character, and our spiritual destiny—is, the Rabbis teach us, our own to fashion.

We are God's partners. God created a physical world: the courses of the stars, the seasons, the orderly growth of nature, all the laws of physics, chemistry, and biology. But we human beings can fashion our own lives with deeds that create a heaven on earth.

11. *Do Jews Believe in Prophecy?*

In every age there have been people who believed that some men and women are gifted with the ability to foretell the future. In ancient times, of course, this superstition was much more widespread. But even in our own modern, sophisticated world there are still those who are attracted to the notion of trying to see beyond the present.

But the great prophets, beginning with Elijah, were not regarded as soothsayers. They were looked upon as recipients of divine visions, often against their will, and certainly not in their own best interest. They had no choice but to rail against the injustices of their age, and to demand the strictest moral standards from the people that claimed to be a people of God. The Hebrew word for "prophet" (**navi** [nah-VEE]) does not suggest the powers of a soothsayer, but rather the courage of a leader who speaks out on God's behalf. Prophets predict, not the inevitable, but the most likely consequences of the wicked misuse of power. When Elijah foretold the tragic climax of Jezebel's life, he was simply affirming the principle that they who sow the wind shall reap the whirlwind. Tradition ascribes greatness to Elijah not because of his gifts as a seer, but because he had the temerity to defy the most powerful and vindictive ruler in Hebrew history.

Jeremiah's prophecies about the doom of Jerusalem always had a big "if" attached to them. If Judah followed a certain course, disaster would follow. There was no magic in his words—only the diagnostic gifts of someone who understood both the basic laws of morality and the complexities of international life. Jeremiah was the spiritual physician who knew the course that his society's moral disease would take.

The prophetic career of Jonah demonstrates precisely how predicted outcomes of history were held to be determined by the moral choices of men and women. Jonah is sent to proclaim God's intention of destroying Nineveh unless the evil Ninevites mend their ways and cease their evil behavior. But the Ninevites actually heed Jonah's warning. Because they repent, God happily saves the city from destruction.

For Jews, the prophetic message is thus, first and foremost, about the relationship between God and ourselves. The prophets insisted that God's covenant with Israel demands strict adherence to God's moral standards. If Israel breaks the covenant, so too will God, abandoning Israel to historical circumstances that will not be good for Israel. But God does not entirely abandon Israel. Rather God waits for Israel to repent. When Israel returns to God's ways, when a moral order is once again established in Israelite society, God reclaims Israel and the covenant is reaffirmed.

So important did this message become in Judaism that the Rabbis initiated the public reading of some portion of a prophetic book at Sabbath and festival services. The reading was called the **Haftarah** [hahf-tah-RAH or hahf-TOE-rah], and was intended as a dose of consolation in the face of the evils we see all around us, no matter what century we inhabit. The Rabbis knew better (as do we) than to believe blindly that the righteous always get their just reward immediately. In the world as we know it, it is often the just who suffer the most; the poor and innocent are often the first to die young. But the prophetic consolation is a call to faith, a guarantee that the world will not always be this way, and a reminder that even in our despair, God stands by us, holding out the promise of a better time.

In Jewish tradition, the greatest prophet was Moses, who is remembered for rescuing Israel from Pharaoh and forging the national character of this band of former slaves, insisting always that he worked only for God and that the Hebrew slaves had to become committed to the God who rescued them and to God's causes.

Hence Jews do believe in the prophets but understand their genius to lie in the moral courage to address the evil of their day and to predict the sorry outcome of a society that abandons its poor or distorts justice. We do not look to the prophets for hints regarding current events or for predictions of events that would occur hundreds or thousands of years after their own lives. To us, the immortality of the prophets is based on their divinely inspired insight into the nature of Israel's covenant with God, not on any mysterious supernatural foresight.

12. Do Jews Believe in Being Saved?

Jews tend not to use the word "salvation," because by now, the term is so firmly associated with the Christian doctrine of being saved from our sins by the coming to earth of Jesus. Judaism has no such belief. We believe that we sin, but believe also that God pardons us for our sins, if we return to God in honest atonement.

But we do believe in salvation in another sense: the sense of redemption. We see the hand of God in history, and believe that we are charged with hastening the dawn of a perfect age of righteousness and justice called the messianic age.

13. Do Jews Believe in God's Grace?

Like "salvation," "grace" too is a word Jews rarely use, because it sounds so Christian to them. But Judaism does believe in "grace," in the sense of God's freely given acts of love toward us. The predominant Christian example of grace is God's so loving the world that He "gave his only begotten son." Jews do not hold that belief, but could easily affirm something similar: God so loved the world, that "God gave us the Torah."

In Christian circles, "grace" is often contrasted with "works." Judaism too believes in "works," by which we mean the mitzvot, or the acts that a life of Torah demands from us. We would say that we are saved (meaning the world will be redeemed) by works (that is, by our fulfilling the many religiously motivated acts that we take to be God's will).

14. *Is Judaism a Spiritual Religion or an Ethnic Identity?*

Judaism is often mistakenly perceived as solely an ethnic identity, a religion that one has to be born into, or one, at least, in which the ties that bind are not so much spiritual or religious as ethnic. To be sure, there are Jews who think of Judaism that way; but they are becoming fewer and fewer.

In the early years of this century, Jews in North America had hailed mostly from eastern Europe, where many of them had exchanged their Jewish faith for trust in socialism. Arriving here from czarist lands, they worked to better society using socialist principles, not religious ones. Socialism had even taught them to view religion as "the opiate of the masses." Yet they knew they were Jews. So they adopted an ethnic view of Judaism. Attending synagogue and having the experience of God was not what they sought. Instead, they enjoyed each other's company, ate old-country food together, told jokes about Europe and the czar, lived in close proximity to each other, and thought that was sufficient to make one a Jew.

In a way they were right, at least for their time. Perhaps we might question whether they were pious Jews, or even good Jews, given their nonreligiousness. But they certainly remained Jews, often fiercely proud Jews, sometimes deriving their socialist principles of justice for all from Jewish teachings. Almost no one crossed religious lines back then, so few people thought to question their definition by noting that you can enter Judaism by choice, not by birth, in which case what you learn and what you select is the religion, not the ethnicity of a prior existence you never had.

Today, large numbers of people are choosing Judaism. Younger Jews by birth, moreover, have less and less recollection of the old-country ethnicity, so if they decide to remain Jews, it will be primarily because they see the spiritual and ethical wisdom of Jewish tradition. Judaism is thus rapidly being redefined not as an ethnic identity, but as a religion.

This is not to say that ethnicity has completely disappeared, or even that it should. There are ethnic foods for holidays and ethnic customs that families retain through the generations. There is a distinctive tradition of Jewish humor and even Jewish values that arose not out of Jewish religious sources like the Bible and the Talmud, but out of the life of the community itself. One of Judaism's strengths is the value it places on all the positive ways in which the Jewish People have remained bonded together through the centuries. Ethnicity per se is beneficial. It prevents our religion from becoming so ethereal that people merely believe in it, but do not live it.

These positive ethnic elements, however, are not inherited, but learned—learned, that is, over time as a Jew in Jewish community. Jews who are born into Judaism as well as those who adopt it later in their lives slowly but surely begin to recognize the appeal of these nonreligious but highly significant aspects of living as a Jew.

On the other hand, ethnicity is not enough. More and more, Jews are asking questions about spirituality, the way we relate to God in day-to-day life. Many Jews do not actually use the word "spirituality," since it is new to the Jewish lexicon, and to some, it "sounds Christian, not Jewish." There is, however, no other word available, so it is convenient to use it.

There are many roads to Jewish spirituality, some familiar to people of other faiths: prayer, meditation, and ritual, for instance, all of which Judaism knows and respects. In addition, there are distinctively *Jewish* ways of the spirit.

Jews sanctify not just time but space, so that the Land of Israel is a remarkably spiritual place for us (see p. 179). To take the road up to Jerusalem invariably sends spiritual thrills up my spine. Jews visit Israel still—as modern-day pilgrims. This is the *spirituality of the Land*.

Then too, there is the Jewish love of blessings in our prayers (see p. 83). Blessings enable us to celebrate God's presence in and through nature and history, both. Living with a blessing on our lips is tantamount to seeking out the beautiful, the promising, and the hopeful, and then praising God who makes these things all around us. This is the *spirituality of blessing.*

Torah too is a source of the spirit. It has been said that study is itself a form of worship, and so it is for Jews, whose prayer book includes whole paragraphs from the Talmud for us to worship with. More Jews study Torah regularly than worship regularly. These are people who find the word of God their deepest inspiration. This is the *spirituality of Torah.*

And last, there are our good deeds, religious obligations we arrive at through study of Torah, and in which we see the hand of God leading us on to a better life. There are Jews who dedicate huge amounts of their time to doing good works, and if pressed hard enough, will tell you that they feel spiritual when they do so. This is the *spirituality of good deeds.*

Do all Jews experience spirituality? No. But along with the positive aspects of ethnicity, spirituality is a thing to be sought.

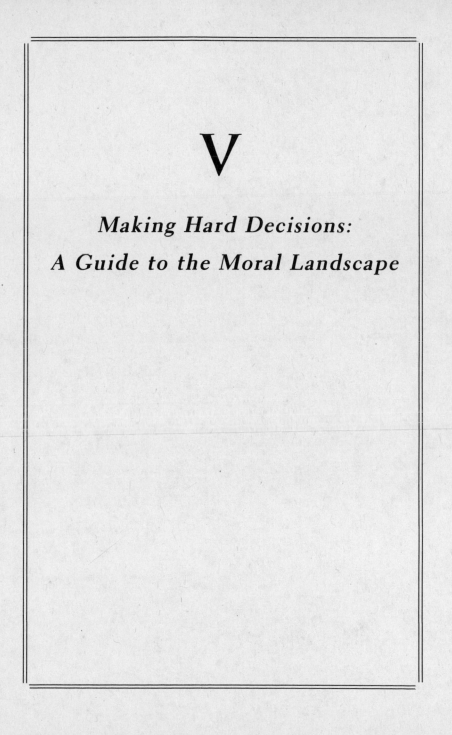

V

Making Hard Decisions:
A Guide to the Moral Landscape

As the twentieth century draws to an end, we can look back on technological progress beyond our wildest imagination. Just one generation ago, Rabbi Kertzer typed this book on a manual Smith Corona typewriter. The only computer available was a dinosaur model that filled a room. By contrast, the computer on which I am typing this revision is a notebook variety that I carry in my briefcase, and it is some ten times more powerful than anything available forty years ago.

We didn't have microwave ovens back then, and there were no digital clocks either. Now everything is controlled by inexpensive microchips, a word no one had heard of when Rabbi Kertzer was writing. Music systems were still called Hi-Fi then; cassette tapes were unknown, let alone Walkmans and CDs.

A better example involving moral decisions is the revolution in medicine and health care. If you thought you were pregnant back then, you had to wait to see if you got your period, and then confirm your condition by a rabbit test that took days to process. You couldn't test in advance to find out the gender of your child-to-be, and without such advances as ultrasound, estimations of whether the fetus was developing normally were largely guesswork. Condoms were common, along with IUDs, but the pill was still about a decade away. No one imagined such things as birth control implants. We didn't have CAT scans and laser surgery either. Most people with poor eyesight still wore glasses back then, though contact lenses—the hard variety, not the soft—were coming on the market.

But technological advance has come at a sacrifice. Able to do things we never imagined doing, we now face moral questions of enormous consequence. It may be easier to live in the modern world, but it is not easier to live morally. The Gulf War of 1991 demonstrated what the arms race and nuclear proliferation might conceivably lead to. Instant television coverage taught us what damage "smart" weapons could do. A doctor has invented a suicide machine, so suicide is easier, but is it right or wrong? The daily mail brings ecological circulars printed on recyclable paper, warning me of global warming and an end to the rain forests. Fish die in polluted rivers, and I worry when I can actually see the air I breathe.

Social movements too challenge us to rethink things we once knew for certain. Our age has discovered the individual person as deserving of dignity and freedom to choose his or her own destiny. That means women are no longer automatically relegated to housework, though they may choose to work in the home—as men can, nowadays; to some extent, corporate boardrooms have been opened to Jews, minorities, and women too. The annual calendar includes not just St. Patrick's Day but Gay Rights Day as well. Animal rights groups tell me I should become a vegetarian. Religiously speaking, people increasingly elect their religion of preference, either converting to a new religion as an adult or deciding to remain whatever it was that one was brought up.

These trends too are packed with moral questions, all the more so as social tendencies speed up or are slowed down by economic and political considerations. Should lesbians and gays be viewed as opting for an alternative life style that is no better and no worse than heterosexuality? Is there some guidance somewhere on matters of sexuality in general? Should Jews be committed to feminism?

Most questions worth considering have no simple answer, and conversely, most questions that can be answered with a simple yes or no are probably not serious questions at all. This section, therefore, charts a moral landscape for Jews, based on Jewish values. Only a sample of issues can be considered here, but we shall see that Judaism has its own distinctive moral tradition. Even if details in specific cases are not clearly at hand, a Jewish overview can often be found.

QUESTIONS IN PART V

1. What Is the Basis for Jewish Moral Decision Making?

Several basic Jewish values underlie most of the questions that follow.

First is the supreme value Jews put on life. When Jews toast, they raise their wine glasses and say **l'chayim** [l'KHAH-yim], "To life." According to the Talmud, life is so important that with only three exceptions, every single Jewish law may be disobeyed if it can be demonstrated that keeping it would be life-threatening. The exceptions are idolatry, murder, and sexual immorality like incest or rape. Under no conditions may Jews agree to abandon God or to murder or rape someone. But by contrast, even though we fast on Yom Kippur, we are duty-bound to eat, even to eat nonkosher foods, if we are sufficiently sick that fasting might endanger our lives. Similarly, Jews circumcise their baby boys, but not if the child is sick and the operation might prove life-threatening.

A second dominant value in Judaism is our emphasis on freedom. The theological message of the Exodus itself is that God's plan for humanity is to set them free. This message is repeated weekly in the Kiddush, the prayer that initiates Shabbat (see p. 209), for the Sabbath is itself a symbol of ultimate freedom from want; and Judaism would be unthinkable without its Passover celebration, which is nothing if not the affirmation that God took us out of bondage, and someday will see the whole world free. We view history itself as a long saga of subject peoples going from slavery and dependence on earthly rulers to liberty and dependence on God alone. The Rabbis discussed what the messianic age or world to come would be like. One of them said, "It will be just like this world, except that no one will be subjugated."

Third, we find Judaism emphasizing human action as the way to save the world. Unlike most Eastern religions, Judaism teaches that the world of our senses is not an illusion. The pain and suffering we see around us are just that: real pain and suffering, which must be eradicated. The Rabbis taught us a lesson by picturing Moses at the shore of the Red Sea, praying for deliverance from the pursuing Egyptian army. "Stop praying," God is imagined to have said. "Do something." With that, one brave man jumps into the raging sea, and only then, because a human being dares to act, do the waters split apart for the Israelites to cross.

From the first century on, children were urged to grow into "good deeds," our only means of deliverance. We differed here from classical Christianity, which emphasized faith, not deeds. By contrast, our tradition pictures God as saying, "It would even be all right if my children forgot me, as long as they keep my commandments." The mystical tradition describes the world as imperfect, awaiting our actions, which accomplish **tikkun olam** [tee-KOON oh-LAHM], literally, "repairing the world." So Jews tend to give to charities, to support organizations that work for peace, and to vote for social programs that will eliminate suffering and disease.

Finally, Judaism strikes a balance between human rights and the rights of other creatures, and even the earth itself. Without a doubt, it gives priority to human needs, both physical and spiritual. But it recognizes animal rights also, and holds that the earth should not be ravaged, since it belongs to God who made it. Still, only humans are made in the image of God, so that humans of every age are to be accorded particular respect, and even after death honor to the deceased is a Jewish mandate.

This balance between different goods is typical of the way Jews answer moral dilemmas. We search our literature for compelling precedents, weigh both sides of the question, and try to arrive at a balanced answer that is fair to all. We prefer making rulings in one case at a time, rather than sweeping generalizations that claim to be universally right in every instance. The prophetic tradition of crying out about general injustice is alive and well among us, but when it comes to acting on those judgments, we prefer the halachic processes of careful legal scrutiny so as to make sure that appropriate moral outrage does not lead to inappropriate moral injustice in any particular instance.

The practicality of Jewish decision making is worth reiterating here. From time to time, in areas where the issue involved is not crucial, the Rabbis rule that we not establish rules that people cannot keep. Even if technically the people are breaking the law, we let them do it, holding that if they realistically cannot be expected to keep it, it is better that they sin in ignorance than knowingly.

2. *Does the Jewish Religion Allow Birth Control or Abortion?*

The Jewish religion has traditionally been opposed to birth control and abortion when practiced for purely selfish reasons. A home without children, Jews believe, is a home without blessing. Our highest fulfillment is in our children and our family life. According to Jewish law, every man and woman has a solemn obligation to bring at least two children into the world. If we cannot have children of our own, we adopt them.

However, the Talmud describes women who used birth control because it was suspected that they would give birth to deformed children, or because if they became pregnant, they might be unable to care for the children they already had, or (finally) because their own mental state made having children impossible. The Rabbis applaud this behavior. Thus early on, Judaism sanctioned birth control under certain conditions: when pregnancy represents a health hazard to the mother or child, or when deformed children might be born. Modern Judaism has extended this concept to include cases of extreme poverty, inadequate living conditions, and threats to the welfare of existing children in the family. Reform Judaism goes so far as to declare that birth control is a necessity under certain family conditions. Most Reform and Conservative rabbis subscribe to the program of planned parenthood.

Moreover, even though having children (by birth or by adoption) is a very important good, it is not the only good. Modern liberal Jews (and modern Orthodox Jews too) have been informed by feminism of the extent to which an undue emphasis on childbearing and mothering as women's primary role may make women into indentured servants in their own homes. Here the Jewish value of freedom enters in. Thus women are encouraged to have children, if they can, but also to pursue other goals. When a couple does have children, husbands are encouraged to share parenthood responsibilities so that the children do not become a burden on the mother only.

A closely related issue is that of therapeutic abortion, prescribed by a physician to save the life or health of a pregnant woman. In Jewish law such an action is considered entirely justified. The life of the mother, Jews believe, is more important than that of the not-yet-born child, both to her husband and to any other children she may have. Technically, the fetus does have some rights—again, we see the Jewish aversion to a position of "all or nothing." It is attached to the mother's womb, and so has the same rights as any other part of her body. She cannot cut off a finger without cause, for instance, and she also cannot cut off the fetus for no reason whatever. If her finger is infected, however, so that her life is at stake, then we do amputate it; and if we fear that the fetus will endanger the woman's life if it comes to term, we perform an abortion. Liberal Jews expand the concept of "endangerment" to include the mother's mental health and the mental health of the family as a whole. They are already alive, and deserve protection against a life of poverty, enslavement to terrible social conditions, and a life of physical or mental suffering that is not in keeping with a soul made in God's image.

The most important consideration in both birth control and abortion is, What is best for the entire family? The sanctity of marriage is not in reproduction. It is in the bond that exists between husband, wife, and the children they want and love.

3. *Do Jews Favor Capital Punishment?*

The Jewish attitude toward capital punishment presents a graphic example of how the Jewish tradition has evolved over the centuries.

The Bible declares unambiguously, "One who takes a life shall be put to death." But very early in Jewish history, there developed among the social and religious leaders of the people a revulsion against legal execution. The literal interpretation of the biblical injunction was hedged with one safeguard after another to protect the accused against miscarriage of justice. Those safeguards finally became so involved that capital punishment virtually ceased to exist.

According to the Talmud, a court of twenty-three judges had been established to judge murder cases and to pass a sentence of death on the guilty. But before they could do so, the prosecutor had to prove that the crime was deliberate and premeditated, and to do that, it was required to produce two witnesses who had actually heard the defendant declare the intention to commit the crime. In addition, the two witnesses had to testify that they had quoted chapter and verse from the Book of Exodus to the would-be murderer, thus warning him or her of the gravity of the offense. Circumstantial evidence was ruled unacceptable in capital cases.

Furthermore, if these virtually impossible conditions were met, and the twenty-three judges voted unanimously for the death sentence, the Talmud ruled that the defendant must be acquitted! The Rabbis reasoned that if not one of the twenty-three could find some extenuating circumstance, the atmosphere of the trial must have been charged with prejudice.

All of these subtleties had just one goal: to leave the biblical law unchanged in letter but modified completely in spirit. The verdict of death was irreversible, after all, and the creators of Jewish law trembled before the possibility of making a mistake.

Since 1954, modern Israel has forbidden capital punishment, except in cases of genocide, acts of terror during war, and grave security violations during wartime, such as the use of explosives. Even so, the death penalty is not mandatory (as of 1992) and has been invoked only once, in the case of Adolf Eichmann, the mass murderer who directed "the final solution," Hitler's war upon the Jews.

4. What Is the Jewish Attitude toward Suicide and Euthanasia (Mercy Killing)?

Throughout the Jewish tradition runs the belief that life is only lent to us. Rabbi Chanina, a great Jewish martyr who was burned at the stake during the Roman persecution, is said to have refused to remove the wet cloth placed in his mouth by his tormentors, although to do so would have hastened his death and ended his horrible agony. To his pleading disciples he explained, "My life is not my own to give or to take. It is God's alone." There are now responsa that prohibit the smoking of cigarettes, on the grounds that there is reason to believe that cigarette smoking is the equivalent of slow but steady suicide.

Legal euthanasia, mercy killing at the request of someone incurably ill and in pain, is also against our tradition. For in this case, another person is being used as an instrument of suicide.

However, we have to look more carefully at these generalizations if we are to grasp the full impact of the Jewish position. As usual, it is balanced.

Take suicide, first. Clearly, the person who commits the

"crime" of suicide is already dead, and cannot be punished by the court. In theory, Judaism deals harshly with the proven suicide anyway, in that Jews who take their own life are buried without honor or eulogy and are mourned without the traditional ceremonial. In fact, however, Jewish tradition establishes the presumption of mitigating circumstances, so as to avoid having to subject the suicide to such humiliation at the time of burial. How do we know it was a suicide? Maybe the person had an accident after all? Maybe mental derangement set in, so that the person was really ill and not in control of his or her own decisions? Maybe the person repented of the act just before death occurred, but it was too late?

We thus avoid rash conclusions when we are faced with apparent self-destruction. In line with the talmudic dictum, "Give everyone the benefit of the doubt," Jewish tradition provides that no person may be deemed a suicide unless there is overwhelming evidence that it was the deliberate act of a man or woman of sound mind. If there is a shadow of doubt, we must assume that the act was accidental, or at least beyond the control of the victim.

In other words, once again we have the attempt to retain the letter of the law in theory, but not in practice. Should people commit suicide? No. We must always strive to do what we can to further God's purposes, not to destroy what God has made, certainly not ourselves, made as we are in God's spiritual image. But if in fact someone fails to live up to the ideal, having been overcome by physical or mental agony, we presume the best, not the worst, and have compassion both for the suicide victim and for the victim's grieving family.

The same balanced judgment is to be found in cases of euthanasia. In general, it is against Jewish law to remove life-sustaining equipment so as to hasten death. But there is no mandate to apply the equipment to start with. A Jewish physician may not turn off the intravenous feeding device that sustains a patient's body, but the same doctor is not duty bound to turn it on or even to refill it when it is empty.

Jewish wisdom tells of a sick and suffering woman who complains to the rabbi that she is in such pain she wishes to die. But God is sustaining her, she observes, well beyond her natural life expectancy.

"What makes God sustain you?" the rabbi asks.

"I pray every day," says the woman; "God must be rewarding me for my piety."

"Then why be so pious?" asks the rabbi. "Stop praying." The woman stopped praying, we are told, and died three days later.

In other words, life is good, precious, holy. But Judaism understands the suffering we go through at our worst times, and cautions that a dignified death is also a good and precious thing. We advise the ideal of retaining life when we can. We recognize exceptions to that rule, and then ring them round with precautionary measures that prevent people from hastily jumping the gun in a bad situation. In the end, we prefer to see life as it should be led, not life that is a living death.

5. *What Is the Jewish Attitude toward War?*

Judaism holds that some wars are just, but it accepts the right of people to be conscientious objectors. At the heart of the Jewish doctrine is the centrality of the Jewish concept of peace (in Hebrew, **shalom** [shah-LOME]). To write about Judaism without using the word *shalom* is tantamount to studying American principles without the Declaration of Independence; or listing America's great rivers, but leaving out the Mississippi. When Jews meet each other on the street, they say "Shalom," the equivalent of the English "Hello." The standard greeting for the Sabbath is **"Shabbat shalom"** [shah-BAHT shah-LOME]—"A peaceful Sabbath to you"—and so anxious are Jews to voice this wish that it is customary to say it to someone not just on the Sabbath but even a day or two before, if you think you may not see that person again before the Sabbath arrives! The **Tefillah** [t'fee-LAH], the most important prayer of the daily synagogue service (see p. 83), ends with a blessing for peace, as does the Grace after Meals (see p. 98), which, in fact, has two petitions for peace. Rashi, our best-known medieval commentator on Jewish tradition, explains the double appearance of a prayer for peace in the Grace after Meals by saying that only peace would be so represented, because "if you have no peace, you have nothing."

In Hebrew, "shalom" is linguistically allied to the root meaning wholeness. The ideal implies harmony among all creatures, the opposite of such things as fragmentation, shattered dreams, and broken hearts.

Commander Arnold Reznikoff, a Jewish chaplain in the United States Navy, notes that all three major Western religions posit peace as their goal, but in different ways. Christianity has traditionally leaned toward a pacifist ideal, seeing its model in such statements as Jesus' instructions to "turn the other check." By contrast, Islam has tended toward the religious use of war to bring about eventual peace. Thus, Islamic nations to this day declare holy wars on their enemies, emulating Mohammed, who fought his way through the Arabian peninsula forcibly converting pagans into Moslems. Judaism takes a middle road. While it does not glorify war in any way, it also does not preach pacifism, in that it does not declare all wars to be unjust. Sometimes people have no choice but to fight.

Nonetheless, we do have our conscientious objectors, who translate the basic doctrine of shalom into a rejection of any resort to violence. Hence, during World War II, American synagogue groups endorsed the position of a number of young Jews who were drafted into military service but claimed they could not in good conscience contravene the principle of nonviolence.

Despite its historic teaching of the sanctity of human life, Judaism has always distinguished some wars as just—not desirable, but just—and perhaps even obligatory, as, for instance, a war of outright self-defense. The Talmud does advise Jews to choose to "be killed rather than to kill," but the reference is not to war. It is to a situation in which a sword is placed against your back and another in your hand with the order to murder another human being or suffer death yourself. "What makes you think your blood is redder than the would-be victim's?" asks the Talmud, as it reminds us that murder is never justified.

But talmudic law does not equate self-defense with murder. Hence, a defensive war against an enemy threatening to kill you is accepted as just. Jewish tradition would thus support the bearing of arms when a nation is engaged in such a war.

An ethical problem arises when two basic principles are in conflict. Jewish religious law affirms that "the law of the land is the law for Jews too." What if one's nation is engaged in an immoral war? What is the obligation, for instance, of a Jewish citizen under a totalitarian regime? The Talmud supplies an answer to the dilemma by distinguishing between "a wicked government" and a "righteous government." In the case of the former, one must obey one's conscience rather than the state.

During the Vietnam War, the question arose among both church and synagogue members whether there could be "*selective* conscientious objection*," which entailed a subjective evaluation of the morality behind a specific war, but not war in general. Most Jews accepted a person's right to make such a claim.

So Judaism does allow for conscientious objection to war, and finds its warrant in the Bible (Deut. 20), which lists those who are able to claim exemption from military service. The list includes those who are too weak for military duty, a condition that the Rabbis interpret to include those who have no stomach for bloodshed.

6. *What Are Some Jewish Guides to Sexuality?*

Though rabbinic Judaism took shape in the midst of the Greco-Roman world, it rejected a good deal of Greco-Roman thought, including the idea that the human soul is good while the human body is evil. Unlike Christianity, therefore, Judaism never looked down upon bodily pleasure, and did not associate sex with sinfulness. Monasticism, chastity, and celibacy never became Jewish ideals. Instead, the Rabbis extolled the state of marriage, partly because of their high regard for raising children, and partly because they believed that God had created human beings with a physical and emotional need for each other.

The Rabbis therefore regarded sex not only as necessary but even as desirable. Husbands and wives whose marital partners vowed not to have intercourse with them could sue for divorce. Husbands whose work took them away from home for long periods of time were admonished to be home often enough to satisfy the sexual urges of their wives. Eventually it even became the custom to consider Shabbat a time when married couples could celebrate their love by having sex together.

On the other hand, the Rabbis were shocked by the sexual laxity that typified some of the pagan cults of their time, so that they cautioned people against sexual wantonness. Their ideal, therefore, was proper sexuality within marriage, and studious modesty in public. Certainly adultery was banned absolutely, in keeping with the Ten Commandments.

The Talmud also discusses rape, noting that the prohibition against rape is one of only three laws that may never be broken, even at the cost of one's life. (The other two are the bans on idolatry and murder.) Moreover, a rapist cannot claim that he was not at fault, that he was seduced, or that he was somehow forced to commit the crime. A rapist is always fully responsible for his act.

The Talmud prohibits premarital sex also, but not with the same degree of vigor as adultery, the other instance of extramarital sex between consenting adults. Even though the Rabbis urged couples to put off having sexual relations until marriage, they were quite open about the fact that people did not always heed their advice in this regard, and unlike adulterers, those who engaged in sex before marriage received no punishment.

To a great extent this ancient Jewish guide to sexuality holds in contemporary society. A modern theology of sex would insist that couples engage in the physical act of sex, but for more than physical reasons. Sex is the most intimate act possible, signifying that the two people engaged in it are intimate not just physically but spiritually as well. They should care deeply about each other and be committed in a special way to each other over a period of time (possibly forever), not just for the moment. The model for Jews is our relationship to God from Mount Sinai on. The Rabbis describe that relationship as a marriage, following the words of Hosea the Prophet, who pictures Israel's idolatry as if Israel is guilty of adultery with other gods. With that theological guideline in mind, we can see briefly how the talmudic rules apply in our time.

Certainly the rabbinic repudiation of rape remains unchanged, and it would be extended to sexual harassment as well. For a manager to speak inappropriately of sex to a secretary, for instance, would also fall under the category of improper speech, literally "contaminating the mouth" in rabbinic parlance, yet another moral guideline. The gift of speech is uniquely human, a further instance of our having been created in the image of God, who, after all, willed the world into being using words. We are to keep our mouths pure, therefore, avoiding such things as slander, lewdness, and inappropriate remarks typical of sexual harassment.

The ban on adultery is also still taken with the greatest of seriousness. Adultery, after all, is equivalent to idolatry, in Hosea's metaphor. Moreover, the family is the central Jewish institution, more important even than the synagogue. In Judaism, adultery is sufficient cause for suing for divorce.

Finally, the Rabbis' unhappiness with premarital sex but their understanding that it was not as grave as the other instances of illicit sexuality mentioned above might be combined with the theology of sex in which sexual partners are expected to be spiritually intimate, to yield the following position. Nowadays with premarital sex the norm, many rabbis emphasize the relative laxity of the ancient approach, and are willing to condone the practice of couples' living together, for instance, as long as their doing so reflects a growing spiritual intimacy that might well lead to marriage.

7. *What Is the Jewish Attitude toward Feminism?*

A preliminary issue is egalitarianism. In talmudic law, women are barred from many commandments to which men are called. For example, women may not serve as witnesses, lead worship, or read the Torah in public services. In addition, they are exempt from many other duties, which they are allowed to adopt, but for which (unlike men) they are not held responsible (like wearing a tallit—a prayer shawl). Orthodoxy retains all of these regulations. In addition, since they are taught to value large families, and since they do not believe in birth control except under exceptional circumstances in which the mother's life might be at stake, women in ultra-Orthodox and Chasidic communities are frequently pregnant and spend much of their time caring for children and homemaking. Modern Orthodoxy, however, and certainly all liberal branches of Judaism have tried in varying degrees to remove the obstacles to women achieving full and equal membership in the Jewish people.

In the past quarter century, considerable progress has been made. It is common now to find women presidents and board members in temples and synagogues. In 1972, the Hebrew Union

College (Reform) ordained its first woman rabbi, and the Reconstructionist Rabbinic College followed suit very shortly thereafter. The Conservative movement voted to admit women as rabbinic candidates in 1983. By 1992, there were approximately two hundred women rabbis, most of them in the Reform movement, where current classes are approximately 50 percent women and 50 percent men. Women may be cantors too, or any other professional person associated with Jewish leadership.

Women note that Jewish law was composed by men for men, so that women are treated as outsiders about whom men pass legislation. For instance, in the marriage and divorce laws adhered to by the conservative end of the Jewish spectrum, men divorce their wives but not the other way around. If a woman wants a divorce, she must persuade her husband to give her one. Failing that she must appeal to a rabbinic court, on which only men sit, and persuade them to make her husband prepare the requisite divorce document. Another instance often cited is the ancient rabbinic law of abandonment, which forbids a Jewish wife to remarry when her husband has disappeared without witnesses to his death. Orthodoxy still retains that law, though it has long tried to mitigate its cruelty by accepting as sufficient the testimony of one witness alone, even though normally two witnesses are required. Reform Judaism, on the other hand, did away with such encumbrances on women over a hundred years ago.

One can appreciate the depth of resentment of modern Jewish women, when, as late as 1970, in a book published in England, Rabbi Immanuel Jakobovitz wrote that "the wife is required by Jewish religious law to 'give the income of her work' and all of her inheritance to her husband, while the husband is only under the obligation to support her throughout her life." The Chief Rabbi of the British Commonwealth quoted this rabbinic law without passing judgment on its equity.

In 1973, the first National Conference of Jewish Women was launched. The following year, the Jewish Feminist Organization was created as a national movement, with the stated goal of "the full, direct, and equal participation of women at all levels of Jewish life—communal, religious, educational, and political." That organization no longer exists, but many Jewish women's organizations and resource centers have grown up in its place all across North America.

Modern Jewish feminism does much more than demand equal access to Jewish responsibility and leadership for women. It has advanced an important critique of Jewish institutions in general, and the synagogue in particular. It raises questions of who has power and why. It challenges the ethics of a system that depends on hierarchical organizations, unilateral decisions, and agendas that exclude the poor and the handicapped. It rejects descriptions of God (such as "great, mighty, and awesome") that assume only masculine role models and suggests that human experience has its masculine and its feminine side, both of which ought to be found in a God of both men and women. It seeks to locate the voice of women in Jewish tradition, so that the role models and interpreters of Judaism are not always men. It creates new rituals to be responsive to women's experience: new moon ceremonies that recognize women's body rhythms, for instance, and covenant ceremonies to mark the birth of a baby girl. It draws our attention to the ways in which our very bodies determine who we are, and the manner in which boys are raised differently from girls, in the hope that rabbis and educators will learn how to speak to and program for both women and men.

Is Judaism in favor of these things? Liberal Judaism certainly is. The feminist critique is heard regularly in the Reform and Reconstructionist seminaries, and increasingly it can be found in the Conservative seminary too. If the very foundation of Judaism is the story of the Exodus, with its theological implication that God wants all people free, it is hard to see how authentic Jewish teaching can object to a proposal that we open our leadership ranks to everyone, that we make women as visible as men, and that we raise consciousness about ways in which our institutional thinking has prevented universal religious and spiritual liberty thus far.

8. *What Is the Jewish Attitude toward Homosexuality?*

The Bible is unalterably opposed to homosexuality, going so far as to declare it "an abomination" (Leviticus 18:22). Rabbinic sources barely discuss the matter, but from what little we have, it is evident that the talmudic Rabbis agree with the Bible. It seems that Jewish authorities were convinced that being gay or lesbian was a misguided use of free choice, in that it ran counter to the Jewish assumption that sexuality should be linked to procreation and the establishment of a family.

The gay rights movement of today has made many Jews question the basis for this classical position. At the very least, it is hard now to believe that sexual orientation is solely a matter of exercising free will. It is certainly difficult to retain the biblical notion that being a gay or lesbian is "an abomination." To the extent that homosexuality can be traced to genetic makeup, the biblical and rabbinic judgment that gays and lesbians have freely selected their sexual preference had to be revised.

Jews have never believed in the literal inerrancy of scripture; that is, Jewish tradition has insisted that the Bible tells us truths, but that these truths are not to be equated with a literal reading of the Bible. The Bible must be interpreted anew by every generation, in the light of postbiblical Jewish teachings and the new insights that we are given with the passing of the years. The Rabbis of antiquity, for instance, regularly altered the plain meaning of a biblical verse in light of the state of knowledge in their own time. Similarly, medieval rabbis felt no need to follow slavishly the advice of every rabbinic predecessor. Even if they had wanted to, that would have been impossible, since Jewish precedents are almost always complex, with rabbis arrayed on both sides of difficult issues. Most modern Jews continue the Jewish tradition of weighing the force of precedent against the evidence of our own age in order to judge the extent to which an ancient opinion should guide our actions today. The case of homosexuality is just one of many instances in which modern Jews have had to come to terms with the conflict between ancient wisdom and contemporary science.

However, there remains the fact that Judaism admonishes people whenever possible to have children and establish a loving, stable family life. Hence rabbis would urge people with heterosexual leanings to follow them. As to genetically determined homosexuality, however, the current tendency in Reform and Reconstructionist Judaism is neither to condemn nor to condone it, but to treat it as a state of being into which some people are born, and therefore not even in the category of being moral or immoral. Conservative and Orthodox Judaism tends still to treat homosexuality in ways that are closer to the biblical model.

The movements that accept homosexuality simply as a given in some people's genetic makeup have passed regulations calling for equal rights for homosexuals and have announced that sexual preference should not be grounds for refusing anyone admission to programs designed to train Jewish leaders, including the cantorate and the rabbinate. The proportion of homosexuals in the Jewish clergy is assumed to be the same as the proportion of homosexuals in the population at large.

Many major cities have synagogues designed to serve gay and lesbian Jews. Some rabbis have designed the equivalent of marriage ceremonies for homosexual couples. More and more, these couples are adopting children so as to raise a family in accordance with the Jewish view that family life is the ideal state of human existence.

9. *What Is the Jewish Attitude toward Money?*

When the socialist revolution broke out in Russia almost a century ago, Jews were in its forefront. But in adopting communism, they were abandoning Judaism. They were reacting to the terrible persecution they had known under the czars. Judaism does not permit unbridled private wealth at the expense of the poor, but it encourages a system in which private property is used to reward hard work, and it demands social responsibility on the part of those who have amassed whatever wealth a society possesses.

The responsibility of the rich to the poor is central to rabbinic legislation. The Bible (Exodus 22:24–25) says, "If you lend money to any of My people, even to the poor among you, you shall not be a creditor, nor impose interest." Moreover, "If you take your neighbor's garment as security, return it by nightfall . . . for that is his only covering. Wherein will he sleep?" Using this verse as their basis, the Rabbis erect the following guidelines for people with money:

1. "If you lend money" really means "When you lend money." Lending to those in need is an ethical obligation.
2. Different degrees of obligation exist. "My people" implies that if members of your own family are poor and others are equally poor, you help your own family first, and then you help others.
3. "Even to the poor" teaches us that first you must lend money to the poor, and only afterward to the rich.

The emphasis was on lending money to the poor so that they would become independent of further doles. Maimonides established the rule that giving charity is required, but he established a hierarchy of charitable acts. Giving in such a way that the recipient does not know who the donor is, for instance, is preferable to letting the recipient know the name of the giver. Giving completely anonymously so that no one knows the name of the giver is better still. Best of all is teaching recipients a trade or establishing them in some independent business so that they can attain the dignity of being self-supporting.

By the Middle Ages, Jews had established a thoroughgoing, economically viable banking system that provided opportunities for Jews whom society increasingly barred from the standard economic pursuits of the day. The system worked to the advantage of society, in that it helped to finance general economic expansion. When historians recall that medieval Jews were in the moneylending business, they are correct. But Jews were not the "Shylocks" or "Fagins" popularized by Shakespeare and Dickens. The reason they loaned money was that they were not allowed to do anything else. They did charge high interest rates, but in fact, non-Jewish moneylenders (like the Italian banks) charged higher. Interest rates were high then because the chances of never being repaid were enormous.

But even as Jews developed their own economic system in which loans were common, medieval Jewish communities saw a parallel expansion of charity funds, not so much to dole out money to the poor for the necessities of life as to establish the indigent as financially independent.

Even the poor were expected to give to those poorer than they.

Underlying the Jewish system of economics is a unique approach to money. Why should we be required to lend our capital at all? Because, says tradition, capital differs from the goods that it buys. The latter are actual things of inherent value that we own; money is not. Money is an arbitrary commodity, useless except for its utilitarian function of enabling us to transfer the real things of the world through complex economic exchange. As one medieval commentator says, "There is no inherent logic why money should even exist, but since it happens to exist, you should at least loan it to others for their welfare."

So money exists as an impersonal utilitarian commodity to be used for the common good. Loans are not only permissible; they are desirable. And in the end Jewish law describes two sorts of loans that we should make.

First, money is to be lent to the poor, especially the poor close to you, your family and friends, lest others have to care for them. Since these poor recipients cannot be expected to be able to repay the principal plus interest, you should waive their interest payments. Second, in a more advanced social stage, money is to be used as interest-bearing loans in business in the hope that social progress will result from healthy financial expansion. And of course, those who benefit from that expansion are especially obliged to care for the poor, both in interest-free loans and in outright gifts to the public relief agencies that can then allot money to those who require it.

Judaism insists that money does not belong to those who have it, for they are mere conduits through whom money passes. They are temporary holders of capital, charged with using it in helpful ways: sustaining the community's funds for the poor; making interest-free loans to those who may someday become independent; and encouraging joint capital ventures in a complex marketplace such as capitalism makes available.

10. *What Is the Jewish Attitude toward the Environment?*

"The earth and all it contains belongs to God," says the psalmist (Ps. 24:1). On the other hand, God creates Adam and Eve and instructs the first human beings to fill the earth and master it (Genesis 1:28). The earth apparently belongs to God and human beings at the same time. How does Judaism balance these two contrary notions?

In essence, Judaism allows us to make proper use of natural resources, but does not allow us to deplete them or to misuse them. Deuteronomy 20:19–20 forbids destroying fruit trees while besieging a city, and rabbinic legislation interprets Leviticus 25:34 so as to protect land outside the city limits from being put to economic use. Similarly, the Rabbis warned against overgrazing the countryside and gave the court the right to intervene if it saw deforestation occurring.

In general, the Jewish principle known as **bal tashchit** [BAHL tahsh-KHEET], "do not destroy," has been cited as a warning against wanton destruction of what God has brought into being. Also, the Jewish emphasis on life has led modern rabbis to issue bans on smoking, polluting the air, and any other misuse of our environment that might destroy life rather than enhance it.

Jewish prayer actually demands that we appreciate nature. Since the earth and all it contains belongs to God, Jews are encouraged to enjoy what God has entrusted to us, but when we do so, we first say a blessing acknowledging the divine origin of what we are enjoying. Upon seeing nature's wonders, the Grand Canyon, for instance, Jews say, "Blessed are You, God, for creating the universe." Observing a pretty flower garden or a white blanket of fallen snow sparkling with sunshine calls forth this blessing: "Blessed are You, God, for having such things as this in Your World." The first blossoms in early spring prompt us to say. "Blessed are You, God, for creating lovely trees that human beings enjoy."

Food too is to be enjoyed only after we make mention of its divine origin. Jews have blessings to say over bread, fruit, vegetables, and even water. The point of these blessings is expressly given in the Talmud. "It is written that the earth and all it contains belongs to God (Ps. 24:1), but it is also written that God has given the earth to human beings (Ps. 115:16). But there is no contradiction between the two verses. The first verse reflects the situation before we say a blessing. The second verse stands for after the blessing has been said."

We may indeed use nature, which God has given to us. But ideally, acts of enjoying it must be preceded by a blessing that reminds us of nature's sanctity and our responsibility as its custodians. We are to resist the temptation to ravage the environment. At the point where our use of nature threatens to do away with life or of the environment itself, we are to remember that what we are destroying is the handiwork of God, and then, as in all cases of teshuvah ("repentance"; see p. 116), we are to do what we can to prevent a continuation of the offense.

11. According to Judaism, Do Animals Have Rights?

Jewish tradition insists that animals do have rights. The laws of keeping kosher (see p. 87) allow us to eat animals, but only if they have been slaughtered in a humane manner. Moreover, we are not permitted to hunt, and the only reason we may kill an animal is for the express purpose of using it for food.

The Torah forbids us to cause "pain to a living thing." We may have pets, but only if we treat them with compassion. Interestingly enough, one Jewish tradition treats kindness to animals as a purer act of goodness than helping one's neighbor, for by definition, it cannot be done in the hope of receiving a reward in return!

Of late, we have become increasingly aware of the existence of animal experiments by scientists. Judaism permits these experiments if it can be demonstrated that human life may be saved eventually as a result of doing them. But it places limitations on the experiments too. Modern-day rabbis oppose experiments that are mere duplications of what has been done before, experiments, that is, about which scientists can just as easily read in the scholarly literature. We oppose also experiments for trivial purposes, that is, for scientific ends other than the enhancement and expansion of life. Jews would thus oppose animal experiments in the cosmetic industry. We would also question the fur industry, in which animals are killed so that people can have beautiful coats. Interestingly enough, the Rabbis did accept the notion of using fur where it was necessary for human warmth and therefore, human health and life, but even there they were ambivalent. Normally a blessing is said when you put on new clothes; but the blessing is omitted if the clothes are made of fur.

The Rabbis warn regularly against becoming so inured to the death of animals that we begin to accept it without hesitation. Even though it may have to occur in certain circumstances, we are cautioned that once we begin to take it lightly, we are on the road to becoming cruel even in our dealings with people, and in any event, cruelty to animals is itself an evil.

Some liberally minded Jews have gone so far as to become vegetarians on the grounds that the meat industry raises animals in conditions that cause the animal pain, so that even if the act of kosher slaughtering is painless, the period leading up to that time is a terrible instance of "pain to a living thing."

12. *Why Do Jews Persist in Remembering the Holocaust?*

Much criticism has been directed against contemporary Jews who seem to have a morbid preoccupation with memories of the Holocaust, the annihilation of six million Jews during World War II. (Many Jews substitute the Hebrew name **Sho'ah** [SHOA-ah] for the English "Holocaust.") The destruction of almost 40 percent of the world Jewish population within less than a decade was a lacerating experience for those who survived. Hundreds of books describe the emotional scars of wives and husbands, parents and children of those who were lost in the Nazi death chambers. For millions of Jews, the manner of the death of their loved ones evokes feelings that time does not heal.

But the question still persists: Is there anything productive in institutionalizing the Holocaust by setting aside a special Holocaust Day each spring? by establishing courses in high schools, universities, synagogues, and centers devoted to Holocaust studies? by creating a worldwide organization to track down the operators of death camps who escaped punishment? Even the liturgy of the synagogue has been transformed by the Holocaust. Prayer books quite generally now call upon worshipers to affirm that "the world is not the same since Auschwitz." Are Jews just being morbid?

There are three reasons why Jews have perpetuated memories of the Holocaust: religious, practical, and moral.

Jew are a history-oriented people. Anniversaries have always figured prominently in our consciousness. Our personal calendar includes not only birthdays and wedding anniversaries but also anniversaries of the death of dear ones. It has always seemed very important to Jews that the dead be remembered. Folk tales speak movingly of tragedies in which people die without anyone to remember them, as if their miserable lives on earth did not matter, as if they had nothing to teach the next generation, no legacy of love worth celebrating.

So Jews recoil with religious anguish at the thought of so many Jews murdered only because they were Jews, whose very names and biographies may now be irretrievably lost to us. At **Yad Vashem** [YAHD vah-SHEM], the Holocaust memorial in Israel, researchers try to piece together these long-lost personal histories. We may see the day when each Jewish family collects a personal story of one person who died, and has it affixed on the wall, thus adopting at least one anonymous victim and ending the ignoble state of anonymity after death.

The religious motive for remembering the Holocaust is therefore to remember the victims and provide them with whatever posthumous dignity we can by rescuing them from invisibility.

Beyond this religious reason for memorializing the Holocaust, there is a practical one. The horrors of the Nazi concentration camps are so mindshattering that we find it excruciating to fix our attention upon them for any extended period. We are psychologically tempted to create the fantasy that the events never actually took place; some academicians have actually written books to that effect, as if they could negate the evidence of tens of thousands of eyewitnesses as well as official Nazi documents confirming the systematic annihilation of six million Jews.

Another problem is that there are those who use the term "Holocaust" for many similar tragedies in world history: the slaughter of Armenians by Turks, the forced march of Native Americans, or Saddam Hussein's attempted annihilation of the Kurds in Iraq. Jews do not minimize these awful events. But we object to the easy way in which people generalize about evil by using a word that denotes a single specific example of nightmarish terror: Hitler's war against the Jews. We believe that a world that recollects evil in general will be tempted to overlook evil in specific cases, and in turn will allow every new specific case to be sanitized as if it were nothing—just "evil" in general all over again.

So the practical reason to remember the Holocaust for what it was is to overcome the human tendency to forget it because it was so terrible, or to generalize about it because it is easier to think about tragedy in general than to face up to specific tragedies in particular.

But the moral reason may be the most important one. When the mass murderer Adolf Eichmann was on trial, the Israelis informed the world that the motive behind the judicial proceedings was not vengeance but the moral education of contemporary women and men. The striking thing about Eichmann was precisely that he was so ordinary, a living symbol of what historian Hannah Arendt called "the banality of evil." Contemplating the events of the Nazi era, we came to see that the sin of omission on the part of the decent peoples of the world was the sin of silence, the refusal to believe that a highly enlightened people like the Germans could permit themselves to be led by a madman into acts of national depravity that culminated in the events of Auschwitz and the other death camps. We had to learn to readjust our vision and take evil seriously once again.

I shall never forget the words of a leading official of the National Council of Churches during an address to an audience of Protestant editors of Sunday School textbooks:

"Sometimes, when I can't sleep, I agonize over this question.

The men who turned on the gas in the Nazi gas chambers—where were they, on a Sunday morning, when they were eleven years old? Were they in church, and what did they learn about Jews that would enable them, without a trace of remorse, to turn the gas on innocent children?"

The moral reason for preserving memories of the Holocaust beyond our lifetime was best expressed by former Israeli prime minister David Ben-Gurion: "We ask the nations of the world not to forget that one million babies, because they happened to be Jews, were murdered. We want the nations of the world to know that there was an intention to exterminate a people. That intention had its roots in anti-Semitism. They should know that anti-Semitism is dangerous and they should be ashamed of it." Jews worry that to fail to remember Hitler is to risk the rise of anti-Semitism once again. We recognize the moral imperative of keeping the Holocaust before the eyes of the world so that anti-Semitism, still alive and well, will someday cease. We recognize too that uprooting anti-Semitism challenges us to correct our own prejudice toward others. Remembering what happened to us, we are driven to make sure nothing similar happens to others. In the end, the moral reason to remember the Holocaust is not only to be sure that Jews are never put in concentration camps again, but also to be sure that the lesson learned from ordinary Nazis turning on poison gas is that anyone is capable of any evil, unless the world remembers to say "No!" whenever and wherever such evil is found.

VI

The Shape of Sacred Space:

Jewish Homes and Homeland

When we want to look up a location, we use a map, but we own many maps. Drivers use highway maps that show interstate connections and toll roads. Vacationers worry about weather maps that predict rain or sunshine. Bicyclers need relief maps that warn how steep an elevation is. Religious people have maps of sacred sites, the places that are spiritual homes, the spots they want to visit before they die.

Jews have three sacred places: our homes (which are our private places), our synagogues or temples (which are our community places), and the Land of Israel (which is the homeland for the Jewish people as a whole). Most of us would say also that certain historical sites are sacred by virtue of what occurred there—Auschwitz, for instance, where so many Jews perished in the Sho'ah (the Holocaust). Cemeteries too are sacred because we honor the dead and say prayers at gravesides. The Rabbis of old taught that places where miracles occurred are sacred too—we say a blessing when we come upon such places: "Blessed are You, Eternal our God . . . who performed miracles for our forebears at this spot in times past." Jews respect the sacred sites of other people too. Christian churches, Moslem mosques, the Bahai Temple in Haifa—all of these deserve our respect for what they mean to others. And finally, there is the earth itself—the Grand Canyon, rain forests, sweeping African veldts, and Asian steppes—all sacred, since "the earth and all it contains belongs to God" (Ps. 30). The Jewish map of sacred sites is obviously vast and complex.

But of all these holy places, it is our homes, our synagogues, and the historical homeland of Israel that are most distinctively "Jewish." This section explains why and how that is so.

Questions in Part VI

1. Why Do Some Jews Maintain Jewish Homes but Rarely Attend Synagogue Worship?
2. What Is a Mezuzah?
3. What Are Some Jewish Symbols that Jews Keep in Their Homes?
4. How Did the Synagogue Begin?
5. What Is the Difference Between a Synagogue, a Shul, and a Temple?
6. Does the Six-Pointed Star of David Have Any Religious Significance?
7. What Are the Most Important Symbols in the Synagogue?
8. How Are Synagogues Organized, and Why Do You Have to Pay to Belong to Them?
9. Why Is Israel Sacred for Jews?
10. Why Does Israel Welcome So Many Immigrants?
11. Is the State of Israel Controlled by Religious Authority?
12. What Is an Israeli Kibbutz?
13. How Is Israel Governed?
14. Is an American Jew's First Loyalty to Israel or to America?
15. Can American Jews Disagree with Israel's Policies?
16. Why Is Jerusalem So Important to the Jewish People?
17. Why Do Jews Say, "Next Year in Jerusalem"?

1. Why Do Some Jews Maintain Jewish Homes but Rarely Attend Synagogue Worship?

Ideally, Jews should take both home and synagogue seriously. In practice, however, there are many Jews who work hard at keeping a Jewish home, but who go to the synagogue only infrequently. They will usually be there for High Holy Day services (Rosh Hashanah and Yom Kippur) and for special occasions like life cycle events, but they do not feel obliged to attend worship regularly. This pattern of observance can seem very strange to Christians who identify religion more closely with church than with home. Jews, by contrast, have frequently identified their own personal religiousness more closely with their home than with their synagogue.

It has been said that if all Jewish houses of worship were to close, Jewish religious life would continue intact, because the religious life would be sustained in our homes; but if Jews stop practicing Judaism in their homes, the synagogues by themselves would not be able to sustain Jewish commitment for more than a generation.

Jews regard their home as a religious sanctuary, with domestic rituals that are as important as communal worship: lighting the Sabbath candles on Friday evenings; blessing our children at the Sabbath table; kindling Chanukah candles, followed by the joy of festival gifts and games; the Passover seder with friends and family gathered to remember the day when we were slaves to Pharaoh. These are no less momentous than synagogue services, and far more

169

central in conveying the inner spirit of Jewish life from generation to generation.

As far back as the American Civil War, we hear of Jewish soldiers in the field who petitioned their commanding officer to let them go into the woods for a Passover seder. They missed it because of its intimate home associations. Interestingly enough, they did not say that they longed for the more sacred Day of Atonement. Surely they would have attended Yom Kippur services if they had not been in the army, but far away in battle what they really missed was not the synagogue, but the warm religious moments of their Jewish home.

2. What Is a Mezuzah?

A **mezuzah** [m'-ZOO-zah] is literally a doorpost, but it has come to signify the small wooden, metal, ceramic, or glass case, usually about three inches in length, that is placed on the doorpost of a Jewish home. The practice goes back to the Bible (Deut. 6:9 and 11:20), which commands us to write the words of God upon our doorposts. Upon entering or leaving their homes, some Jews even kiss their fingers, and then transfer the kiss by softly touching the mezuzah with their hand.

The mezuzah is usually set at an angle, about five feet from the floor, to the right of the entrance. In some homes we find them inside the home as well, on the doorpost of every room where people live—bedrooms and even the living room, but not bathrooms or storage rooms. Nowadays, they appear in entranceways of Jewish institutions too: the Israeli parliament, for instance, or the headquarters of Jewish organizations.

Inside the case is a tiny parchment on which are inscribed fifteen verses from the book of Deuteronomy: Deut. 6:4–9, and 11:13–21. The first sentence is the watchword of Israel (see p. 83): *Shema yisra'el Adonai Eloheinu Adonai echad*—"Hear O Israel! The Eternal is our God; the Eternal is One." The inscription continues with the command to "love the Eternal your God with all your heart, with all your soul, and with all your might," and ends with a reminder that God's laws must be instilled in our children.

The custom goes back very far. Archaeologists have discovered mezuzah parchments nearly two thousand years old.

Those who live in the house see the mezuzah as a constant reminder of God's presence. It functions as a visible sign that the home is Jewish, that the lives of those who live there should be marked by the love of God and the values that such love implies.

3. *What Are Some Jewish Symbols that Jews Keep in Their Homes?*

Jewish homes look, feel, and sound unique because they are decorated with Jewish objects and outfitted with Jewish sights and sounds: such things as a Passover seder dish, a wine cup for Friday night Shabbat dinner, a tray for the Shabbat challah loaf, candlesticks, and even a tablecloth embroidered with Sabbath or festival motifs (see p. 209 for details regarding these things).

One reason we need such items is for our children. It has been said that we remember only 10 percent of what we hear, up to 20 percent of what we see, and nearly 80 percent of what we do. Jewish objects that are displayed as evident loving reminders of Jewish identity are far more likely to produce Jewish commitment than mere words, especially if the objects are ritual items that are held, waved, smelled, and eaten.

In the 1930s and 1940s, every Jewish kitchen displayed a blue metal box big enough to hold in one hand. It was a little bank in which Jews dropped coins, even at the height of the depression. From time to time, someone came by to collect the money, which went to buy land in what would someday be the State of Israel. Some people have told me that they remained Jewish as adults largely on account of their parents' commitment to "feeding the blue box." They watched it grow weekly and marveled that even though their family had little money, some of what they had went to establish a Jewish state.

Jewish objects are important for Jewish adults too. They symbolize the Jewish values that we hope our home will stand for. In addition to the ritual objects, many Jews like to have some form of Jewish art on their walls, cassettes and CDs of Jewish music for their stereo, pictures taken at family life-cycle celebrations such as a bar or bat mitzvah, and if they have traveled to Israel, some visible reminders of their journey.

4. How Did the Synagogue Begin?

We do not know for sure how the synagogue began. The earliest synagogues are probably a little over two thousand years old, but they may not then have become the kind of institution that synagogues are today. The word *synagogue* comcs from a Greek word meaning "coming together," and one early Hebrew word for a synagogue—still used, in fact—is **bet hakenesset** [BAYT hah-k'NES-set], which means the same thing: "a place of gathering." So a synagogue has always been more than a place of prayer. It probably began as a communal center where public events could be discussed and where the local governing body could meet, a sort of town hall. In time, however, it became also the place where worship occurred, and where the word of God was read and preached. It thus attracted two other Hebrew titles: **bet hatefillah** [BAYT hah-t'fee-LAH], meaning "a place of prayer," and **bet hamidrash** [BAYT hah-meed-RAHSH], "a place of study." Synagogues still function in these three ways. They are places where Jews go to discuss communal events and to meet one another, places for public worship, and places of study—not just Sunday schools for children, but study groups of all kinds for adults anxious to study Torah in all its guises.

Some of our earliest reports of synagogues come from Christian scriptures, in which we find Jesus and Paul in attendance. Other evidence in recent years comes from inscriptions on ancient walls that archaeologists excavate, informing us that synagogues back then had lay presidents and wealthy donors, some of whom were women. Many ancient synagogues were outfitted with beautiful mosaic floors and wall paintings. Many, but not all, faced Jerusalem. The only necessary furniture in a synagogue was an ark to hold the Torah scrolls (see p. 40), but the ark was often moveable, so that it could be placed in the main room for services but kept outside when people were gathering for some other purpose, a town meeting, for instance.

5. What Is the Difference between a Synagogue, a Shul, and a Temple?

The words *synagogue* and *temple* are largely interchangeable. The word **shul** [shool] is simply a Yiddish term (adapted from German) for synagogue. Yiddish is the folk language Jews developed while they lived in northern and eastern Europe (see p. 97); Yiddish has practically disappeared by now, but a few Yiddish words, including shul, are still used, especially by Orthodox and Conservative Jews, who speak of "going to shul."

If *shul* is derived from German, *synagogue* comes from Greek, and *temple* from Latin. Medieval Jews would never have called their place of worship a temple, because they believed that word should be reserved for the one single Temple in Jerusalem, the place where sacrifices had once been offered, until the Romans destroyed it in the year 70 C.E. They thought that God would someday rebuild the Temple as part of the messianic age, and they anticipated being brought back home to Jerusalem from their places of exile. They even expected to reinstate the ancient system of animal sacrifice. Orthodox Judaism still teaches that.

By the nineteenth century, however, modern Jews who no

longer believed that the Temple would be restored and who considered the countries in which they lived to be their home rather than a place of exile felt free to rename their synagogue "temple," often as a symbolic reminder that they neither expected nor wanted the Jerusalem Temple to be rebuilt.

Frequently, therefore, "synagogue" refers to an Orthodox, Conservative, or Reconstructionist place of worship, while the "temple" is the parallel Reform institution. But this distinction is not universally applicable. In some communities the temple is Conservative while the Reform congregation is called a synagogue. The word "synagogue" is in vogue today. Most new congregations do not call themselves "temples."

In either case, the temple or synagogue is the focal point of all Jewish community life. In addition to containing a sanctuary for worship, it serves as the home of religious education, youth activities, social action, and communal affairs. For many centuries, the synagogue also contained a hostel for wayfarers. Nowadays, synagogues often host soup kitchens for the homeless.

6. *Does the Six-Pointed Star of David Have Any Religious Significance?*

The six-pointed Star of David, made up of two superimposed triangles pointing in opposite directions, is the single symbol most commonly associated with Jews and Judaism. People have even begun calling it a Jewish star. Jews call it a **Magen David** [mah-GAYN dah-VEED], meaning "shield of David." Surprisingly, however, the star did not arise within Judaism, and until recently, it has had no particularly Jewish religious meaning. It was once used also by Moslems and Christians and it was sometimes associated not with David but with Solomon. Jewish mystics of the sixteenth century, however, saw deeper significance in it, and gradually it took on symbolic importance for Jews.

About three hundred years ago in central Europe, it became a favorite architectural design on synagogues, largely because the six straight lines of the star were easy to chisel in the stone walls. Since the star was now an evident part of Jewish buildings, the fiction arose that it must be an ancient and revered Jewish symbol.

Whatever its origin, the Star of David really is distinctively Jewish now. The Nazis ordered it worn by Jews as a "badge of shame." The growth of Zionism in the last seventy-five years gave it national significance. The flag of modern Israel is a white banner with two horizontal blue bars, and between them a blue Star of David.

7. What Are the Most Important Symbols in the Synagogue?

Several of the symbols found in the synagogue are as old as the Jewish religion. Most are connected to worship and are placed in the room where prayer services are held. Unlike Catholics, but like Protestants, Jews call that entire room the *sanctuary*.

The most conspicuous symbol there is the *ark*, an artistically designed cabinet usually built into the eastern wall so that Jews who face it during prayer are simultaneously facing the holy city of Jerusalem. The Torah scrolls are kept there. In the Middle Ages, Jews tried to make their ark look like the tabernacle that the Israelites built on their journey from Egypt to the promised land. Using the book of Exodus as their blueprint, they designed an ark equipped with all the things mentioned in the biblical narrative. Over the doors, they placed a curtain. Sometimes the Ten Commandments were engraved inside the doors, since it was believed that the tabernacle had held the tablets brought down from Mount Sinai by Moses. Exodus said also that two angels called "cherubim" were perched above the ark, so synagogue builders designed some animal-like representations of the angels, usually lions or deer, which they affixed above the doors. Last, they placed an eternal light (**ner tamid** [NAYR tah-MEED]) between the cherubim.

Nowadays, synagogues have modern arks as well, usually without cherubim. But you will still see an eternal light, its flame that never dies standing for the continuity of Jewish tradition and God's eternal presence. The first two words of each of the Ten Commandments may also be prominent, as a visible symbol of the Torah, the very cornerstone of Judaism. You may also find other words or phrases in evidence, one such favorite being the rabbinic aphorism "Know before whom you stand," words of advice to worshipers who read the apt reminder as they turn in prayer to God.

Another prominent symbol may be a seven-branched candelabrum, the **menorah** [m'NOE-rah], which was central to the worship in the ancient Temple in Jerusalem. Orthodox synagogues sometimes avoid decorating their sanctuaries with this symbol, or if they do use it they alter it in some way so as to make it manifestly different from the one used in the ancient Temple. In that way they avoid the implication that the synagogue and its worship have taken the place of the Temple cult for all time, rather than (as they believe) only for an interim period until the end of history when the cult will be reestablished. Non-Orthodox Jews, however, may more easily adopt the menorah for their sanctuary design, precisely because they do not expect a return to Temple days.

A desk or table for reading Torah will stand out prominently as well. Especially in northern Europe, when synagogues became too large to expect everyone in them to be able to hear the Torah being read, the worship space was outfitted with such a desk in the middle of the room. When it came time to read the Torah publicly, the scrolls were ritually marched from the ark to the desk. Since it was customary for several people to stand around the reader when the Torah was being read, the desk was built on a large raised platform big enough to hold five or six people. We customarily call the platform by its Hebrew name, **bimah** [BEE-mah or bee-MAH]. Modern synagogues that use a microphone need not worry about having a central reader's desk and have moved the reading back to the front of the room. Interestingly enough, however, in many places the people miss the Torah being marched through the congregation; in those places they march the Torah all around the room in a large circle, bring it back to the front of the room, and only then read it. The ritualized circuit is called a **hakafah** [hah-kah-FAH]; as the Torah passes, people may touch it with their prayer book (or tsitsit; see p. 92) or kiss it as a sign of love and respect for what it contains.

The Torah scrolls are decorated. Like the high priest of old, each scroll is provided with a *breastplate*, a decorated metal plate that hangs upon it. It may have other jewelry as well, including a pencil-shaped object with a sculpted hand at one end. This is the pointer, called a **yad** [yahd]; Torah readers use it instead of their finger to keep their place as they read. No one ever touches the actual words inside the Torah scroll with their finger, since the oil on our fingers might eventually deface the script.

Most modern synagogues also use the arts for symbolic ends. Murals, showcases, and wall hangings may display Jewish symbols or Bible stories. The lions of Judah, symbol of the biblical king David, are seen in some Orthodox synagogues. Memorial plaques are also usually in evidence. The names of deceased members or relatives of members are engraved on them, and at the anniversary of their deaths (called their **yahrtzeit** [YAHR-tzite]) lights beside the plaques are turned on. Next to the plaques, you will usually see a memorial to the victims of the Holocaust so that the millions who have no one to remember them can be honored in their death by all present.

8. How Are Synagogues Organized, and Why do You Have to Pay to Belong to Them?

In North America, synagogues are completely autonomous. Any group of Jews can start one and apply for membership in one of the large denominations (Reform, Conservative, Orthodox, or Reconstructionist movement). A potential congregation will be accepted into a denomination if it adheres to the principles for which the movement stands.

Rabbis are hired by congregations and given contracts. On the other hand, rabbis see themselves as owing allegiance not only to the congregation that hires them but also to the larger community—Jewish and general. And in addition, above all, rabbis make decisions based on their understanding of Jewish tradition and God's will. Many rabbis have, in fact, resigned or been fired for taking stands on moral issues that conflict with the opinion or policy of the synagogue board. The best-known example is the case of Rabbi David Einhorn, who had to leave his Baltimore congregation during the Civil War because he opposed slavery.

Synagogues are organized democratically. They have elected boards that make decisions. In all but some Orthodox congregations, women as well as men may be board members and synagogue presidents.

Synagogues are supported only by dues that members pay, in accordance with rules for payment laid down by the board. There are no central organizations that support synagogues; on the contrary—synagogues collect extra money from their members to support national synagogue bodies, like the Reform movement's Union of American Hebrew Congregations, the Conservative United Synagogue Movement, and the Federation of Reconstructionist Congregations and Havurot. These national bodies use their allotment for such things as maintaining social action agencies and developing national curricula for synagogue schools.

Usually synagogues have a fair-share system that obliges people to pay what they can afford and allows people to pay small amounts or even nothing at all if that is all they can afford.

Besides the rabbi, synagogues usually have other professional workers, including a cantor, who is trained particularly in Judaism's rich musical heritage, and who leads much of the worship service (see p. 79). Some large synagogues also have full-time educators who direct the religious school, temple administrators who make sure the synagogue runs smoothly, and part-time teachers for religious school classes.

9. Why Is Israel Sacred for Jews?

The Hebrew Bible makes it clear that from the very beginning, Jews considered their destiny intimately and necessarily interwoven with the Land of Israel. God tells the first Jew, Abraham, "Leave your land, the land of your birth, and go to the land that I will show you." The rest of the Torah assumes that the covenant between God and Israel includes the deeding of the Land of Israel to the people of Israel. Israel was charged with keeping God's ways there, under the threat that if its members sinned, they would pollute the Land, and the Land would "spew you out." Clearly, they held the Land to be sacred in and of itself, and therefore not to be profaned by evil or injustice. When the Southern Kingdom of Judah was destroyed, it was not the war with all its death and destruction that the biblical author remembered above all else. It was the fact that Jews were taken out of the Land into exile, a fate worse than death to him, for as the psalmist says of the exiles, "Our tormenters asked of us mirth: 'Sing us one of the songs of Zion!' How shall we sing God's song in a foreign land?"

Later still, the Rabbis held that there were different degrees of holiness in the Land. The holiest place was the central room of the

Temple sanctuary, called the Holy of Holies, where only the high priest was allowed entrance, and only on the holiest day of the year, Yom Kippur. Holiness then radiated out in lesser and lesser degrees, the way ripples spread out from a rock thrown into the water. Around the Holy of Holies was the Temple building as a whole, which was the second most holy site. Jerusalem, the city where the Temple stood, was slightly less holy than that, and eventually, the last ripple of holiness was the Land of Israel from border to border, all of which is certainly less sacred than the Temple, or even than Jerusalem, but is still holy—as opposed to territory outside the borders, which the Rabbis believed was not holy at all.

Jews therefore trace the idea of Israel's holiness back to our very origins. Unquestionably, Jews find something indefinably sacred about that land we call Israel. It is our homeland, just as our family abode and our synagogue are our homes.

10. *Why Does Israel Welcome So Many Immigrants?*

In the harbor at Haifa, Israel, an old steamer rests at anchor. It has outlived its usefulness, but despite the crowded port, the ship has been left there as a historic symbol: a monument to homelessness.

It is the famous ship the *Exodus*, which in 1947 carried a load of refugees from Europe to Palestine, only to be turned back by the British authorities and forced to take its hapless human cargo to a port in Germany. The *Exodus* is a reminder of other vessels, too, which plunged to the bottom of the sea with their human cargo of men, women, and children: all refugees without a port.

The tragedies of the 1940s were a repetition of history. In the 1490s too, thousands of Jews fleeing from the Spanish Inquisition perished in the depths of the sea or on escape routes over land.

These and similar experiences have made Jews "allergic" to immigration quotas and border restrictions. When the State of Israel was founded, therefore, even though it was economically unsound to absorb as many immigrants as there were inhabitants, all barriers to Jewish immigration were removed. Not only were the doors opened wide, but the citizens of Israel imposed heavy taxes upon themselves to pay for transporting immigrants into their land. The keystone to Israel's constitution became the Law of Return, which gives every Jew the right at any time to relocate to Israel, which is to say, to "go home" to the land God showed Abraham and Sarah four thousand years ago. In free countries, such as the United States and Canada, Jews feel quite at home where they are. But in most of the world, Jews have not been free, and for them, Israel has been a haven, the only place where they knew they would be welcome no matter what.

Israel's immigration policy has been determined not only by the fact that Jews worldwide have sought asylum but by the parallel fact that even the free countries of the world closed their gates to Jewish refugees escaping Hitler; they and others like them discovered that they could go either to Israel, or nowhere.

Each wave of immigrants to Israel is called an **aliyah** [ah-lee-YAH or ah-LEE-yah], meaning "a group of people who go up," as if Israel were the highest point on the globe. (There are people who will tell you that Jerusalem actually is a little closer to heaven, and I must admit, whenever I go there I half suspect they are right.) The early aliyahs that settled the country around the turn of the twentieth century were composed of Jews fleeing from czarist Russia, whose foreign minister had boasted that he would get rid of every single Jew in his own lifetime, and from Poland, where post–World War I nationalism produced bloody anti-Jewish riots. Almost immediately after Israel was founded, however, Jews being persecuted in Arab lands were airlifted to the new Jewish State, where they joined another recent aliyah, Jews saved from the Nazi concentration camps and interned in British displaced persons camps thereafter, while they waited for a country that would take them in.

The latest examples of Jews in search of a haven—the most recent aliyahs, that is—are the enormous Russian Jewish population suddenly set free by the crumbling Soviet empire, and the entire body of Ethiopian Jewry, who had been systematically tormented for decades but were flown to Israel in 1991, in a miraculous twenty-four-hour airlift.

The basis for Israel's open-door policy, then, lies in its citizens' realization that it must always be ready to save Jewish lives. From time to time, a small party of right-wing religious fanatics there agitates for a change in the Law of Return (see p. 188), whereby automatic Israel citizenship would be granted only to people who could prove they are Jews by very strict Orthodox standards—but not, therefore, to many Reform, Conservative, and Reconstructionist Jews. Yet the overwhelming majority of the citizens of Israel believe that every Jew who wants to settle in the Jewish state has an inalienable, God-given right to do so. The Israeli government can no more deny Jews the right of entrance to the Land than it can bar their entry to a house of worship.

11. Is the State of Israel Controlled by Religious Authority?

The modern State of Israel is not a theocracy: it is not governed by the rabbinate of Jerusalem or by any other religious leaders. Its government is democratically elected by all the citizens (including non-Jews). The laws of the Jewish state are therefore civil, not religious.

This does not mean that the laws do not favor a Jewish ambience throughout the country. Israel was created, after all, as a *Jewish* state; it observes Jewish holidays, for instance, much as the United States observes Christmas and Good Friday, even though, technically, it is not a Christian country. Such institutions as the Jewish Sabbath and festivals are an integral part of community life, even though people are free to decide for themselves how to observe these days, or for that matter whether to observe them at all.

Like Catholic priests and Protestant ministers in America, rabbis may run for office in Israel. But their religious office entitles them to no special political standing. There is no religious test for office. Prime ministers and cabinet members may be synagogue-goers, and then again, they may not. Several delegates to the Knesset (parliament) are Arabs, who may be Moslems, Christians, another religion still, or no religion at all. With one important exception, therefore, Israel, like the United States, practices separation of church and state. This vital exception is the set of laws that governs personal status like marriage and religious identity; here, every religious population is governed by its own religious rules. Christians decide what is a valid baptism, for instance; Moslems decide what constitutes a proper Moslem funeral; and Jews decide such things as the rules of converting to Judaism or how a Jew must be married. Christians and Moslems are therefore granted religious autonomy, freed from whatever opinions the Jewish majority might have.

But the Jewish decisions in such matters rest with an Orthodox establishment. That means that the religious status of Jews is determined by an "established church" comparable to the Church of England, at the head of which sit two chief rabbis, one for the Ashkenazim and one for the Sephardim. They work closely with Orthodox religious parties in the government, insisting that their Orthodox understanding of Jewish law must govern the personal and religious lives of all Jews, even those who are not Orthodox.

The inevitable result is increasing friction between the population at large and the Orthodox religious leaders who constitute the official religious establishment, as the Orthodox have consistently pressured the civil government for a greater say in public life. On the Sabbath, for instance, the nation's official day of rest, public buses and train service grind to a halt, and in most municipalities, movies and soccer matches are banned. Similarly, dietary laws are observed in all state institutions, including the armed forces.

Those who support these state-buttressed religious observances believe that the system preserves the right of religious conscience. An Orthodox youth who is drafted into the army, they argue, has the right to follow religious principles in the matter of diet. Therefore the kosher laws must apply to army food. Similarly, the strict Sabbath enforcement, it is claimed, will not interfere with the nonobservant, but will insure full freedom of conscience to the Orthodox.

Those who oppose government backing for religious ritual are concerned with the principle of freedom of choice for the non-Orthodox and, increasingly, with their claim that Orthodoxy is not the only valid interpretation of Judaism. They would prefer a system in which Judaism as a religion is taken seriously, but liberal Jews are accepted as authentic interpreters of the Jewish tradition. They also fear the rising influence of the Orthodox, who often have the swing vote in a political system that depends on coalition governments, to the point that secular politicians offer larger and larger concessions to the Orthodox to guarantee their votes.

The consequences may be minor or major, depending on the particular issue under consideration. The curtailing of bus service on the only day of the week when workers can travel to see relatives and friends, or when they can escape from the summer's heat to the beach, arouses deep resentment on the part of most Israelis. Reform and Conservative Jews object especially to the refusal of the state to recognize Jewish marriages and conversions performed by non-Orthodox rabbis. The greatest source of conflict has been the right wing's insistence that the Bible gives Jews the right, even the obligation, to settle in traditionally Arab neighborhoods, buying out long-term Arab residents if necessary and expelling Arab tenants.

The official form of religious expression now found in Israel is an extremely narrow interpretation of Jewish tradition. No sermons are preached in the synagogues of Jerusalem. The functions of the rabbis are almost exclusively ritualistic. A chaplain of an Israeli hospital does not visit the patients; he supervises the kitchen to check on its adherence to the laws of keeping kosher. This rigid view of religion has divided the Israelis into two camps: the Orthodox and the secular. With official support for liberal Jewry lacking, it has been difficult offering Israeli citizens a Jewish religious alternative. (The state pays Orthodox rabbis, for instance, but Conservative and Reform rabbis have to hold another job to earn a living, and then practice their rabbinic calling on the side.)

Eventually, a broader interpretation of religion will have to develop, something more in consonance with the traditional spirit of Judaism. Such a development is already leading to a head-on clash between the Orthodox and the rest of the population, and the probable result is the eventual separation of institutional religion and the state—not just in theory, but in practice also.

This does not mean that Israel will abandon its distinctively religious character. For as ancient tradition says, "The Land of Israel is inseparable from the religion of Israel."

The teachings of Moses, Isaiah, Rabbi Akiba, and Moses Maimonides, it is hoped, will continue to be the cornerstone of Israel's culture as they have been the cornerstone of Judaism's proud heritage through the centuries.

12. *What Is an Israeli Kibbutz?*

At the turn of the twentieth century, a few dozen hardy pioneers laid the foundations for the modern State of Israel with a group of cooperative agricultural settlements known as **kibbutzim** [kee-boot-SEEM]. A **kibbutz** [kee-BOOTS or ki-BUTS] is a farm colony run on a share-and-share-alike basis, quite similar to the Christian utopian settlements established in the United States during the nineteenth century or some of the Amish and Mennonite communities. All members share equally in the work according to their individual talents and capacities; and all receive an equal share of the benefits.

The kibbutzim performed a vitally important function in the early years of colonization in Israel. Life was austere, and the pioneers could look forward to little beyond a minimum of economic security and the peace of mind that comes from seeing the fruits of toil and sacrifice. Only hardy spirits, fired by idealism, would undertake this kind of life. And it was this idealism that made possible the completely cooperative living of the kibbutz.

The kibbutz founders were usually secular Jews who had merged the Jewish messianic ideal with the idealistic expectations of socialism. But the kibbutz is not a commune in the way the Soviet communes were, in that there has never been any compulsion about joining or staying on one. Those who try it and find it unappealing leave for neighboring free enterprise settlements, or for city life.

The kibbutzim are governed by leaders who are democratically elected by the membership. There is no centralized authority over all the kibbutzim, though they are loosely allied in networks that make cooperation feasible.

After the State of Israel was established, the agricultural cooperatives declined in importance. The newcomers from Europe, and particularly those from the Arab countries, had little appetite for "covered wagon" life, and knew nothing at all about socialism. In recent years, the popularity of kibbutz life has decreased even more. In most cases, kibbutzim have failed to remain economically self-sufficient, and in general, the socialist basis for Israel's economy has shifted to a free market system.

The idealism of the kibbutzim that still exist may be as fervent as ever, but life has become more comfortable in all but the newest settlements, and the extremes of collective life have been modified. For example, individuals are usually permitted their own personal allowances to spend as they see fit. On one kibbutz, I asked someone whether his wristwatch belonged to him. Yes, it had come out of savings. But repairs to the watch were the responsibility of the group. "What about saving money to bring relatives from Russia?" I asked. That, too, was a group responsibility. If the members of the kibbutz approved of such a request, they would subsidize immigration together.

In their search for economic viability, kibbutzim have become more than agricultural communities. They also manufacture a good many products.

Some kibbutzim are returning to religion, now that the radical socialism of the founding generation has abated. From the beginning, there were some Orthodox kibbutzim, of course, but they were the exception. By 1990, there were two new Reform kibbutzim, and a Conservative one too, instances of a renewal of religious life even in the settlements that once prided themselves on keeping no religious ritual at all.

As Israel has become increasingly urban, the kibbutzim have assumed a more modest place in the economy, but they should be credited with contributing much to the spiritual character of the Israeli people. The dignity of labor and the willingness to sacrifice the comforts of the present for the future are dominant characteristics of Israel's way of life.

13. *How Is Israel Governed?*

Israel is a democracy. Its government structure is close to the British or French parliamentary system, with supreme authority vested in the Knesset, a body of representatives elected by the people. As in Britain, France, or Canada, the party or coalition of parties that receives the most elected delegates tries to form a government. If it fails to govern because a majority of delegates vote against its proposals, it may have to call a new election. In other countries similar systems have proved very stable. Israel's system has not.

Unlike the United States, which has only two political parties, Israel has many, which are constantly banding together in blocs so as to increase their leverage. The religious bloc, for example, consists of those parties that want to see Israel governed by Orthodox Jewish law. Another large coalition is called Labor (stemming from Israel's socialist origins), and a third cluster of parties (more to the right) is known as Likud.

The number of parliamentary seats held by each of the political parties is based on the proportion of votes that a party receives at the polls. For years, the Labor coalition dominated, since the majority of Israel's citizens had vivid memories of eastern Europe, where they or their parents had adopted socialist economic principles as part of their reaction against czarist persecution of Jews. By 1980, however, Likud had turned the tables, and along with the religious parties, managed to form a government. But the Likud coalition proved shaky. Both the religious bloc and some equally right-wing but nonreligious groups kept threatening to leave the coalition unless their own extremist agendas were satisfied. In order to placate the religious parties and the fringe groups on the far right, and thus to avoid calling another election that they might lose, the Likud bloc gave in on a number of issues, such as funding more and more Orthodox schools, exempting Orthodox men studying in those schools from military duty, refusing to recognize liberal rabbis in Israel, increasing the number of settlements in the territories occupied by Israeli forces since the 1967 Six-Day War, and even threatening to change the Law of Return.

The Law of Return has been the backbone of Israel's moral right to existence. The state was founded to provide a home for the Jews who managed to survive the Holocaust but who were still languishing in displaced-person camps because no country would admit them. In addition, millions of Jews who had already died in Hitler's death camps would have been saved if the free nations of the West (such as the United States and Canada) had not refused to admit them as immigrants, thereby forcing them to remain in the countries overrun by the Nazis. Israel's very first law, therefore, promised that in the future any Jews being persecuted anywhere in the world would finally have a home that would take them in. They would automatically be permitted to "return" to their ancestral land. That law is still in effect. It is considered sacrosanct by Jews everywhere. It has saved Jews from Yemen, Ethiopia, Syria, Iraq, and a score of other places.

In the late 1980s, however, the religious parties advocated changing the Law of Return to admit only those Jews who could prove their Jewish status according to strict Orthodox standards. People who had been converted to Judaism by non-Orthodox rabbis, for instance, as well as their children, would not be admitted.

The Likud-religious alliance failed to institutionalize this change, however, so that the Law of Return remained in force.

The largest body of recent beneficiaries of the Law of Return has been Jews from what was once the Soviet Union. Under Stalin, especially, but also under Khrushchev and his successors, anti-Semitism was used by the Soviet state to justify the harsh conditions in the communist system. Jews were blamed for economic failure, and even featured in show trials designed to divert the attention of the population at large from the real failures of the communist system. When the Iron Curtain finally fell in 1990, Jews were among the first to flee the empire that had dealt them decades of grief. Other countries had immigration laws that limited the number of Jews they could take in. But Israel gladly welcomed all who arrived.

This influx of Russian Jews into Israel changed the balance of power. Along with others who rejected Likud policies—Israelis who did not favor settlements in the West Bank, for instance—these new immigrants voted successfully to return the Labor bloc to power.

Israel has a president too, but the presidency of Israel is an honorary office, bestowed upon a beloved elder or public figure who officiates in an honorary way at state events, much as the queen or king presides over England.

14. *Is an American Jew's First Loyalty to Israel or to America?*

When Napoleon conquered Europe, he freed Jews from the ghettoes and summoned an assembly of Jewish delegates to Paris, where they were to answer several questions. First and foremost, Napoleon wanted to know if these Jews would regard themselves as French citizens, loyal to France. The notables were quick to respond that they were a religion like other religions, and that their political loyalty was indeed to the French government. Behind their willingness to pledge loyalty to Napoleon was the talmudic dictum, "The law of the land is the law." As long as Jews are ruled by a just government, they are obliged to follow that government's laws. Hence, American Jews are loyal to the United States, Canadian Jews to Canada, and so forth.

But the State of Israel is the Jewish *ancestral* home, the birthplace of our faith and our Bible. It is the sacred center for the Jewish soul, a source of Jewish culture and Torah. In recent years, Israel has been the sole haven for over three million Jews. Surely it is not surprising that Israel has unique religious meaning for us.

American Jews will therefore continue to watch the development of the Jewish state with passionate concern, and to offer moral and material aid to it. Like many Americans who retain strong attachments to the land of their ancestors, Jews feel particularly strongly about Israel, especially since many believe it faces the constant possibility of being destroyed by its enemies on all sides. Whereas France or England can confidently expect to remain French or British, if Israel loses a war to those who have sworn to drive its Jewish citizens into the sea, Israel and one-quarter of the world Jewish population might well perish. So Jews expend an enormous amount of energy worrying about Israel's destiny.

Still, an American Jew's political loyalty is to the United States. The messianic age for which we yearn depends on applying to whatever country we inhabit the prophetic principles of justice, compassion, and peace.

15. *Can American Jews Disagree with Israel's Policies?*

American Jews can and do disagree with many things Israel does, just as we can and do feel pride in other policies of the same government. It is possible to differentiate three items from each other: the Land of Israel; the State of Israel; and any particular government of that state.

We believe the *Land* to be sacred: It is the place to which God summoned the first Jews, Abraham and Sarah; the land to which the Israelites returned from their slavery under Pharaoh; and the religious center of the world for Jews everywhere.

The *state* is the third Jewish Commonwealth, a revival of Jewish independence after some two thousand years of subjugation. The Zionists were right to see a Jewish state as a necessary haven for persecuted Jews everywhere, and a spiritual center where Hebrew would be revived as a living language, where Jewish culture would flourish, and where a new era of Jewish creativity would be launched. The existence of the Land and the state is a matter on which Jews cannot compromise.

The *government*, however, is just a political institution made of human beings who may or who may not pursue wise and just policies. Americans who claim allegiance to the United States feel no compunction about voting out an administration in which it loses confidence, and Israelis do the same in elections to the Knesset. Jews outside Israel cannot vote, of course, but they can exercise influence in other ways.

Jews in North America, for instance, can let their will be known through American or Canadian Jewish organizations or through extensions of Israeli organizations that exist here. They can even be represented in debates in Israel itself, not in the Knesset, where only Israelis sit, but in something called the World Zionist

Organization, a loose federation of Jewish groups worldwide, all of whom consider themselves Zionists but are willing to criticize Israeli governments without compromising their firm support of a Jewish Land and a Jewish state.

16. Why Is Jerusalem So Important to the Jewish People?

For the past three thousand years, Jews have lived in the City of David, hallowing it not only as the national capital of their homeland but as the spiritual center of their faith as well. Jerusalem has actually been seen as the very center of the universe itself, the gathering place of the faithful "at the end of days," when messianic redemption comes for all humanity.

Three times a day, 365 days a year, for some two thousand years, Jews have prayed for the well-being of Jerusalem. In our marriage ceremony, grooms and brides exchange vows with the blessing that joy will return to the Holy City. Mourners at a graveside are comforted with the prayer that they will be consoled along with those "who mourn for Jerusalem." From time immemorial, the pious would arrange for burial in the consecrated earth of the Holy City. And on Passover, we still conclude our seder liturgy with the chant, "Next year in Jerusalem!" (See next question.)

That Jerusalem has always been the center of the Jew's sacred map is clear from one of the ways that Jews have traditionally signed letters: not "Sincerely," or even "Send my regards to the family," but "Pray for the welfare of Jerusalem."

There were times when Jerusalem held relatively few Jewish inhabitants, but these were brief interludes in Jewish history, when the Jewish population was expelled by foreign invaders; it was never a situation that Jews chose willingly. While they were "outside the Land" (as they referred to their situation), they said they were in "exile" (**galut** [ga-LOOT]), merely awaiting the opportunity to return home. Jews thus never abandoned their moral claim to Jerusalem.

Aside from historical and religious attachments to Jerusalem, Jews cite legal and political grounds for their claim to the Holy City. Few people realize that the majority of its population has been Jewish since 1844. In 1922, the ratio of Jewish to Moslem inhabitants was three to one, and in 1948, the year of Israel's birth, Jerusalem's Jews outnumbered its Moslem population by one hundred thousand to forty thousand. Jerusalem was then (as it had always been) the capital city for Jews, whereas Arabs regarded Ramle as the center of their administration.

When Jordanian troops invaded Jerusalem in 1948, the Jewish defenders were exiled beyond the old city's walls. From 1948 to 1967, Jews were denied access to their holy places, including the ancient Temple's western wall (known as the **kotel** [KOE-tel]), the only part of the Temple complex still standing, and the most sacred site in all of Judaism. In addition, Jewish gravestones on the Mount of Olives were used as pavingstones for sidewalks, and scores of synagogues where Jews had prayed for centuries were demolished.

The political problems of today derive from the fact that Christians and Moslems too consider Jerusalem sacred. For Islam, it is one of three holy sites, the other two being Mecca and Medina, in Saudi Arabia. Mohammed is said to have flown through the air of Arabia to the spot in Jerusalem where the Dome of the Rock now stands. Christian pilgrims visit the places where Jesus preached and walked; at Easter they follow the Stations of the Cross that are marked on the exterior walls of the houses that enclose the Via Dolorosa, an ancient Roman street that winds through Jerusalem on its way to the Church of the Holy Sepulchre. Arab Moslems and Arab Christians along with Jews thus share the old walled city, each group zealously anxious to preserve its sacred sites.

With the Six-Day War of 1967, old Jerusalem fell into Israeli hands. Jewish sites were rebuilt or renovated; Moslem and Christian sites were handed over to their respective religious communities. All three faiths were thus guaranteed free access to their own religious shrines.

For many years, the three groups lived in relative harmony. Tourists flocked to the ancient Arab market; Jewish bookstores opened alongside Arab shops; enormous amounts of money were spent beautifying the city and building relations among its diverse inhabitants. In the 1980s, however, hostility broke out on both sides, as right-wing Jewish religious settlers claimed the right to more of the city than they already had, and an insurrection of Arabs in the West Bank territories spread to Jerusalem as well.

Honoring their claim that a united Jerusalem has always been the Jewish capital city, and fearing a repetition of the days when Jewish sacred sites were desecrated and Jews prohibited from visiting them, Jewish authorities have steadfastly refused to give up the city. On the other hand, even during the worst periods of unrest, Jewish courts have been equally unwavering in their support of the right of Christians and Arabs to control the access to and destiny of their own religious landmarks.

But as late as 1992, Jerusalem, the city of peace, still enjoyed a shaky peace at best. People of all faiths pray that the peace negotiations between Israel and its neighbors begun in 1991 will successfully resolve Jerusalem's many tensions. All visitors to Jerusalem have the right to come away thinking that this place is holy. If there is a place where heaven touches the earth, it is surely Jerusalem.

17. Why Do Jews Say, "Next Year in Jerusalem"?

Since the Middle Ages, "Next year in Jerusalem!" has constituted the final line of the Passover seder ceremony. As such, it has symbolized the inherent hopefulness of Judaism. No matter how bad the times, Jews have counseled against despair, holding out the promise instead that a better time will come. That better time was associated with a better place, the ideal spot on the face of the earth, from a Jewish perspective: Jerusalem.

For many years, and still today among many Jews, that promise is taken literally. In the difficult days of the dying Second Jewish Commonwealth, Jews found themselves forced to leave the land of Israel and settle elsewhere. Some left of their own free will, searching for a place to raise families in peace and earn their bread in quiet dignity. Others were carried away captive to Rome by the victorious Roman general Titus. (Indeed, to this day, on Rome's Arch of Titus you can see a pictorial record of Titus' victory parade with Jewish slaves in tow. Many Jews will not walk through the arch, in pious protest against the event.)

The Rabbis recognized the need for Jewish settlements elsewhere; indeed many of them joined the stream of emigres, and from that day to this Jews have lived both inside and outside the Holy Land. But theologically, traditional Jewish thought differentiated the two sites. "Outside the Land" was said to constitute, at best, a temporary place of settlement. The Rabbis called it **galut** [ga-LOOT], "exile," and looked ahead to the messianic age when Jews would return home.

The hardest blow of all was the Roman destruction of Jerusalem. The Temple was destroyed in the war of 70 C.E., and after a short-lived but very bloody rebellion in 135, the entire city was declared a pagan center, outfitted with a new Latin name, and declared off-limits for Jews. To be sure, by the end of the century Jews had returned anyway, but the city remained in ruins. The Jewish religious imagination thus arrived at a vision of the end of days. The messiah would arrive and, together with the Jews returning from the four corners of the earth, would restore Jerusalem to its pristine purity.

In the years of the Crusades especially, hopes for a return ran high, partly because all of Europe was stirred by messianic expectation brought on by the millennium, and partly because the Crusaders had killed so many German Jews that Jews needed some promise, however tenuous, to get them through each day. It was at that time, therefore, that Jews added "Next year in Jerusalem" to their Passover liturgy. This year might be unbearable; but perhaps next year would see the promised end arrive.

By the nineteenth century, however, Jews were beginning to receive civil rights in Europe. In North America, separation of church and state promised a speedy acceptance of Jews and Judaism guaranteed by law. The medieval notion of "living in exile" hardly fit these new developments. Reform Jews even began thinking that the so-called exile from Israel had actually been part of God's plan to send Jews out on a mission to bring monotheism and ethics to early pagan society, and later still, to work with other monotheistic religions to effect a perfect world made over in the vision of the prophets. Considering themselves at home wherever they lived, they ceased hoping for a return to Jerusalem. They would work for God's ultimate reign wherever fortune had flung them.

Nowadays, Jews are divided on the issue of "living in exile." Orthodox Jews still tend to believe that no matter how well we are received in this land or that, only Israel is our ultimate home. While living outside it, these Jews are duty bound to be good citizens, and they may even decide to stay where they are as they await the messiah's arrival. But when they say, "Next year in Jerusalem," they still mean it in much the same way that a medieval Jew did.

Liberal Jews, on the other hand, take the phrase metaphorically. There is no single doctrine of what it means to them. Rather, it may mean different things to different people. In general, they continue to believe, with their nineteenth-century forebears, that along with their non-Jewish neighbors, they are working for a better time for all the world. Jerusalem is the symbol of that better time. "Next year in Jerusalem" conveys the hope that someday all humanity will bask in a world that is all Jerusalem: Jerusalem the peaceful, Jerusalem the golden, Jerusalem where the sun beats down but the air is cool, Jerusalem that sometimes does seem a little closer to heaven.

VII

The Shape of Sacred Time:

Festivals and Fasts

The festive year includes a judicious mixture of joyful celebration and spiritual solemnity, deftly interwoven. Passover is a time for children's games—but it is also an occasion to pray "for life and peace." On Simchat Torah, we literally dance around the sanctuary cradling the scrolls of Torah in our arms, but at the same time we plead, "O God, do not forsake us." And even Yom Kippur, the most solemn day of fasting, is associated with a large family dinner in advance and a community break-fast following.

The sacred calendar of the Jewish year is largely a matter of atmosphere, a feeling created (and even contrived) to establish a mood unique to each festive or solemn day. To live each such day to the full is to be deeply in touch with what it is to be human, for the sacred calendar gives us pause to rejoice, to grieve, to be sorry, and to celebrate. Some days are intensely personal; others are communal, inviting us to affirm our ties to family, friends, the Jewish People, and the world entire.

Actually, each holy day represents more than a single day or even a cluster of days. The High Holy Days of Rosh Hashanah and Yom Kippur, for instance, are announced a month before they actually arrive, by the daily blowing of the shofar (the ram's horn) at morning worship. Similarly, the feast of Passover is anticipated at least two weeks in advance by special synagogue readings that announce the arrival of the month in which Passover falls, reminding people to begin the cleansing process, both moral and physical, associated with the holiday. A sense of expectancy builds, until finally, by the eve of Passover, both home and family are spiritually prepared for the great event.

The day before any holy day is especially filled with anticipation. Technically, it is called **erev** [EH-rev], meaning "the eve of" the holy day. Jews often use the term *erev* for the actual evening that the day begins as well. Thus **erev Shabbat** [EH-rev shah-BAHT or EH-rev SHAH-b's], for instance, "the eve of the Sabbath," though technically all day Friday, is a word most Jews reserve for Friday evening alone.

The close of each festival brings reminiscence: in the case of Passover, the beauty of this year's seder, and the special guests with whom it was shared; for the High Holy Days, the sound of the shofar, heard once again this year, and now silent for another twelve months, or the twenty-four-hour fast just ended, and the invigorated feeling that you have begun life all over again, freed of the errors of the past, ready to launch a new chapter in the book of life.

More than mere celebrations or even commemorations, Jewish holidays serve as object lessons in Judaism's most important ideals: thanksgiving, freedom, learning, sacrifice, repentance. Holy days dramatize these values in songs, rituals, and altered states of consciousness that far exceed the minimal effect that words alone convey. Abstract values, after all, are always difficult to teach. A love of learning is transmitted more abundantly through the pageantry of the Torah processional on the feast of Simchat Torah than it would possibly be in a classroom lesson. And respect for the earth as the source of our food comes clearly to mind as a child stands in a sukkah (the booth we build for Sukkot), looking up through a rickety roof covered with autumn produce and waving the traditional lulav and etrog (species of vegetation, principally a palm branch and a lemonlike citrus fruit) to indicate that all we have comes from God.

The festivals also serve the very useful function of strengthening family and group bonds. Be it fast or feast, a Jewish holy day is the season of homecoming: home with one's family or friends, and if that is impossible, home with other Jews. A Jewish executive doing business in London exerts every possible means to rejoin family at the seder table, be it in Boston or Seattle. But if that proves impossible, an invitation will likely arrive from someone.

During the second century, Rabbi Akiba was asked, "In the prophecies of Isaiah, God announces, 'I despise your feasts.' Why then, do you celebrate them?" The Rabbi replied: "You will notice that God said, '*your* feasts' and not '*my* feasts.' If the festive days are used for human benefit alone, they are worthless. But if they are attached to things divine, they have value."

QUESTIONS IN PART VII

1. Why Does the Jewish Day Begin at Sunset?
2. Why Do Jewish Holidays Fall on Different Days Each Year?
3. Why Do Jews Fast on Certain Days?
4. What Is Shabbat?
5. Why Do Some Jews Keep Only One Day of a Holy Day, While Others Keep Two?
6. What Are the High Holy Days?
7. What Is Sukkot?
8. What Is Simchat Torah?
9. What Are Chanukah and Purim?
10. What Is Passover?
11. What Is Shavuot?
12. What Are the Rest of the Feasts and Fasts that Mark the Jewish Calendar?
13. Are There Modern Holidays in Judaism?

1. Why Does the Jewish Day Begin at Sunset?

The custom of reckoning the day from sunset to sunset is based on the story of Creation as depicted in Genesis: "There was evening, and there was morning, a first day." The evening came first. Thus, each new day begins with the sunset of the one before. The Sabbath is ushered in as the sun sets on Friday. And if Passover falls on April 9 (for instance), the celebration actually begins on the evening of the eighth.

During the period of the First Commonwealth (before 586 B.C.E.) the day was reckoned not by hours but by watches. The night was divided into three: the early watch, the middle watch, and the morning watch. (Hence such biblical sayings as "Watcher, what of the night?") The day was divided into forenoon and afternoon.

When the Jews returned to Palestine after their Babylonian exile (536 B.C.E.), they brought back with them the Babylonian astronomy and way of reckoning time. But they still clung to a rather curious way of dividing the daylight hours: An hour was a twelfth part of daylight—longer in summer than winter.

This lack of exactitude is still followed with regard to Sabbaths, festivals, and fasts, for Jewish tradition stretches the day a little: A few minutes are added at either end—and even an hour or two by the highly punctilious. It is considered unseemly to begin the Sabbath and other holy days at the last moment, or to end them at the earliest opportunity.

In the Jewish tradition, therefore, an ordinary Sabbath is calculated from one moment of sunset to the next. The day consists of exactly twenty-four hours only twice a year, during the equinoxes. At other times it is a few minutes longer or shorter, depending on the season.

Orthodox Jews measure time by the actual moment of sunset. Some Chasidic Jews actually place an advertisement on the front page of every Friday's *New York Times*, telling interested readers the precise time for Sabbath candle lighting! Their Yom Kippur fast that falls in early autumn may last twenty-six or twenty-seven hours, as long as it takes to go from sunset to sunset.

Reform Jews, however, measure time on the basis of human action, defining both feast and fast days more or less arbitrarily from the time the family sits down to dinner, whether or not night has actually fallen. For them, the human act of declaring the day holy takes priority over the astronomical event of the sun's going down, as mathematical precision yields to the needs of the spirit.

2. Why Do Jewish Holidays Fall on Different Days Each Year?

Jewish holidays are reckoned on the Jewish calendar, which differs from the Gregorian calendar used by most of the Western world.

The main difference is that the twelve months of the Jewish year actually correspond to the lunar cycle of the moon as it circles the earth. It takes the moon roughly twenty-nine and one-half days to complete each orbit, at the end of which time a new moon can be observed in the skies, and a new Jewish month begins. The problem is that twelve such months add up to a year that is only 354 days long. If we started a new year every 354 days, our years would be out of sync with the earth's orbit around the sun. Soon spring harvest festivals would come in the dead of winter!

The Gregorian calendar has a similar problem, but not as pronounced. The actual solar year is closer to 365¼ days, not 365. To make up the deficit of one-quarter day every year, the calendar is thus adjusted by adding an extra day every four years. We call that year a leap year. The Jewish calendar does the same thing, but on a grander scale. To make up the deficit of roughly eleven and one-quarter days each year, it adds an extra month seven times in every nineteen years.

So the Jewish calendar is always in flux relative to the Gregorian calendar. Holy days will fall earlier and earlier until eventually a whole month gets added, and the holy days will suddenly fall very late in the season the next year. Of course their Jewish dates are always the same; only the corresponding English date differs.

Most of the names of the Jewish months are actually Babylonian in origin. Only remnants of old Hebrew names are found in the Bible.

Rosh Hashanah ushers in the Jewish New Year. In September 1990, Rosh Hashanah marked the beginning of the Jewish year 5751. According to tradition, the year 1 was the year of Creation, though modern Jews accept fully the scientific evidence that the universe is much older than that.

Of the three major Western faiths Judaism alone reckons its calendar not from an event in its own history, but from what it considers the birth date of all humanity.

3. Why Do Jews Fast on Certain Days?

Fasting has four distinct purposes in the Jewish faith: mourning, self-denial, petition, and penitence.

Good examples of fasting as mourning are several minor fasts that some Jews, especially the Orthodox, observe. The most important of these is the Day of Lamentation, **Tisha Be'av** [tish-AH b'AHV], in August. It commemorates the destruction of both of the temples of Jerusalem.

On the Day of Atonement, however, fasting functions as penitence for the sins we have committed during the past year, and as voluntary self-denial, symbolizing our ability to conquer our physical appetites and concentrate instead on making a moral accounting of our character and behavior.

Jews rarely fast for petitionary purposes anymore, but in antiquity, especially, communal fasts would be declared to beseech God to end a drought or to prevent impending destruction by enemies. The Book of Esther tells that when Haman threatened to destroy the Jews of Persia, Queen Esther undertook to save her people and sent word to them, "Fast for me." Among very observant Jews, the day before the Feast of Purim is still marked by fasting.

Although asceticism is generally frowned upon in Jewish tradition, it has been the custom among very pious Jews to fast on many occasions throughout the year, particularly on certain Mondays or Thursdays, when, according to tradition, additional penitential prayers are recited.

4. *What Is Shabbat?*

Shabbat [shah-BAHT] is the Hebrew word for the Sabbath. Shabbat is more than just one institution among many, for Jews. It is the very heart of the Jewish religion.

A historian could write two histories of the Jews, one bearing little resemblance to the other. The external history—that is, how we have fared socially and politically through the years—has known its share of grief. But our spiritual history is another story. Spiritually, we have managed to create a way of life that provides internal well-being even in the midst of external anguish.

Without a doubt, Shabbat has been at the very heart of this well-being. It has been said that "more than Israel has kept Shabbat, Shabbat has kept Israel." The calendar that charts Jewish spiritual history is virtually a series of weekdays spent in preparation for Shabbat.

This is no mere figure of speech. At the turn of the century, the journalist/reformer Jacob Riis visited Jewish immigrants on New York's Lower East Side. Poverty there was as abundant as anything American cities know today. Population density was so great that people lived several to every room, and tumbled off onto the fire escapes, hallways, porches, almost anywhere, including (in one case at least) a coal cellar, which one rather stately new immigrant Jew called home. Riis photographed this unknown man, for all eternity to see. There he is, at his Friday night Shabbat dinner. He has put on his single set of good clothes and spent what money he made on the traditional Shabbat loaf of bread, called **challah** [KHAH-lah]. No matter how hard he worked during the week, on Shabbat he rested; and no matter what insults came his way as he struggled through the work week, on Shabbat he reclaimed his divine right to dignity. The other six days were a means to an end: One worked only to be able to reap the joys of the Sabbath, a sanctified moment in time when to all intents and purposes, the world stopped.

It is easy to mistake Shabbat as a day hemmed in by all kinds of restrictions, and indeed it can become that. According to talmudic legislation, a series of perfectly ordinary modern-day actions that do not seem to us to require any physical labor are nonetheless classified as work that is forbidden on Shabbat. Driving a car, buying a newspaper, even writing a letter—these are all contemporary violations of Shabbat law. But those who keep Shabbat see it not as a time when they are prevented from performing minor tasks, but as a twenty-four-hour period when they can enjoy a world of complete serenity, beauty, and peace.

Jews on the Orthodox end of the spectrum therefore maintain all the ancient regulations as they apply to modern life, believing that God wants nothing less from them, and aware also that without such self-discipline, the sanctity of Shabbat tranquility will elude their grasp. Reform Jews, on the other hand, choose selectively among the Shabbat regulations, believing that it is the spirit of the law that God demands, not its every letter. They elect to keep those aspects of Shabbat legislation that are supportive of Shabbat spirituality, but pass over other rules that would only get in the way of Shabbat holiness.

Gardening, for instance, is forbidden by the letter of the law, since gardening involves planting, making a furrow, and ripping off dead leaves—all of which are forbidden forms of Sabbath work. In antiquity, keeping a garden was a job, not a hobby. But Reform Jews who are weekend gardeners may think of nothing more restful, more satisfying, and more spiritual than caring for the soil of God's good earth and producing a harvest of home-grown vegetables. They will happily devote a beautiful summer Shabbat to gardening. However, they may have decided on principle not to shop on Shabbat, even for gardening supplies, which they are careful to have on hand by Friday night; fighting traffic and crowds at gardening centers is not conducive to Shabbat rest.

All Jews, therefore, whether liberal or Orthodox, concur in

this: Shabbat is a time for spiritual refreshment, and for a break in the routine of daily labor. It is a reminder that the need for making a living must not blind us to the need for living.

Traditionally, Shabbat is also a day for family memories: when children who have grown up and moved out rejoin their family circle; when visits can be made to parents and grandparents in nursing homes; when family (and friends who are virtually family) can gather to recall old memories in an ambience guaranteed to create positive new ones.

Shabbat begins with a dinner complete with guests—and with grandeur. Marking the Shabbat, there are special foods, like twisted loaves of bread (the challah); wine or grape juice for the Sabbath blessing (called **Kiddush** [kee-DOOSH or KID-ish); a fresh white tablecloth; flickering white candles; the best china and silverware that we own; flowers in a polished vase; and young and old alike who have temporarily traded in their jeans and sweatshirts for something special. All present share in the feeling of oneness. If children are present, their parents may bless them.

The glow of Shabbat candles reflects a deeper glow within the hearts of those who see them; tradition has it that God sends us an extra soul on Shabbat. Perhaps that is where the glow comes from.

The Sabbath's character has evolved with the centuries. Some medieval Jewish sects pressed for the observance of a somber Sabbath. The Karaites, a group of scriptural literalists, insisted that God wanted the Shabbat to be lifeless and lightless, since the Bible said, "You shall kindle no flame on the Sabbath day." But rabbinic tradition prevailed, and the day became known for its Sabbath joy. Abraham Heschel quotes an old tradition, saying, " 'You shall kindle no flame' refers to the flame of anger." Shabbat calls for even tempers and pleasant dispositions, for spiritual joy, based on such enduring values as learning and love, family and friends, and a preoccupation with things of the soul.

The Sabbath is also a day of synagogue worship. The Orthodox usher in the Sabbath before sundown on Friday, and attend services before dinner. Reform and Conservative Jews eat dinner first and then attend a late evening service, which is followed by an **oneg Shabbat** [OH-neg shah-BAHT], an hour of sociability after worship. "Oneg Shabbat" means "Sabbath joy." There is Saturday morning worship as well, and in traditional synagogues people return for afternoon services too. The Torah is read on Sabbath morning and afternoon services, and in some Reform synagogues it is read Friday night as well.

Saturday morning services often focus on a bar or bat mitzvah (see p. 246), so many of the people present are visitors for the occasion rather than regular members of the synagogue community. Much of the available time is devoted to the bar or bat mitzvah ritual. As an option for the regular members who wish to celebrate the joy of Shabbat in a more intimate and traditional way, many synagogues have developed a parallel Shabbat morning service, or even a "learners' service," at which people who want to become regular worshipers can learn how to follow and even lead Shabbat worship. These services usually feature study, discussion of the Torah reading, and song; both dress and style are more informal than what is required in the main sanctuary.

As Shabbat begins at home, it ends there too, with a colorful ceremony called **Havdalah** [hahv-dah-LAH or hahv-DAH-lah], in which wine, sweet-smelling spices, and a braided candle are used to bid farewell to Shabbat and to mark reentry into the world of ordinary time.

Although the rituals for Shabbat differ somewhat among the various wings of American Judaism, their prayers everywhere are variations of a single theme, contained in this age-old Jewish prayer for Shabbat: "Our God and God of ages past, may our rest be acceptable to You; hallow us by Your commandments; satisfy us with Your goodness; gladden us with Your salvation; and purify our hearts to serve You in truth. . . ."

There are few prayers more eloquent or more descriptive of Shabbat than this traditional Reform version of the Kiddush (the prayer over wine or grape juice that initiates Shabbat): "Let us praise God with this symbol of joy, and give God thanks for the blessings of the past week: for life and strength, for home and love and friendship, for the discipline of our trials and temptations, for the happiness that has come to us out of our labors. You have ennobled us, O God, with the blessings of work, and in love You have sanctified us by Sabbath rest and worship."

5. Why Do Some Jews Keep Only One Day of a Holy Day, While Others Keep Two?

The months of the Jewish calendar follow the natural cycle of the moon as it orbits around the earth. Every twenty-nine and one-half days or so, it begins a new orbit, and a new month begins. Nowadays, we have organized the calendar according to mathematical formulas, but originally, Jews depended on people actually seeing the new moon in the sky. When the new moon was sighted, witnesses would so testify to the court in Jerusalem, and a new month would be declared. Messengers would then be sent to outlying cities telling them that the new month had begun. Since the moon's orbit is neither exactly twenty-nine days nor exactly thirty, but something in between, it was possible for the month to begin on one of two days, either the thirtieth day after the last month had begun, or the thirty-first. Until the messengers arrived, it was impossible for people to know which one it was.

Imagine the case of Passover, a holy day that falls on the fifteenth of the Hebrew month of Nisan. If you lived far away from Jerusalem, you would have arrived at the twenty-ninth day of the month prior without knowing whether the next day should be the thirtieth and last day of the month or the first day of Nisan. Keeping both options in mind, you would have started counting the days to Passover. Finally you get to what is either the thirteenth or the fourteenth day of Nisan. If it is the fourteenth, you need to begin Passover that night with a traditional seder ceremony. If it is only the thirteenth, you have to treat tonight and tomorrow as regular days, but celebrate your seder the next night. In antiquity, then, the messengers reached some Jews in time to let them resolve the puzzle, but some Jews had to act without knowing exactly what day of the month it was. The former kept only one day of the holiday, because they knew what day it was. The latter played it safe, and celebrated two days, knowing that in retrospect, only one would have been accurate, but that they would at least have marked the right day.

Eventually, the calendrical system was computed mathematically, so that no messengers were needed. Everyone could know in advance for years and years to come exactly when the new months began and also when each holy day should be kept. In faraway places like Babylonia, however, the tradition of observing two days was so strong that people continued keeping them. Eventually, Jews in the Land of Israel adopted the practice of keeping one day, while Jews elsewhere kept two.

Reform Jews have adopted Israel's approach, arguing that the keeping of two days, one of which is the wrong one, is surely illogical in an age when we have a calendar that tells us which day is which. Other Jews retain both days out of a love for tradition.

6. What Are the High Holy Days?

The High Holy Days are **Rosh Hashanah** [ROSH hah-SHAH-nah or ROSH hah-shah-NAH] (the Jewish New Year) and **Yom Kippur** [yuhm KIP'r or YOME kee-POOR] (the Day of Atonement), ten days later. The ten-day period in between is known as the Ten Days of Repentance, when we "pass in judgment before the heavenly throne." During this period, tradition holds, God looks into our hearts to examine our deeds and our motives. But God is not alone in passing judgment. We Jews too sit in judgment upon ourselves, comparing our conduct during the past year with the better selves we had hoped to become when just one year ago we marked the last High Holy Days by promising to mend our ways and overcome our weaknesses. The resolve to do better with our life—literally, "to return to God" and thus to repent—is called **teshuvah** [t'shoo-VAH or TSHOO-vah]. Teshuvah is a prime Jewish value, especially in the High Holy Day season. The concept carries with it a metaphor of space and of direction. Teshuvah implies returning in the sense of "re-turning," turning again to God. Sin is in that sense like turning one's back on God and on God's ways. To begin anew is simply to turn around and find the warming glow of the divine simply awaiting our re-turn.

The most important symbol of Rosh Hashanah is the **shofar** [sho-FAHR or SHO-fahr], or ram's horn, which is sounded during worship on the New Year. In ancient times, the shofar was an instrument of communication. In the hills of Judea it was possible to reach the entire country in a matter of moments with shofar calls from a row of mountain peaks. In the Rosh Hashanah services, the shofar is the New Year's call to repent for our misdeeds of the past year; to return to God with contrite and humble spirit; and to distinguish between the trivial and the important in life, so that the next twelve months may be richer in service to God and humanity.

In spite of the solemn nature of the Rosh Hashanah message, an air of happy expectancy is an almost tangible reality in home and synagogue, since the dominant emotion of the Ten Days of Repentance is born of our faith in God's compassion and forgiveness. As at other hallmark occasions that demarcate Jewish sacred time, Rosh Hashanah too thus features this significant blessing: thanks to God "for having kept us in health, sustained us, and enabled us to reach this day." As a symbol of the sweetness that we hope will mark the new year, in the prayers that accompany the breaking of bread, we dip the bread along with some sweet apples in honey. Traditionally, Jews do not wish each other a "happy" new year; the traditional greeting for the new year is **shanah tovah** [shah-NAH toe-VAH]— "a good year."

Among the variety of meanings that Jews assign to Rosh Hashanah is the "the birthday of the world"—the very anniversary of Creation itself. And among the day's prayers is one looking to the day when "all humanity shall come to serve You"—when, that is, every man, woman, and child of every race and nation will be joined in universal harmony with God.

The climax of the High Holy Day period arrives with Yom Kippur, the Day of Atonement, a solemn day of fasting and confession of sin. Do Jews believe in sin? Yes indeed—not in the innate sinfulness of human nature, but in the human propensity to choose wrongly, to delude even ourselves, and to hurt even those we love best. Jewish confessions, however, are communal, not private; they are liturgical staples that everyone says together, rather than personal soul-searching shared only by a single solitary soul with God. That is not to say that each of us is not responsible for private soul-searching before our Maker; indeed, more than one medieval master insisted that all our communal confessions are useless, if we do not, each of us, dare to stand before God alone to make restitution for our errors on earth in the year just past. But nonetheless, Judaism has bequeathed us as mandatory not a personal but a communal confession, indicative of the communal responsibility we are to take for one another. Part of that prayer is as follows:

> For the sin that we have committed under stress or through choice;
> For the sin that we have committed in stubbornness or in error;
> For the sin that we have committed in the evil meditations of the heart;
> For the sin that we have committed by word of mouth;
> For the sin that we have committed by abuse of power;
> For the sin that we have committed by exploitation of neighbors;
> For all these sins, O God of forgiveness, bear with us, pardon us, forgive us!

Yom Kippur is marked by twenty-four hours of prayer and fasting. On it, the synagogue interior is transformed by the use of white, a symbol of both purity and (since people are buried in white shrouds) death. This is the day to face up to one's sins, after all, and therefore to their consequences: We shall emerge from the day purified by repentance, not, we hope, so accustomed to evil that we are morally and ethically dead. The cloths on the readers' desk and Torah covers are white this day. So too are the robes of the rabbi and the cantor. In some congregations the people wearing skullcaps (kippot) will have replaced their usual black or multicolored ones with white ones. "Though your sins be as scarlet, I will wash them white as snow," said Isaiah.

Kol Nidre [kole need-RAY or kole NID-ray], along with the Shema (see p. 83) one of the most famous prayer in all of Judaism, opens the evening service, which is often called by that prayer's name: "the Kol Nidre service." The theologian Franz Rosenzweig tells us that as a youth he was so assimilated into German culture that in 1913, he decided to be baptized. However, that year he attended one Kol Nidre service. Upon hearing the age-old strains of the Kol Nidre chant, he was reborn to Judaism instead, to the extent that he gave his life to developing a Jewish philosophy that would help recover Judaism for others like himself.

Kol Nidre is an ancient prayer for absolution, composed in ancient Aramaic (see p. 98). It asks God to release us from vows undertaken but not fulfilled. These vows refer only to our unfulfilled promises to God, not those we make to human beings. All the prayers of Yom Kippur cannot absolve us from sins against our neighbor: Only a forgiving neighbor can accomplish that.

What moves people, at any rate, is the music, not the words. The Kol Nidre chant is one of the oldest of our traditional melodies. Since the tune matches the Aramaic original, the prayer is sung in the original language, not in translation, so it is unlikely that many people know exactly what the words mean. But they are moved, almost to tears, as they listen to the cantor's singing. People rise as all the Torah scrolls are taken from the ark, and stand throughout the prayer as congregants selected for this honor hold the scrolls in their arms. It is hard to describe the solemnity with which the people in the overflowing sanctuary listen to this tune, year after year.

But solemn as Yom Kippur may be, it builds toward a joyful

climax, born of the thought of forgiveness. We believe that "God is close to those who are contrite." In the words of the Yom Kippur ritual, "You desire not the death of the wicked, but that they return from their sin and live." Careful observers can watch the promise of forgiveness build regularly through the day, until at the very last service (as the sun is setting in the evening of Yom Kippur day), one of the confessional prayers is replaced with a prayer that says, "God, you reach out your hand to those who sin." That service is called **Ne'illah** [n'ee-LAH or n'EE-lah], "The Closing of the Gates." Recollecting the closing of the Temple gates when Yom Kippur ended in ancient times, the service evokes also the metaphoric gates of our lives. The gates of our sinful past will close forever; new gates to a better self will open shortly. As the Chasidic saying has it, "God allows some doors in our lives to be closed, but only while opening others."

Judaism stresses that prayer is not the sole avenue of God's grace. Equally important, in God's eyes, are deeds of love and compassion. Many Jews therefore take advantage of the day to reflect on the past year, to tell neighbors and family members that they are sorry for any hurt they may have caused them in the year past, and to resolve to live better lives in the year ahead.

A story is told of Rabbi Israel Salanter, one of the most distinguished Orthodox rabbis of the nineteenth century. One Yom Kippur eve the rabbi failed to appear for worship to intone the sacred Kol Nidre prayer. His congregation was worried, for it was inconceivable that their saintly rabbi would be late or absent on this holiest of days! A search party was organized to scour the countryside. After a long search they found their rabbi in the barn of a Christian neighbor. On his way to worship, he had come upon one of his neighbor's calves lost and tangled in the brush. Tenderly he freed it and led the calf back to its stall. The night of Yom Kippur that year, the rabbi's prayer was an act of mercy.

In our shrinking world, we are all becoming a single interdependent community. Geographic vastness has been shrunk by jet travel and satellite television; localized battles threaten to become world wars, and regional economies affect global markets. More than ever before, we realize just how completely a world-communal responsibility has become the lot of us all. The Rabbis of old used to say, "All Israelites are responsible for one another." Modern Judaism would say that all human beings are responsible for one another. The High Holy Days that begin with the anniversary of the birthday of the world remind us of our worldwide mission to be sure the earth and its inhabitants are not wiped out by the ultimate sin of turning from God and gratifying selfish whims at the expense of the very continuity of the human race. "To save one person," says our tradition, "is to save the world; and to destroy one person is to destroy everyone." Never has that been more true than today!

7. *What Is Sukkot?* ✓

Sukkot [soo-KOTE] (the Festival of Tabernacles, or "Booths") falls five days after the Day of Atonement and continues for eight days (seven for Reform Jews). In biblical days, it was the most impressive celebratory event of the entire year, far eclipsing even Rosh Hashanah and Yom Kippur in popular stature. Nowadays, synagogues fill up on the High Holy Days. Originally, it was Sukkot that drew the multitudes. First-century Rabbis tell us, "Anyone who has not seen the joy of Sukkot has never seen real rejoicing!" Sukkot marked the autumn harvest and looked ahead to winter rains, without which the spring harvest would fail.

Sukkot is filled with rich and colorful symbols, most notably the **sukkah** [soo-KAH or SUH-Kah] itself (pl., **sukkot,** whence the holiday gets its name). A sukkah is a booth or hut, something like a four-sided lean-to, built in suburban backyards, on apartment fire escapes, and even atop roofs! Synagogues build communal sukkot that everyone can enjoy.

The sukkah is a deliberately improvised structure, just a few two-by-fours hammered together, with a roof of leaves, cornstalks, and branches. The roof must not be solid, for those in the sukkah are to be able to see the sky at all times. The interior of the sukkah is decorated with autumn fruit and vegetables, generally tied to strings and hung from the branches. During the week of Sukkot, some Jews try to eat all their meals there. Others simply spend a few minutes each day in the sukkah, usually saying some traditional prayers associated with the lulav and etrog (see below).

The symbolism of the sukkah is multifaceted. Originally, it represented the booths established in the fields by workers who lived temporarily in the midst of the fruit they were harvesting, so as to make full use of their time in the field collecting the ripe fruit and vegetables before they rotted. It is harder in a city environment to imagine what it must have been like knowing that if the harvest failed, you would go hungry the next winter. But even the most hardened urban dweller gets some sense of our dependence on nature, just by sitting in the sukkah—looking up at the sky, for instance, instead of our usual ceilings, or getting drenched by a sudden downpour during dinner.

Open to nature, surrounded on all sides by reminders of our inherent connectedness to the earth and its produce, we experience the sukkah today as a contemporary reminder of our need to protect the earth and the ecosystem on which we all depend.

Our fragile mortality completes the symbolism of the sukkah. The Rabbis saw in it a replica of the temporary dwellings used by the Israelites in their forty years of wandering through the wilderness. The pilgrimage of our individual lives is not unlike that forty-year period, in that we too face life-threatening situations at every step of our way: illness, accidents, all the things we never plan but must endure. The sukkah is a temporary, makeshift booth, which a violent storm may well knock down, just as the storms of life may signal an unexpected end to our years on earth. Prescribed reading for the Sukkot is the biblical Book of Ecclesiastes, whose author bemoans human vanity and calls instead for dependence on God as the sole foundation on which a meaningful life may be built.

Two other symbols mark the festival of Sukkot: the citron, known as an **etrog** [ET-roag] (a fruit that is cousin to the lemon);

and the **lulav** [LOO-lahv], a palm branch to which myrtle and willow sprigs have been attached. Each plant has its symbolic meaning, but overall, like the sukkah, they recall our dependence on nature and the foolish self-delusion that any of us is strong enough, talented enough, lucky enough, or smart enough to "go it alone."

Festival worship services are held in the synagogue on the first two days and the last two days of Sukkot (the first and last day in the Reform ritual). The most memorable part of the service is the occasion for the congregants to march in a procession around the sanctuary, bearing the lulav and the etrog, chanting ancient prayers that culminate in pleas to God to save us. Each plea is punctuated with the Hebrew word "Save!"—*Hoshana*, familiar to Christian readers of the Gospels as "Hosanna."

8. *What Is Simchat Torah?*

The one-day festival of **Simchat Torah** [sim-KHAT toe-RAH or SIM-khs TOF-rah] is celebrated the very day after Sukkot ends and is often misunderstood as an extension of Sukkot. In reality, however, it is a festival in its own right. It marks the day when the weekly readings of Torah are completed for one year and begun again for the next.

On Simchat Torah, the worshipers read the last chapters of the Torah's final book (Deuteronomy) and immediately afterward, the first chapter of Genesis. Our study of Torah never ends, this ritual declares.

On the eve of Simchat Torah an elaborate service is held. All the Torah scrolls are removed from the ark and given to members of the congregation. All the worshipers, young and old, take their turn carrying a scroll in a procession around the sanctuary. The children carry flags and receive candies and fruit. People touch or kiss the scrolls as they are carried around the room. The entire event occurs with great singing, and even dancing, as the people carrying the scrolls break into spontaneous dances of joy.

During the morning worship, the ceremony is repeated in a somewhat more sedate vein. All adult worshipers are given the opportunity to be called to the Torah to say the blessing over the Torah reading, and when they are through, the children are gathered together to receive a collective blessing in a memorable ambience of love and joy.

9. *What Are Chanukah and Purim?*

Chanukah [KHAH-noo-kah or KHAH-nuh-kuh] and **Purim** [POO-rim] are two so-called "minor" holidays, falling in December and in February or March, respectively. They are called "minor" not because they are not celebrated with vigor, but because they are postbiblical in origin, and because we do not cancel work obligations on account of them. The "major" Jewish holidays are like Shabbat, in that Jews are bidden to refrain from work on them. On Chanukah and Purim, however, aside from the special practices associated with the days, we go about our regular business.

Chanukah and Purim are mirror images of each other. While Purim commemorates the rescue of the Jews as a people from physical destruction, Chanukah marks the rescue of Judaism as a faith from obliteration.

Chanukah is popularly known as the Feast of Lights, though its Hebrew title more accurately means "Dedication." It commemorates the Jewish people's victory in the first recorded battle for religious liberty.

Chanukah recalls the Maccabees, who in 167 B.C.E. led a small guerrilla army of Jews against the overwhelming might of their Syrian rulers in a struggle to the death for the right to worship God in their own traditional way. It is a valiant story. But Jewish tradition was hesitant about transforming a military triumph into a religious celebration.

The Rabbis therefore preferred to emphasize the spiritual aspects of the Maccabean war. Hence the title "Chanukah," which means "dedication" and refers to the rededication of the ancient Temple, a final spiritual act in which the victorious Jewish army cleansed the Temple of the idols with which the Syrians had stocked it while their army was occupying the Temple mount. For similar reasons, synagogue services during Chanukah call for a reading from the prophet Zechariah, who warns that deliverance comes "not by might, nor by power, but my My [God's] spirit." The Rabbis thus commemorated the military victory by obliterating its military character. They chose not to include the account of the war in their sacred scriptures, and the tale they told each other to explain Chanukah's existence said simply that after the war was over, a miracle occurred—not the miraculous victory against all odds, but a miracle by which the eternal light of the Temple precinct, which had been put out by the Syrians, was rekindled and remained burning for eight days, even though the oil available was sufficient only for one. Eight days later new oil arrived by messenger, and the miracle ceased. That is why Chanukah lasts eight days.

At its best, Chanukah thus celebrates rededication, the light of hope, God's miraculous presence in our lives, and the will to solve the problems that beset us without recourse to military means.

Though Chanukah may be "minor" in theory, more Jews keep Chanukah than any other Jewish festival! Partly, that is because it falls so close to Christmas; for better or for worse, it has been built up to balance Christmas in a Christian society. Like Christmas, it too has been commercialized by televised Chanukah greetings between programs and an avalanche of gift-giving. Partly, however, its inherent beauty gives it immeasurable richness. In the depth of winter, for eight straight evenings, the entire family gathers to light candles of hope, after which its members exchange gifts. Ideally, they share the night, eating special foods (see p. 94), playing Chanukah games, or just remaining together around the Chanukah lights instead of scattering off to meetings, homework, and tomorrow's paperwork—the bane of modern existence.

Candles are lit in a specially designed eight-branch Chanukah candelabrum known as a **menorah** [m'NOE-rah]. One candle is lit the first evening, two the second, and so on until all eight are kindled. In each case an extra candle is lit first, and is used to kindle the other tapers. In ancient times it was suggested that the order of kindling be reversed: eight candles the first night, seven the second, and so forth. But the Rabbis clung to the procedure that has now become fixed; the lights increase steadily, to reflect Israel's faith in a brighter future.

The candles are to be placed in a window so that passersby may see them and be reminded of the miracle by which Israel was saved. But the lights are not to be used for any purpose other than being seen. They are sacred witnesses to God's presence in history.

The extra candle was also endowed with special meaning. Its flame gives of itself to create an additional flame without losing any of its own brightness. Thus we too may give of our love to others without losing anything for ourselves.

Purim too celebrates deliverance from ancient foes—in this case, from the archetypal enemy of the Jewish people, Haman, a character in the biblical Book of Esther. According to the story, Haman, who controls the government under the Persian king, Aha-suerus, becomes fanatically angry when a Jew named Mordecai refuses to bow down to him. He therefore plots to kill all the Jews in the empire. Meanwhile, Mordecai's cousin, Esther, has joined the king's harem as his latest wife. In the end, Esther convinces the king that Haman, not Mordecai, is the enemy, and the Jews are saved. The date that Haman was to destroy the Jews had been arrived at by drawing lots—in Hebrew, *purim*—hence the name of the holiday. The main religious event of the day is a communal reading of the Purim story from a scroll (in Hebrew a **Megillah** [m'gee-LAH or m'GIL-ah].

If Chanukah is a time for family warmth and home celebra-tion, Purim is a wild and public display of unrestricted joy, high-lighted by carnivals and nonsense. The festival falls in the middle of the Hebrew month of Adar [ah-DAHR], usually some time in February or March. As the Talmud puts it, looking ahead gleefully on the very first day of the new month to the celebrations yet to occur, "It is Adar; be happy!"

For centuries, Jews have gathered in the synagogue on the eve of Purim to hear the dramatic events read from the Megillah. Whenever Haman's name is mentioned, people stamp their feet, hoot, howl, and bang on noisemakers to express their condemnation. People come in costume, wondering what the rabbi and cantor will wear. ("Can you believe last year they conducted services dressed as Peter Pan and Tinker Bell?")

Because it seems to take forever to read through the Megillah, some congregations skip a chapter here and there. The length of the Megillah reading is the source of a popular Jewish expression. Upon hearing a detailed account of something that never seems to end, a Jew might plead, "Just tell the main points, not the whole Megillah!"

Purim has become a time for religious school carnivals and masquerade parties for adults and children alike. In rabbinic seminaries students devote the day to spoofs on their professors. Jewish magazines often publish tongue-in-cheek parodies of Jewish institutions or public figures.

10. *What Is Passover?*

Passover, or **Pesach** [PEH-sakh] as it is called in Hebrew, is the outstanding home festival in Jewish life. It is the Feast of Freedom, commemorating Israel's deliverance from Egyptian bondage.

Passover is celebrated for eight days (seven days by Reform Jews, and by Jews living in Israel) during the first month of spring.

The rituals of Passover are largely home ceremonials. The Bible recollects that the departing Hebrew slaves fled before allowing their bread to rise. As a result, throughout the festival Jews eat only unleavened bread called **matzah** [MAHT-sah], that is, bread that is made without yeast and not allowed to rise. On the night before the holiday begins, some Jews collect the last bit of leaven—bread and foodstuffs that have risen—and ritually burn it the next morning.

The highlight of the Passover celebration is the **seder** [SAY-der] service—a family banquet held on the first and second evenings of Passover (Reform Jews have only one seder, on the first night). The seder is an elaborate ritual. The table is decorated with fruit and flowers, the best china and candlesticks, and other marks of festivity. A wine cup beside each place setting is used for the four cups of wine (or grape juice), each one a symbol of joy and gratitude for God's saving acts in history.

Essentially the ceremony consists of elaborating on the story of the Exodus, using various symbols, especially foods (see p. 94), for illustration and dramatization. The youngest child at the table poses four questions to the adults, referring to the special Passover foods and asking why this night differs from all other nights of the year. The answer emerges as the evening ritual unfolds.

The ritual is carried in a book known as the **Haggadah** [hah-GAH-dah or hah-gah-DAH]. It describes the familiar tale of Egyptian slavery, Pharaoh's obstinate refusal to let the Israelites go, and the miracle of redemption. But it contains also poetry and songs from two thousand years of Jewish life and lore. The ritual calls for eating or pointing to symbolic foods, each with its own interpretation: parsley sprigs to designate the hope of springtime growth; an egg roasted until it browns, to represent the ancient temple sacrifice once offered on this holiday; hard-boiled eggs as a reminder of life that transcends death; salt water to recollect the tears of the Jewish slaves; horseradish as bitter herbs, a reminder of the bitterness of servitude; and matzah itself, the unleavened bread such as that which our ancestors ate on their way to freedom.

An important part of the Passover is the tradition of sharing our blessings. Custom thus dictates that guests be invited to the family table. The symbolic highlight of the evening occurs when the door is opened, as if to invite Elijah the prophet to arrive with news that the long years of waiting for redemption are over.

The feast of Passover is symbolic of our most cherished ideal, freedom. It is an annual reminder that the work of liberation is never ended. "In each generation, Jews must regard themselves as if they personally had been delivered from the hands of the Egyptians," declares the Haggadah.

11. *What Is Shavuot?*

Shavuot [shah-voo-OTE] is the Festival of Weeks, a name derived from the fact that the date of Shavuot is determined by counting seven weeks from the Feast of Passover. If you count the day on each end of the sequence, you get fifty days; hence, Shavuot is also known as Pentecost, from the Greek word *pentecoste*, meaning "fiftieth." Unlike Sukkot and Passover, it is observed for only two days (only one in the Reform Movement).

Originally Shavuot was an agricultural festival. The barley harvest that had ripened around Passover would have ended, but the wheat harvest would just have begun. When the Temple still stood, Jews celebrated the harvest by offering its first sheaves back to God. But celebrating the harvest was only one layer of meaning for Shavuot. Over the years, it was endowed with another: the anniversary of the giving of Torah.

The Book of Exodus is read on Shavuot, including the chapter containing the Ten Commandments. The general theme of the day is our traditional love of learning. The Book of Ruth, the story of a Moabite woman's devotion to her adopted Jewish faith, is also featured then.

Unlike Sukkot and Passover, Shavuot has no colorful home ceremony that attracts attention: we build no sukkah on it and hold no seder then. Nonetheless, Shavuot is not without its own attractiveness. In many circles, it is celebrated by a marathon study session from dusk to dawn. Those who can manage stay awake all night long as people take turns leading a discussion of Jewish texts. More commonly, Shavuot has become a time for Confirmation. In Reform Judaism particularly, it is thus a sort of graduation from religious school for those who have continued their Jewish education beyond their bar or bat mitzvah age of thirteen. Customs vary, but generally the graduating class prepares the liturgy for the occasion, and its members receive a blessing from the rabbi as they go forth from their final formal class in the religious school structure.

12. What Are the Rest of the Feasts and Fasts that Mark the Jewish Calendar?

In addition to the major religious days in the Jewish calendar, some Jews, especially the Orthodox, observe two traditional periods of mourning commemorating ancient disasters. The weeks immediately following Passover are associated with Roman persecution, including the martyrdom of Rabbis, and as a result, no weddings or other festive affairs are scheduled then. The thirty-third day of that period, however, is an exception to the rule. Known as **Lag Ba'omer** [lahg bah-OH-mehr], it is given over entirely to festivity. Many Jewish nursery schools and day schools celebrate Lag Ba'omer as a day of spring picnics and an occasion to honor teachers.

Another three-week period of mourning is observed every summer in commemoration of the destruction of the ancient Temple. This season is climaxed by the fast day called the Ninth of Av (the Hebrew date), or **Tisha Be'av** [tish-AH b'AHV] in Hebrew. Special synagogue services that day feature the chanting of the Book of Lamentations in a plaintive minor key. The same sad melody is used in the services on the Sabbath preceding the fast. The following Sabbath is called the Sabbath of Consolation. The synagogue is decked in white and the congregation reads the fortieth chapter of Isaiah, where God instructs the prophet, "Comfort, O comfort My people."

Tu Bishvat [too bish-VAHT], the Jewish Arbor Day, usually falls in February and marks the tree-planting season of ancient Israel.

Custom dictates that fruits distinctive to Israel be eaten. In modern Israel, schoolchildren, each bearing a young sapling, take part in a ceremonial planting of trees. Because reforestation is an important Israeli goal, the annual planting ceremonies have become very festive occasions.

The first day of each Hebrew month (**Rosh Chodesh** [rosh KHOE-desh]) is a semiholiday on which the new moon is greeted with special religious ceremonial. In ancient times it was seen especially as a women's holiday, since the moon is a natural symbol of a woman's menstrual cycle. Today, Rosh Chodesh has been revived in some circles as a women's festival, a day on which women meet to pray and study together.

13. *Are There Modern Holidays in Judaism?*

The Jewish calendar has always changed with time, reflecting the changing destiny of the Jews who keep it. Biblical Jews knew nothing of Purim or Chanukah, and their most important holidays were the three harvest festivals of Sukkot, Passover, and Shavuot. The Rabbis added Chanukah and Purim and converted the harvest festivals into holidays rich with historical allusions. The fall of the Temple left its impact on medieval Jewry in the form of mourning periods, especially the Ninth of Av. And today it is the twin events of the Holocaust and the birth of the modern State of Israel that have resulted in the addition of new holy days to our modern calendar.

The Holocaust (**Sho'ah** [SHOA-ah]) is recollected on **Yom Hashoah** [yome hah-SHOA-ah], or Holocaust Day, an annual event falling some time in the spring (as with the traditional holidays, Yom Hashoah falls every year on the same Hebrew date, but a different English date). A second occasion of commemoration is the night of November 9, *Kristallnacht*. On that date in 1938, Hitler began the process that would lead to the systematic murder of the Jewish people. The night of November 9 is remembered as the time the Nazis engineered widespread attacks on Jewish businesses, houses, and synagogues, smashing glass windows and torching the premises. Hence the name—*Kristallnacht* (in German), meaning "the night of broken glass."

Israel Independence Day (**Yom Ha'atsma'ut** in Hebrew [yome hah-ahts-mah-OOT]) falls later in the spring, just a few weeks after Yom Hashoah. In Israel, it is preceded by **Yom Hazikaron** [yome hah-zee-kah-RONE], Remembrance Day, the Israeli equivalent of Veterans' Day, honoring the fallen soldiers from all the Israeli wars. Another holiday associated with modern Israel is Jerusalem Day (**Yom Yerushalayim** [yome y'roo-shah-LAH-yeem). Until 1967, the old city of Jerusalem was in the hands of hostile Jordanians who expelled the Jewish inhabitants and destroyed Jewish spiritual sites, such as graveyards and medieval synagogues. In 1967, the Israelis retook the city as part of the Six-Day War. The twenty-eighth day of the Hebrew month of Iyar, Jerusalem Day, marks the unification of old and new Jerusalem under Jewish control.

American Jews have yet to develop standard ways of marking these days. Though they are all noted on the calendar, not all of them are observed by everyone, and even those who do keep these days do so in different ways. Yom Hashoah is usually a time for memorial services, often in conjunction with Christian churches that mark the date as well. Israel Independence Day often features parades and festivities of a secular nature, but it is also recognized by religious authorities as a day for special prayers, particularly among Conservative Jews, who have taken great care to grant Israel Independence Day the importance it is due.

VIII

Growing Up and Growing Old:

The Shape of a Jewish Life

Like other religions, Judaism too marks the important occasions that shape a human life. From birth to death, Jews stop to take note of the important signposts of growing up and growing older. But the Jewish system is uniquely Jewish in that it is tied to Jewish values, especially the life of Torah. In one way or another, the most important life-cycle occasions celebrate the sanctity of human life and the privilege of sharing a covenant with God.

The Torah is itself analogous to human life. It begins with Genesis, which chronicles the birth of the world, and continues with stories consumed with the problem of births and family rearing. Cain kills Abel; Abraham almost kills Isaac; Sarah and Rebekah almost never bear children at all; Rebekah finally has twins who fight in utero, even as they prepare to leave her womb. Rachel's children, Joseph and Benjamin, are favored over Leah's. Genesis ends with Father Jacob blessing his children and predicting their destiny as the twelve tribes of Israel. Clearly, Genesis is what its name implies, a set of stories about human beginnings. So too, our life cycle begins with birth.

Exodus, by contrast, features fully formed adults at work in the world. The twelve tribes, fully grown, are enslaved in Egypt, and then freed by God and brought to Mount Sinai to reestablish the covenant as consenting adults. Rabbinic tradition even likens the Sinai experience to a marriage between Israel and God. So if Genesis brings us childhood, Exodus portrays for us young adulthood, complete with marriage and adult commitments.

Leviticus is almost totally consumed with legislation, most of it priestly and detailed at one and the same time. We have left the grand stories of Exodus and Sinai far behind, and are now deep in the details of what life as an Israelite really is all about. Here we find the rules of curing the sick, of recovering from childbirth, of proper and improper sex partners, and so forth. Truth be told, the last half of Exodus had already turned toward the details of Israelite society, its civil and criminal legislation, for instance, and the incredibly complex blueprint for the desert tabernacle, which was to be the focus of Israel's life of the spirit.

This near obsession with tiny detail that follows immediately upon the marriage of God and Israel at Sinai mirrors precisely the way in which in our own lives we must grapple with all the details of home-making, job-hunting, and rule-keeping in the real world. Wedding day is one thing, but you cannot live eternally on the blissful high of that magnificent occasion. You eventually discover how complicated ordinary life really is. The Israelites too had to wander off from Sinai and begin the task of learning all the rules of the sacred society that they were charged with becoming. So the end of Exodus and all of Leviticus give us the very ordinariness of actual adulthood, its endless responsibilities, its lengthy lists of things to do, and its many rules that society imposes on its members.

The fourth book of the Torah is Numbers. It is a story of forty years of wandering through the desert. The Israelites had hoped to reach the promised land much earlier. Instead they are forced to wait until the first generation dies. Only the second generation will be fit enough to enter the Land of Israel. The theme of wandering characterizes our late adulthood. Early on, we are so busy with the obvious tasks of raising families, succeeding at work, and establishing a home that we have precious little time even to think about what we are doing. But then comes midlife crisis, a backward-looking pause in which we inquire if what we have been so busy doing was really worth it. Looking ahead, we note we have just about forty years left of life. If our adult life thus far has offered few choices, relatively speaking, we now discover that, within reason, we will be increasingly able to do almost anything we like. We will have forty years of wandering—changing careers, perhaps; going back to school; finding a hobby or learning to appreciate leisure time; maybe even traveling. In the book of Numbers, people rebel; they complain; they try to find themselves in a vast desert without signposts or obvious directions to take. Similarly, our mid-to-late-adult life will be led with few signposts to guide us. We choose our lives and lead them as best we can, sometimes rebelling or murmuring but eventually, we hope, finding a path that takes us out of the desert and into that period late in life when we can look back on a life well led.

At last we reach Deuteronomy. Most of the book is a retrospective look at Israel's history from Exodus to Sinai, from desert wandering to the moment when the people stand poised at last to enter the promised land. Our old age too gives us the chance to look back and tell our story, to paste the pictures of our lives in a photo album that will outlive the people pictured in it and display the shape of the lives we manufactured. But Deuteronomy stops before anyone actually enters the promised land. Its last vignette is the death of Moses, just as the last act of our own life cycle will be our death. What promised land there is awaits us only on the other side of this life.

Jewish ritual gives us the chance to mark important occasions as we grow from childhood to adulthood, from youth to old age, and when we eventually pass from this world. It will reflect the Torah's implicit recognition that life is a journey through Genesis, Exodus, Leviticus, Numbers, and Deuteronomy. Each stage in that journey is important.

QUESTIONS IN PART VIII

1. *Is Having Children Valued in Judaism?*
2. *Why Do Jews Practice Circumcision? What Parallel Ceremony Is Used for Baby Girls?*
3. *How Is a Baby Named in Jewish Families?*
4. *Do Jews Always Name a Child After a Deceased Relative?*
5. *What Is Pidyon Haben?*
6. *What Are Bar and Bat Mitzvah?*
7. *Do Jews Have Confirmation Services?*
8. *How Do Jews Get Married?*
9. *Do Rabbis Perform Weddings When a Jew Marries a Non-Jew?*
10. *What Is the Jewish Attitude toward Divorce?*
11. *How Are People Buried in Judaism?*
12. *What Mourning Customs Do Jews Follow?*
13. *Do Jews Have a Confession, Deathbed or Otherwise?*
14. *How Can Friends Appropriately Extend Comfort to a Jewish Family in Mourning?*
15. *How Do People Choose to Become Jews?*

1. Is Having Children Valued in Judaism?

The stories of Genesis demonstrate on one hand how important continuity through the generations is in Jewish tradition, even as they illustrate the fact that not all of us are able to have children of our own. Ideally, however, family life ranks among the highest values for Jews. The Rabbis urged people to get married and have children, at least one boy and one girl.

On the other hand, we are told of one Rabbi who did not marry, and who maintained that he was not fit for marriage. His decision is not treated as sinful. Rather, the Rabbis recognized that the ideal of marriage was not right for everyone, even though for the vast majority of people it remained the preferred way of life.

Jews today who can bear their own children do so in accord with Jewish values. Those who cannot try to adopt children. Judaism does not distinguish between children living with the parents who bore them and children who are adopted, except that in traditional circles, mostly Orthodox, adopted children might have to go through the process of ritual conversion (see p. 263). In either case, by birth or by adoption, the arrival of the child is greeted with great joy, and with the exception of the added conversion ritual among traditionalists, the same ceremonies will apply to the one as apply to the other.

2. Why Do Jews Practice Circumcision? What Parallel Ceremony Is Used for Baby Girls?

The circumcision of a male child on the eighth day of his life is probably the oldest rite in the Jewish religion. It was practiced by the patriarchs even before the Torah existed and is so deeply ingrained in the tradition that no postponement is permitted either for the Sabbath or even for the Day of Atonement. Only if it is suspected that the baby's health is in jeopardy is the ceremony deferred.

Judaism has considered the rite of circumcision an external symbol binding the child to his faith. It is not a sacrament that inducts the infant into Judaism; his birth accomplishes that. But it is a sacred act that celebrates this little boy's status as one who is in covenant with God. Circumcision thus confirms the child's status as a Jew and defines the nature of that status as continuing the covenantal relationship with God that began with Abraham and continues ever afterward. Appropriately, the Hebrew term for circumcision is **brit milah** [BREET mee-LAH], literally, "the covenant of circumcision." Jews often refer to it simply by the Yiddish word, **B'ris**.

Since antiquity, the professional circumcisor (known as a **mohel** [MOE-hayl]) has been highly regarded in the Jewish community. A series of stringent requirements for the licensing of a mohel exist. A mohel need not be a physician or a rabbi; in fact, most usually are neither. But all **mohalim** [pl., moe-hah-LEEM] have specialized training guaranteeing that they are thoroughly versed in the medical complexities of the operation and the sanitary conditions that even this relatively simple procedure demands. In addition, they are expected to be religiously motivated in their work. Performing a brit milah matters to them, because it is the act by which the covenant continues generation after generation.

Some parents prefer that the circumcision be performed by a physician, however, and nowadays, many Jewish doctors, especially obstetricians and pediatricians, take special training in the religious rules and values so that they can be licensed as a mohel too. The Reform movement, especially, has devised a national licensing program for men and women who want to perform circumcisions not only as doctors but as committed Jews who want to celebrate the continuity of the Jewish covenant.

The ceremonial liturgy that surrounds brit milah may be led by the mohel or by a rabbi who is in attendance, or both. Part of the rite calls for parental involvement as well. It usually is held in the parents' living room.

In the traditional ceremony, the child is brought into the room and greeted by the guests with the time-honored biblical words, "Blessed be he who comes." (Christians will readily recognize this phrase as messianic, and indeed, the medieval Jewish community also intended it as a messianic greeting. It was added to the circumcision rite as if to utter the hope that the messiah had been born and was here being greeted by those assembled.) During the operation, the child is held by a man known as the sandek [SAHN-deck], the Jewish equivalent of the godparent.

The circumcision usually takes almost no time at all. The mohel quickly completes it and recites a blessing, at which time the father of the infant says a benediction praising God for instructing him "to bring the child into the covenant of Abraham our father." Onlookers respond, "May the boy grow into the life of Torah, marriage, and good deeds." Other prayers include the blessing over wine (some of which is put on the child's lips); a petition for the child's health; and the bestowing of his Hebrew name.

The ceremony is clearly a male ritual, and has become more and more so through the years. Originally, the child was held by his mother during the operation, not by a male godfather. It was the practice for centuries to offer wine to both mother and father after the blessing was recited, at which time a prayer for the mother's recovery from childbirth was the norm. But by the sixteenth century,

*home/partner/family

at the very latest, the mother had been relegated to a back room, or even to a different building, her home, while the men attended the ceremony at the synagogue.

The result of all this is a certain ambivalence about the ritual today, especially among circles of liberal Jews who value gender equality. On the one hand, it is nearly unthinkable after all these centuries not to have your son circumcised. But on the other hand, the fact that only boys can be circumcised and the evolution of the ritual into a men-only affair make it equally impossible for these modern Jews to go through the rite as it has come down to us.

Some liberal Jews, therefore, have altered the traditional rite. The Reform movement, for example, emphasizes the *brit* (the covenant aspect) and plays down the *milah* (the actual operation of circumcision). There is a single eighth-day liturgy for boys and for girls, a common "Covenant Ceremony" in which boys and girls are inducted into the "covenant of Abraham and Sarah." The only difference is that in the boy's rite, as the liturgical words are recited, a mohel or physician performs the operation.

Most Jewish life-cycle events are followed by celebrations, usually with a lot of food being served. Such a meal is called a **se'udat mitzvah** (s'oo-DAHT mits-VAH), meaning a religiously commanded banquet. The joy of a life-cycle occasion thus spills over into the social life of friends and family, in that the celebrants are urged to throw a party, and those who are near and dear to them consider it a religious duty to absent themselves from work or other responsibilities to attend. Thus, the brit milah does not end with the liturgy alone. It continues with an hour or two of eating and celebrating together, as a way of welcoming a new member into the Jewish community and its covenant with God.

3. How Is a Baby Named in Jewish Families?

A lot of old-country traditions gave the prerogative of naming children to either the father or the mother, but nowadays, in North America, these customs have all but disappeared.

It is usual for children to be given both a Hebrew and an English name. Traditionally, the Hebrew name employs the father's name too, by designating the child as either **ben** ("son of") or **bat** ("daughter of")—for example, Avraham *ben* Moshe (meaning, Abraham son of Moses), or Rachel *bat* Moshe (meaning Rachel daughter of Moses). Many modern liberal Jews employ the mother's name as well, by adding her name with the Hebrew prefix *ve* [v'], which means "and"—Avraham ben Moshe veSarah (Abraham son of Moses and Sarah), for instance.

You will find some Jews who are given the same name as their father, David Sanders, for instance, and then known formally as David Sanders, Jr. But having your father's name with the word "junior" affixed is very rare among Jews.

The Hebrew name is often changed considerably from the actual name of the person you are named after, and Jews often strive to find some relationship between the English and the Hebrew. Thus if you are named after your deceased aunt whose traditional European name was the Yiddish "Chaya," but if your parents did not like the old fashioned "Chaya," you might have been given the Hebrew biblical name, "Channah" (which at least begins with the same Hebrew sound, "Ch"), and the English equivalent, "Hannah"; or if they didn't like Hannah either, you might still be "Channah" in Hebrew, but Helen in English—at least the sound of the initial letter remains almost the same.

The traditional custom also is to name boy babies on the eighth day, at the time of circumcision. If circumcision is postponed, the naming of the baby is also delayed. Among Orthodox and many

Conservative Jews in the United States, a baby girl is named by the father in the synagogue on the Sabbath following her birth. Reform Jews name boys and girls at the same time, and in the same way. Some communities like to name them at a Friday night synagogue service. Others emphasize the common covenant ceremony that exists for boys and girls, a modification of the traditional liturgy for brit milah (see p. 242), and name both boys and girls at such a ceremony held in the parents' home on the eighth day.

4. Do Jews Always Name a Child after a Deceased Relative?

The custom of naming a child after a relative who has died exists only among the Ashkenazic Jews of eastern and central Europe. Among the Sephardic or Mediterranean Jews, children are quite often named after living grandparents.

In Jewish tradition, the name given to a child usually has some meaning. To call a boy Abraham is to associate him either with a character trait of the patriarch Abraham, or with the beautiful things remembered about another Abraham, a deceased uncle perhaps, after whom he is being named. Similarly, a girl may be called Ruth in the hope that she will live up to the loyalty and devotion of the biblical Ruth. Parents do not name a child after a ne'er-do-well relative, because they do not want to associate the youngster with that person's blemishes. For the same reason, it is possible that a child will not be named after a brother or sister who died in childhood or early youth.

In biblical times it was customary to give children names entirely unrelated to those of relatives, living or dead. Jacob, for example, did not name any of his children or grandchildren Abraham or Isaac.

The Ashkenazic custom of not using the name of a living relative dates back to a superstition of the Middle Ages. It was thought that the angel of death, appearing with a summons, might serve it on the child instead of on the older relative and so bring about premature death.

Even though the rabbis recognized this fear as based on superstition, they made no attempt to discourage the custom. There were many reasons to encourage memorializing the name of an honored grandparent, uncle, or aunt whose qualities the parents would like to see reborn in their child.

5. *What Is Pidyon Haben?*

Pidyon Haben [pid-YONE hah-BEN or PID-y'n hah-BEN], the redemption of the firstborn, is a ceremonial rite observed mostly by Orthodox Jews when the first child born into a family is a boy.

This ritual, which takes place on the thirty-first day after the birth of the baby, is one of the oldest in the Hebrew tradition. It reaches far back to the dawn of Jewish history, when the firstborn son was usually charged with the religious ritual of the household.

According to the Torah, the firstborn of the Israelites were consecrated to God's service when the firstborn of the Egyptians were smitten. Instead of being killed, after all, these Hebrew firstborn children were saved, but since God had saved them, it was as if they belonged to God. Theoretically, that meant they would be charged with the ritual duties entailed by ancient biblical law. But after the Exodus the duties of sanctuary worship were turned over to the priestly caste known as **kohanim** [koe-hah-NEEM] (sing., **Kohen** [koe-HAYN or KOE-hayn])—the descendants of Aaron, and to the Levites, their assistants (see p. 81). The firstborn were thus relieved of their ritual responsibilities. But theoretically, they had to acquire exemption from their status of still belonging to God. We might say they had to enter the real world by being ritually transferred from their sacred state to the ordinary status of every other Israelite. Pidyon Haben is the Jewish ritual by which this is accomplished.

The ceremony is very brief. It takes the form of a little drama. The Kohen (or priest) is given five silver dollars. He holds them over the child's head and offers the father his choice of the child or the money. The father chooses the child, and the priest takes the money. Later, the Kohen donates the redemption sum to charity.

If the father of the baby is a Kohen or Levite, or the mother a daughter of one, the family is exempted from the ritual.

Conservative and Orthodox Judaism still encourage the rite of Pidyon Haben. In its stress on egalitarianism, however, Reform Judaism stopped recognizing distinctions between the ancient classes of priest, Levite, and "ordinary" Israelite. Since the rite of Pidyon Haben assumes the continuing validity of status differentiation, Reform Judaism eliminated the rite altogether. Some Reform Jews still practice it, but not very many.

In traditional circles, the firstborn son is charged with one duty that remains with him throughout his life. Each year, on the day before Passover, such a firstborn son is supposed to fast, in sympathy with the fact that his ancestors, the firstborn Hebrew slaves, had not been killed in the tenth plague. Interestingly enough, however, the Jewish emphasis on study and celebration intervene to annul his obligation to fast. Whenever you finish studying a tractate of Talmud, you are supposed to celebrate with a party called a **siyyum** [see-YOOM] (see p. 48). Firstborn sons are therefore urged to study the last page of a Talmudic tractate on the day of this fast. Except for exceptionally important fast days, a religious feast clearly takes precedence over a fast. Thus the firstborn child avoids the fast by a symbolic affirmation of the life-sustaining merit of learning.

6. What Are Bar Mitzvah and Bat Mitzvah?

A boy who reaches his thirteenth birthday is a **bar mitzvah** [BAHR meets-VAH or bahr MITS-vah], literally a responsible man. Technically, from that day on, in Jewish tradition, he is answerable for the religious duties of an adult. (Of course, modern Jews do not really expect such answerability from a teenager. Once people were married at the age of fourteen or fifteen! Things have changed since then.) Traditional Jews recognize no such status for girls, even though traditional women too are charged with adult duties. Liberal Jews, however, have generalized the status of bar mitzvah to girls as well as boys, and recognize the female equivalent, **bat mitzvah** [BAHT meets-VAH or baht MITS-vah], a responsible woman. Technically, girls are said to reach that status somewhat earlier than boys, in their twelfth year, because girls mature faster than boys do. However, for ritual purposes most liberal congregations that celebrate the bat mitzvah of their congregants do so on their thirteenth birthday, just as they do for boys.

Until the Middle Ages, people reached the age of responsibility without any ceremony or ritual fanfare at all. Nowadays, however, bar and bat mitzvah have become dramatic public spectacles, so much so, that the terms "bar mitzvah" and "bat mitzvah," which originally meant simply being of a certain age, now refers to the ceremony that celebrates the child's getting there. On the Sabbath corresponding to their thirteenth birthday, Jewish children are given an honor reserved for adults: They are summoned to lead the congregation in prayer. At the very least, they will recite the blessings that accompany the reading of Torah, and they will probably proclaim or chant part of the Torah reading aloud for the congregation. They may also recite or chant the lesson from the Prophets, called the **Haftarah** [hahf-tah-RAH or hahf-TOE-rah].

Measured in the broad span of Jewish history, the ceremony of bar mitzvah is of recent origin. Tradition associates it with an eighth-century rabbi's son, but it was probably unknown before the fourteenth century. The equivalent ceremony for girls is attributed to Mordecai Kaplan, the founder of Reconstructionism, who initiated the breakthrough for his daughter, Judith, in 1922.

In many old European Jewish communities, it was customary for the bar mitzvah to deliver a scholarly discourse on the intricacies of talmudic law, with which he was, by the age of thirteen, very familiar. It was not uncommon to hear as part of the bar mitzvah address a thoughtful analysis of such themes as civil and criminal courts, the problem of free will, or the laws of marriage. Today too, a bar or bat mitzvah speech is the norm, usually a discussion of some theme in the Torah portion that the child has studied and now reads before the congregation.

As with other life-cycle events, this one too is the opportunity for festive celebration with friends and family. Modern Jews have vested bat and bar mitzvah with remarkable depth of meaning. People who belong to no synagogue usually join one to make sure their children will "receive a bar or bat mitzvah," as they put it, or (very colloquially) "to have their children bar or bat mitzvahed." Children are enrolled in special bar or bat mitzvah classes. By the time the big day arrives, tension and expectation run high. Families are reunited from all over; friends whom the parents may not have seen in years arrive from far away. It is a time when parents come to terms with life, looking back over the thirteen years of raising their child and ahead to adolescence and young adulthood, which they hope will treat their children kindly. It is a time of taking stock, remembering grandparents who did not live to see this day, perhaps, or just wondering how it is that the years passed by so quickly.

But adults too can celebrate a bar or bat mitzvah. In fact, increasingly, they are choosing to do so. To begin with, until 1922, no young women had the opportunity to celebrate their coming of age as adult Jews, and even after that it was decades until bat mitzvah became the norm. So women reclaiming their full status as Jews often elect to have a bat mitzvah. Most temples have adult bat mitzvah classes for them.

Reform Jewish men may join as well. Some of them choose to do so because they grew up in the classical period of Reform Judaism, when bar mitzvah was replaced with Confirmation (see next question). Of course, Reform Jews have reinstated bar mitzvah (and adopted bat mitzvah) by now, but that innovation came too late for these men who had no bar mitzvah when they were thirteen.

Finally, more and more Jews have chosen Judaism as adults,

long after their thirteenth birthday. They too make up the rolls of modern men and women studying for adult bar or bat mitzvah.

There is even a practice of giving a second bar or bat mitzvah to people who turn eighty-three, exactly seventy years after their first one. It is as if we reach the life expectancy of seventy and then start counting a second time. For instance, Judith Kaplan Eisenstein, the first woman to celebrate a bat mitzvah, did it all over again in 1992.

Bat or bar mitzvah is not just for teenagers.

7. Do Jews Have Confirmation Services?

In the nineteenth century Reform Judaism introduced the group Confirmation service as a substitute for the individual bar mitzvah ritual, extending this practice to girls as well as boys as the first step in preparation for full membership in the congregation.

Confirmation services were scheduled for fifteen-or sixteen-year-olds, since it was felt that thirteen was too young for modern youths to take on the responsibilities of adulthood. Originally the Confirmation ceremony was held at various times of the year. But eventually the practice was linked to Shavuot, the festival commemorating the giving of the Torah.

Confirmation has been universally adopted by Reform congregations, and by some Conservative and Reconstructionist synagogues as well. At the same time, Reform Judaism has recovered the bar or bat mitzvah ceremony, for both boys and girls. Jewish children thus have two "graduations" of sorts. First, just as they are entering puberty they celebrate an individual bar or bat mitzvah, in which they take on adult responsibility for their actions and are given the symbolic adult duty of leading worship. They are then encouraged to remain in religious school for two or three more years, at which time they celebrate a class graduation marking their group status as the next generation to stand at Sinai receiving the Torah as their Jewish heritage.

Confirmation practices vary widely, but generally speaking the class as a whole designs the liturgy for the day and its members take turns leading it. One by one they may walk to the ark, where the rabbi blesses them. As a class, too, they may receive a charge relating their Jewish learning to the world in which they live. The class may give a gift to the synagogue. A class picture will probably be taken, forever to appear with those of previous classes along a corridor in the building. Shavuot services will be followed by a party honoring the graduates.

8. How Do Jews Get Married?

Nothing is as wonderfully celebrative as a Jewish wedding. In fact, Jews often refer to it merely as a **simchah** [SIM-khah], meaning a joyous event. People will say, "I'll see you at the simchah." If the wedding was particularly joyful with plenty of dancing and good feeling, people might even say, "It was especially **simchadik** [SIM-khah-dik], a Yiddish word meaning "joyous beyond description." (A bar or bat mitzvah might be referred to in the same way.)

The joyous feeling refers especially to the party following the religious ceremony, since even the party has religious significance. Traditionally, part of the religious ritual (the seven wedding blessings with which the marriage rite concludes) is repeated at the party. The food need not be expensive, and the decor need not be lavish, but the happiness should be patent and potent.

The wedding ceremony has two parts. First, after an optional procession, the bride and groom commit themselves to each other in a section of the service called **Kiddushin** [kee-doo-SHEEN], which means "sanctification." In Kiddushin, two people become sanctified to each other, and enter a new stage of sanctification before God as well. All of Judaism is based on the idea of each and every Jew being committed to God ever since Sinai. That eternal commitment through the ages is what we mean by the covenant that binds us to

God, and vice versa. In Kiddushin, two people vow to pursue their covenantal commitments together rather than singly. They will keep a Jewish home, raise Jewish children (should they be blessed with them), and make joint decisions on such important matters as giving to charity, joining a synagogue, and working for worthy causes—all of which are covenantal responsibilities. The highlight of Kiddushin, therefore, is the exchange of rings between bride and groom, along with the accompanying vow, "By means of this ring, you are sanctified to me, according to the law of Moses and Israel."

The second part of the ceremony features seven benedictions, which are called, in fact, **Sheva Berachot** [SHEH-vah b'rah-KHOTE], "the Seven Blessings." They praise God for creating man and woman and express the hope that the bride and groom will be happy together. To emphasize the joy that everyone hopes will be theirs, these blessings use two wonderful images. First, the bride and groom are likened to Adam and Eve living in the paradise that was the Garden of Eden. But almost immediately the metaphor changes. They are now likened to inhabitants of the messianic world to come, listening to the sounds of joyful singing and dancing in the utopian society of Jerusalem restored.

In between the two parts of the ceremony, the officiating rabbi usually addresses the couple.

There are other customs associated with this basic ritual. These include the **chupah** [KHOO-pah], the canopy under which the marriage vows are taken; a cup of wine from which bride and groom both sip to symbolize their sharing of life that begins this day; the religious marriage document, called a **ketubah** [k'TOO-bah]; and a ritual smashing of a glass underfoot at the very end of the ceremony. Immediately after the glass is shattered, the entire congregation shouts "**Maz'l tov**," [MAH-z'l tuff or mah-ZAHL-TOVE], which means "congratulations," but also, "May you enjoy good fortune." *Maz'l* is a Yiddishized form of the old Hebrew word for a constellation ("mazal"), and *tov* means good, so literally, we wish the couple an auspicious beginning to their life together.

Each of these traditional symbols is endowed with a variety of meanings.

The chupah (canopy) is a symbol of the privacy to which the newly wed couple is entitled, a visual reminder of the home they will make together. It is becoming increasingly common to improvise a temporary canopy made from the tallit, a prayer shawl (see p. 91), tied to a pole at each of the four corners, and held over the couple's heads by friends.

The ring is a symbol of perfection and eternity, the circle without beginning or end. Traditionally the ring was to be unadorned with precious stones, but many Reform weddings allow any kind of ring the couple wishes. The traditional emphasis on simplicity, however, is typical of the Jewish tradition of equality, in that an unadorned ring minimizes the difference between a poor and a wealthy bridal pair.

The sharing of a single cup of wine by the bride and groom is a reminder of their common destiny, for henceforth their lives will be inseparable. Often two cups are shared, one in the Kiddushin part of the service and one during the Seven Blessings. In some circles, it has been customary to consider the first cup as the cup of shared joy, and the second as the cup of mutual sacrifice. As they will rejoice together, so too they will sacrifice for each other, willingly sharing life's burdens as they are encountered.

The breaking of the glass climaxes the traditional service and is interpreted in many ways. The broken glass conjures up Judaism's symbol of human fragmentation and destruction: the fall of the Temple, a symbol of the sorrows of Israel. It is a reminder also that even at the height of our joy, we reserve a little sadness for those whose lives were not or are not as happy as our own. In the midst of their greatest joy, bride and groom thus consider the sorrows of life, sobered by the thought of their own responsibility to others.

Modern practice in most liberal synagogues is egalitarian, in that two rings are exchanged, and both bride and groom say (to each other), "You are sanctified to me." Orthodox custom still follows ancient precedent in that only the groom hands a ring to the bride, and only he says the formula of sanctification. Traditional ceremonies, especially among the Orthodox, also feature other customs that have been handed down through the ages: the practice of the bride walking seven times in a circle around the groom, for instance, and **bedecken** [b'DEH-k'n] a ceremonial veiling of the bride by the groom.

Other things that you may see are largely a matter of local practice rather than of Jewish law. In each country where Jews have settled they have adopted, in addition to their required religious rites, some of the nonreligious customs of their non-Jewish neighbors. Processional, attendants, and order of procession are matters of local custom rather than Jewish law.

Judaism insists that marriage is not just a private matter, but one in which the entire community has a stake. In old European Jewish communities, for example, every wedding was more than a family affair. No wedding invitations were sent out, because the entire community considered it a religious obligation to attend. If a bride was too poor to afford a trousseau, a collection was made on the eve of the Sabbath for her. In fact, even though weddings are not performed on the Sabbath, one famous sixteenth century rabbi notes that he cheated just a bit and married a couple after sundown Friday night. His reasoning was that the bride was so poor she had been unable to put together a dowry; moreover, she was an orphan, and had no one to arrange a marriage for her (in those days, all marriages were arranged). The rabbi located a distant relative who agreed under pressure to put up a modest dowry, and then he found a prospective husband. Fearful that the relative would back out of the agreement if he had too much time to think about it, the rabbi married the couple as soon as he could, even though the Sabbath had just begun. He reasoned that the good deed of providing a fuller life for the orphan took precedence over a few minutes of Shabbat.

Nonetheless, weddings are not performed on Sabbaths and

holidays, because marriage entails a change in status, a sort of being reborn into a new stage of life, and halachah (Jewish law) forbids what it calls "making over a person" on days reserved only for rest and the personal sanctification of time.

9. Do Rabbis Perform Weddings When a Jew Marries A Non-Jew?

By and large, rabbis do not perform weddings between Jews and non-Jews, though some Reform rabbis do. In both cases, rabbis follow their own conscientious reading of what Jewish tradition licenses them to do and what it does not. Rabbis may refuse to officiate at such marriages for a number of reasons, but usually because as much as they might want to do so, they feel constrained by the dictates of Jewish tradition, which provides a Jewish ceremony with Jewish commitments for a Jewish bride and groom. These rabbis feel that they cannot expect or even ask a non-Jew to make those commitments, and yet they know that the Jewish ceremony presupposes that precisely those commitments have been made. They know that their decision will be unpopular, and they would usually much prefer to be able to say "Yes," and enjoy the warm gratitude that they would get from the couple sitting in front of them. But respecting the integrity of both Judaism and the religion of the non-Jewish partner, most rabbis refuse nonetheless, insisting that they would be compromising both Judaism and the religious commitment of the non-Jewish member of the couple were they to choose the easy path of agreeing to perform the wedding.

The rabbis who agree to perform such weddings usually do so only in certain circumstances. Since a Jewish wedding carries with it the couple's commitment to establishing a Jewish home and providing a Jewish education and household ambience for any children they might have, these rabbis generally insist at the very least that the couple study Judaism together for a period of time, and that they agree in all good conscience to the commitments that their marriage will entail. They will not, therefore, marry two people if one of them is a believing non-Jew; to do so would be to ask the non-Jew to honor commitments contrary to his or her own religious integrity.

Respecting both Judaism and Christianity means that even the rabbis who do perform interreligious marriages will not co-officiate with non-Jewish clergy, since one or the other or both officiants would have to sacrifice religious integrity to do so.

A tiny minority of rabbis—really a minuscule number—go beyond the guidelines mentioned above. They are usually people who have virtually left the rabbinate for other work, and who round out their income by taking advantage of prospective intermarried couples who will pay anything to get the ceremony they want. To protect themselves against unscrupulous treatment, couples contemplating marriage should always deal directly with congregational rabbis known for their integrity.

Both the Conservative and the Reform movements operate a network of outreach offices located in many major cities. Their personnel are expert in dealing with interreligious couples at all stages of their relationship: from people contemplating engagement to people long-married with children. Outreach workers can direct such couples to rabbis who can be of help to them.

10. *What Is the Jewish Attitude toward Divorce?*

Until relatively recently, divorce was rare in the Jewish community. Nonetheless, the social forces that make a successful marriage more difficult for everyone make it equally exacting for Jews as well, so that the Jewish divorce rate is now similar to that of the population at large. While Judaism prefers that marriages last forever, Jewish sources agree that when differences between husband and wife make living together intolerable, a divorce should not only be permitted but encouraged. There should be no stigma whatsoever to a marriage that did not work out. A love-filled home, our teachers tell us, is a sanctuary; a loveless home is a sacrilege.

In the strict letter of Jewish law, divorce is easy to obtain (though this has no bearing on the civil divorce requirements of most countries). Traditionally, the husband prepares a divorce document called a **get** [pronounced as it looks, like the English word "get"] and hands it to his wife before witnesses. A knife is used to slash the get twice down the middle in the form of an X—an act highly symbolic of the ripped ties that divorce entails.

Emphasis is always on counseling with the possibility of reconciliation and renewed understanding between husband and wife. The welfare of any children is considered, as well as the happiness of the parents. But in the Jewish tradition it is considered a greater evil for youngsters to be reared in a home without peace and mutual respect than to have to face their parents' divorce. When two people can find no common basis to continue their marriage despite repeated and genuine efforts to make a life together, Judaism both sanctions and approves their divorce.

A divorced person who wishes to do so is encouraged to remarry, and is treated exactly as any unmarried person. However, traditional Jewish law forbids a woman to remarry if she does not have a religious divorce. If she does so, any children she might have in a later marriage are forbidden by biblical and rabbinic law from marrying another Jew. To be sure, it is mostly the Orthodox who insist on this punitive regulation, but after they grow up, such children might want to marry an Orthodox partner, so all rabbis try to guard against second marriages without a prior Jewish divorce.

Many Orthodox and some Conservative rabbis will refuse to perform a marriage ceremony for a divorced woman who cannot prove that she received a get. They will therefore also refuse to do so for a man who cannot prove that he has delivered a get to his former wife.

Reform Judaism does not require that a woman being remarried have a religious divorce first. Rather, it accepts a civil divorce as both sufficient and binding. Reform rabbis will officiate at a Jewish divorce ceremony if the couple requests it, and will even encourage such a ceremony, hoping that the couple will agree to participate in it. But they are in no position to demand it. Similarly, they will encourage a woman about to be married to acquire a divorce document from her former husband, if she can. But if she cannot, the rabbi will marry her anyway.

11. *How Are People Buried in Judaism?*

For generations, Jewish families have observed a fixed pattern of mourning. According to Orthodox tradition, burial must take place without delay; only if a Sabbath or holy day intervenes may the body remain unburied for longer than twenty-four hours. This rule has been somewhat relaxed in Conservative and Reform practice, but a lengthy wake, or having the deceased "lie in state" for any length of time, is foreign to Judaism.

The funeral arrangements must be as simple as possible. Jewish law forbids elaborate funerals on the principle that all of us are equal in death. Ideally, the shroud consists of a simple linen vestment; the coffin is plain wood, without adornment. The ancient Rabbis insisted on this "democracy in death," so that no poor family would be embarrassed or forced into excessive expenditures because of the ostentatious funerals of its wealthy neighbors.

At Orthodox Jewish funerals flowers are not permitted and instrumental music may not be played, since both are considered symbols of joy inappropriate in mourning. Liberal Jews tend to agree, especially with regard to the flowers, since spending money on flowers runs contrary to the principle of keeping the funeral simple. Donations to charity in the memory of the deceased, however, are encouraged, since philanthropy is such a high priority in the Jewish scale of values. Hence, it is common to urge people to take the money that they might otherwise have spent on flowers and give it instead to some charity that had special meaning for the person who has died.

Cremation of the dead is also alien to Jewish tradition, for though Judaism stresses that our souls are more important than our bodies, our tradition frowns upon the deliberate destruction of "human beings made in the image of God." On the other hand, Reform Judaism does permit cremation, suggesting that "the ashes be buried in a Jewish cemetery."

Funerals are short, usually featuring a chapel service at which the deceased is eulogized, and then a graveside ritual. Before the chapel service, immediate relatives (parents, children, brothers and sisters, and the spouse) affix a black ribbon to their clothes and in a brief ceremony called **Keriyah** [KREE-yah], meaning "cutting," have it cut by the rabbi or funeral director, as a sign of the torn fabric of their lives, now that they have lost a loved one. Orthodox Jews may even require that the actual clothes themselves be torn on the occasion.

12. *What Mourning Customs Do Jews Follow?*

As a religion with traditions reaching back scores of centuries, Judaism has created a pattern of customs designed to help us face humanity's greatest crisis: the end of life.

The first period of mourning, called **Shiva** [SHIH-vah] (meaning "seven," that is, seven days of mourning), begins immediately after the funeral. Actually, there are only six or even fewer days, since mourning is forbidden on the Sabbath and holidays. Moreover, if a holiday falls during this period of mourning, Shiva is not resumed thereafter. Many Reform Jews have limited the period of Shiva to only the first three days.

The obligation to "sit Shiva" is limited to the immediate relatives. Traditionally, they do not leave their home, except for Sabbath worship. A large candle burns steadily for all seven days. Daily worship is conducted in the Shiva home, so that the next of kin may say the mourners' prayer known as the **Kaddish** [KAH-dish] (see p. 83). In Orthodox tradition, only men recite the Kaddish. Among liberal Jews Kaddish is recited by women too.

The Kaddish prayer is the most distinctive feature of the Jewish observance of mourning. Its words are Aramaic, not Hebrew, and in its usual form, it contains no direct reference to death or the dead. Beginning with the words, "Magnified and sanctified is God's name," it is an affirmation of faith in the wisdom of God's decrees, and a fervent prayer for the speedy arrival of the final reign of God.

During the week of Shiva friends and neighbors visit the family, offering whatever consolation and practical help they can. They bring food, so that mourners do not have to prepare meals for themselves. One of the greatest mitzvot, or good deeds (see p. 71), that Jews can perform is to contribute to the mourners' first meal, a meal known literally as "the meal of recovery." The Talmud suggests that the food be brought in simple baskets, again to prevent competition among the neighbors who might be tempted to outdo each other. People continue to bring food throughout the Shiva period.

After the first week, a general period of mourning continues for eleven months, during which the Kaddish is repeated daily (some mourners continue the practice only on Sabbaths, and Reform Jews say the Kaddish for a whole year). The first thirty days, including the days of Shiva, have particular solemnity, and sometimes a special memorial service is held on the thirtieth day. At a convenient time before the first anniversary a memorial stone is unveiled at the graveside.

After the first year, anyone who has ever been a mourner

recites a special memorial prayer, **Yizkor** [YIZ-kore], at synagogue services on Yom Kippur (the Day of Atonement) and on the last days of Passover, Sukkot, and Shavuot. Also, on the anniversary of the death, a day known as **Yahrtzeit** [YAHR-tzite], the family recites the Kaddish again and lights a candle in memory of the deceased.

In addition to these religious rituals there are several secondary Jewish mourning customs, some of which are found more frequently than others. Especially in traditional circles, for instance, it is usual to cover all the mirrors in a house of mourning, a practice meant to symbolize that in this time of grief, the mourners have no interest in such normal concerns as how they appear to others. Upon leaving the cemetery the members of the funeral procession wash their hands and toss a twig or grass over their shoulders, clearly a remnant of old forms of magical thinking. And in most Orthodox services, even today, nonmourners leave the synagogue during Yizkor, lest their presence there result in the death of a living relative—as if mourning might be "contagious."

Our mourning rituals are intended to emphasize basic Jewish values. They strengthen the solidarity of family and friends, and they impress upon the bereaved the message of the funeral liturgy, "to number our days that we may get us a heart of wisdom." Finally, they do honor to the dead, in keeping with Judaism's insistence that human life is sacred, so that those who were once alive should not be forgotten or treated with disrespect.

13. Do Jews Have a Confession, Deathbed or Otherwise?

Judaism has known both an individual confession and a collective one. The individual confession was common from antiquity to the Middle Ages, some particularly pious people saying one every day. Eventually, however, the practice emerged of requiring a personal confession only twice in a lifetime: immediately before marriage and just before death. Nowadays, the marriage confession is rarely observed, and even the deathbed confession is not very common.

However, the communal confession of sin is said annually by all Jews as part of the Yom Kippur liturgy (see p. 216).

The Jewish confession is an outpouring of the heart directly to God, without human mediation. A witness is present at the deathbed act of contrition, but he or she need not be a rabbi. No one, neither rabbi nor any other dignitary, has the power to transmit God's absolution.

On the other hand, confession of sin to a sympathetic listener obviously has psychological and religious value. It happens that many rabbis receive such confidences from their congregants. But our tradition does not consider such conversations as instruments of atonement. Rabbis cannot pardon sins, or even be the vehicle for the pardon that God grants. Pardon comes only from God, and directly to the person seeking it. Judaism insists that God does not want the death of those who sin, but only their sincere atonement.

If the sin was committed against another human being, only restitution and requesting forgiveness from the aggrieved party can effect atonement. A sin against God can be forgiven only through sincere repentance, and an honest resolve to avoid repeating the transgression in the future.

Maimonides pointed out that God does not need the confession, but that sinners do, in order to know themselves better.

The deathbed formula of confession begins with a prayer for healing and continues with these words: "but if my death be fully determined by You, I will accept it. . . . May my death be an atonement for all my iniquities against you. . . . Make known to me the path of life, for in Your presence is the fullness of joy. . . . O God who is parent to those who have no parents, protect my beloved family with whose souls my own is knit. Into Your hand I commend my spirit. . . . Amen, amen!" Then follows the affirmation of Israel's faith, the Shema: "Hear O Israel, the Eternal is God, the Eternal is One."

14. How Can Friends Appropriately Extend Comfort to a Jewish Family in Mourning?

Funeral notices involving a Jewish family frequently include the request: "Instead of flowers, please send donations to . . ." It is appropriate, therefore, to find out if the deceased had a favorite charity, or simply to make a donation to a favorite good cause of your own, either a Jewish cause such as the synagogue to which the deceased belonged, or a nonsectarian charity, connected, perhaps, with the cause of death: a cancer research organization, for example, if the deceased died of cancer. In addition, you may bring food for the mourners during the mourning period known as Shiva (the days when they remain at home receiving visitors). Find out, therefore, where they are "sitting shiva," and for how long, and make a condolence call, bringing a basket of food or a homemade meal. If you decide on the latter, you will want to know in advance if the mourners "keep kosher" (see p. 87), that is, if they follow the Jewish dietary rules. You can play it safe by bringing a fruit basket or a vegetarian dish, that is, a dish that contains no meat, chicken, or seafood.

Always, of course, a personal letter or a simple condolence card is an appropriate note of comfort to the bereaved.

15. *How Do People Choose to Become Jews?*

The majority of people who are Jews were born to Jewish parents. But conversion to Judaism is more frequent than ever before. Often, the immediate motivating factor is an interreligious marriage and the desire of the non-Jewish partner to share the faith of his or her spouse. Similarly, if children are born to such a couple, the non-Jew may at that time decide on Judaism as the religion of choice, so as to raise children without the ambiguity of two religions in the household. Not infrequently, however, rabbis are approached by non-Jewish men and women who on their own and without any connection to a proposed marriage have the sense that Judaism offers them the best medium of religious expression, and who then study it, and eventually adopt it as their faith.

Conversion is a process, not simply a one-time act that magically changes people from one thing to another. There are certain predictable stages: a period of uncommitted investigation marked by study and dialogue; then a period of "trying it on for size," as potential converts begin seriously considering what it will be like to live as a Jew. Then will come the decision, and the official ceremony. But even after the ceremony, people choosing Judaism as their faith should anticipate a normal period of adjustment as they go through the process of redefining things they once took for granted: things like buying Christmas trees and having Christmas dinner.

Conversion to a new religion does not suddenly make you over into something altogether new; it does not deny all that you have been before; it does not cut you off from old family ties. It does offer you the opportunity to add a new dimension to your life, but that happens only slowly, over time.

The formal steps to conversion are not formidable. In the Orthodox ritual converts appear before a panel of three rabbis, and declare: (1) that they know the responsibilities of Jewish law and sincerely intend to fulfill them; and (2) that they reject those tenets of their former faith that are not in keeping with Judaism. Ritually speaking, both men and women go to a ritual bath called a **mikvah** [MIK-vah], where they immerse in the water as a sign of being reborn into their Jewish faith. In addition, men who have not yet been circumcised undergo circumcision.

Reform and Conservative Judaism put more emphasis on the idea that those who choose Judaism do so only if they have studied it sufficiently to know that they can wholeheartedly embrace it, and that they have no conflicting religious loyalties to another faith. They emphasize Jewish study in general, not simply Jewish law, and define Jewish responsibility more broadly than simply following the letter of the law as contained in Jewish law codes. Before accepting Judaism candidates will generally have completed an intensive course of study, including the Bible, the prayer book, Hebrew, life-cycle customs and rituals, holiday and Sabbath observances, and Jewish history.

Modern converts to Judaism often learn more about their new faith than people who were born Jewish and who may take Judaism for granted. People considering conversion in conjunction with marriage should therefore attend an Introduction to Judaism class with their Jewish spouse or spouse-to-be, so that both can grow together in their newly shared Jewish identity.

Among liberal Jews, the actual ritual varies from synagogue to synagogue, rabbi to rabbi. Reform Judaism stresses knowledge of Judaism and spiritual commitment rather than the traditional ceremony, so that ritual immersion and circumcision may be treated as options.

Reform and Conservative Judaism operate a network of offices called Outreach (Reform) and *Keruv* [Kay-ROOV] (Conservative) with professionals who work with people seeking information about conversion, and with intermarried families interested in learning how better to deal with the challenges that such dual-faith families face.

Orthodox tradition calls for the new initiate to attend the synagogue on the Sabbath following conversion. If he is a man, he is called to the reading of the Torah, and a special blessing is recited: "May he who blessed our ancestor, Abraham, the first convert, and said to him: 'Walk before Me and be righteous,' bless and give courage to this convert who enters the fold." He is then given a Hebrew name for use in all ritual acts.

Reform and Conservative converts are welcomed into the Jewish community also, but in a variety of ways, many of which are the result of Outreach programs designed to continue the process by which Jews by choice become familiar with the Jewish community.

IX

Judaism and Christianity:

The Double Helix of Western History

When scientists uncovered the structure of DNA, they charted it as a double helix: two parallel spiraling lines that curve around each other, held together by chemical bonds that can break and rejoin. Judaism and Christianity are like a double helix. Throughout history, Jews and Christians have been intertwined, intermittently loving and hating each other, more often the latter, but never oblivious to each other's existence. Christianity grew out of Judaism and defined itself with reference to those Jewish beliefs and practices that it accepted and those it did not. Judaism spawned Christianity and worried incessantly about how to retain its independence in what became largely a hostile Christian world.

Typical of Jewry's uneasy existence in that Christian world is an event from the days of Charlemagne, when a group of Jews settled in the southern part of France, finding peace and security as tillers of the land. Pope Stephen III marked the occasion in a noteworthy epistle to the Bishop of Narbonne: "With deep regret and mortal anxiety we have heard from you that the Jewish people are on Christian soil and in enjoyment of full equality with Christians."

In the succeeding centuries the Jews of Europe and the Americas were destined to remain a minority group in a civilization that was predominantly Christian. It was not a happy world for any religious minority: for the Protestants in Catholic France, the Catholics in early Virginia, the dissident followers of Roger Williams in Massachusetts, the nonconformists in Calvin's Geneva. For a dozen centuries Jews suffered every kind of persecution, ranging from unimportant social slurs to the tortures of the rack.

Jews, in turn, built an emotional barrier between themselves and the Christian community. Even if the gates were open, they preferred not to venture out into the "Gentile" world.

A few shafts of light did burst through the darkness—for example, there were forward-looking Catholics and Protestants who fought for Jewish civil rights in the eighteenth and nineteenth centuries. But a realistic approach to an understanding of Jewish-Christian relations must bear in mind more than a thousand years of conflict.

Fortunately, we are beyond all that today. Vatican II recognized the Jewish covenant with God as eternal and equal to that which Christians enjoy. Except in evangelical and fundamentalist circles, the harsh Protestant triumphalism of many of the church leaders who founded America is disappearing. Christians and Jews now work together creating a single shared community based on mutual respect and profound understanding.

Nevertheless, group memories run deep. The centuries of Christian teaching that the Jews are despised because they rejected the Savior (himself a Jew), and of Jewish suspicion and fear of Christians, are not easily erased. We have much hate to unlearn before the vital lessons of love and amity can fully penetrate the deepest layers of our psyches.

But we are "unlearning" very quickly. Seeing ourselves as united against such common enemies as injustice, poverty, and oppression, we have discovered how much we share and how much also our successful mission in the world depends on recognizing that we share it. The differences that divide Jews from Christians are not as significant as the ideals we cherish together. We shall remain what we are—different—but we are developing a creative partnership whereby we work side by side, each of us with God's blessing, fostering mutual respect without compromising matters of principle.

The Fascism and Nazism of the 1930s and 1940s seem far behind us now, even though neo-Nazi fringe groups have not disappeared. The menace of communism has also become a thing of the past. But secularity is still dominant, so that the call for a spiritual approach to life, with its concern for the sanctity of the individual, is as timely as ever.

There are still areas of tension between Jews and Christians, particularly in regard to recent developments in Israel. Many Christians who are staunch supporters of Israel champion the rights of Palestinian Arabs as well; as they see it, the Middle East conflict is about two groups, both of whom deserve their own state. Jews may even agree on the issue of Arab rights, but are apt to say that Christians do not take the military threat to Israel seriously. Victims of Arab terrorism since their state's inception, Israelis and hence Jews are wary about settling the age-old Arab-Israeli dispute by installing an Arab terrorist group only a few miles from Israel's busiest cities.

Still, even as we differ, the lines of communication have steadily improved. Jewish-Christian dialogue has moved us to a higher level of mutual understanding than ever before.

This final section addresses the particularly siblinglike relationship between Jews and Christians. It asks questions that reflect the unique history of Jews and Christians, living together now in North America, after two thousand years of intertwined involvement in each other's destiny. Christians can understand Judaism better than other faiths, because we have so much in common. But for the same reason, Christians may also wonder more about Judaism, which remains doggedly persistent in retaining its own independence as a faith. Most of the questions pertinent here have arisen elsewhere in this book. But there are a few "left over." This concluding chapter addresses those remaining specifically Christian concerns about Jews and Judaism.

QUESTIONS IN PART IX

1. *What Do Jews Believe about Jesus?*
2. *Do Christianity and Judaism Agree on Anything? On What Points Do They Differ?*
3. *Does Judaism Accept Converts?*
4. *If Christians Can Pray in Synagogues, Why Can't Jews Pray in Churches?*
5. *Can Jews Celebrate Christmas?*

1. What Do Jews Believe about Jesus?

Jesus' ministry on earth coincided with the lives of the early Rabbis known as Pharisees (see p. 18). Jews therefore see Jesus as a historical personality whose work and teachings parallel those of other wonder-working Jewish leaders of the time, especially in Galilee, the northern part of the land that Jesus called home. Jews can identify positively with many of Jesus' parables and with the morality explicit in his teachings and implicit in his actions. We recognize as innately Jewish his announcement of the coming of God's reign and his concern that the men and women of his day should prepare themselves for membership in it. And we see in his crucifixion yet one more example of the cruel Roman regime that led both Jesus and the other Jewish leaders like him to hope or even to believe that the reign of God must be close at hand. The Romans crucified Jesus just as they tortured Rabbi Akiba to death, because they feared the revolutionary effect of their doctrine of love and justice.

But Jews stop short of identifying Jesus as in any way divine. Simply put, Jews do not believe that God had a son or appeared in human form. We thus do not accept Jesus as the Christ, as our Lord, as the son of God, as the word of God incarnate, or as our savior. These and other ways in which Christianity has expressed its faith in Jesus as more than just a man, even a great man, are what Judaism has consistently denied.

Moreover, Jews do not quote Jesus as a model, not because we cannot identify with much that he said, but because his life and death are so intrinsically central to Christianity. Appropriately, Jesus belongs at the very heart of Christianity, not of Judaism. Were we to point to Jesus' behavior or teachings as our guide in life, we would feel as if we were crossing the boundary from Judaism to Christianity. The Lord's Prayer, for instance, has nothing in it with which Jews would not agree. It is a prayer for the coming of God's reign, a doctrine taught by every Rabbi of the first and second century. But we would not say the Lord's Prayer, since it is part of Christian liturgy, associated firmly with the bedrock of Christian faith. Similarly, Jesus is known to have preached the Golden Rule. But we do not cite Jesus to the effect that we should love our neighbors as ourselves, even though we agree that we should. Instead, we have our own daily prayer called the **Kaddish** [KAH-dish] (see p. 83), which parallels the Lord's Prayer and was formulated about the same time. We say that prayer every day. Similarly, Jesus was not the only person to acknowledge the Golden Rule. A contemporary, Hillel, one of the great Pharisees, is known to have preached it also, and we cite his version as our own.

It is always hard to second-guess history, but it is interesting to imagine what would have happened if the life of Jesus had not been appropriated by Christianity. What would have happened if he had been remembered only as the Jew he was, but not as the Savior? His life and work might in that case have been retained by Jewish sources. He might well have remained a Jewish moral hero like the Pharisees of the time, who were much like him. But precisely because Jesus was recognized by Christians as the Christ, he could not be recognized as a Jewish role model by those Jews who did not accept his divinity.

People sometimes ask why Jews do not accept Jesus as their savior. Jews answer that question by pointing to the unrelieved misery in the world as we know it, and say that classical Jewish doctrine teaches that the messiah will arrive only once, and will be recognizable by the fact that the world's suffering will be ended then. As long as we see hunger, inequality, and injustice in the world, we are forced to conclude that the messiah has not yet arrived. That answer will not convince a believing Christian, however, and it is not intended to. It is merely a response to the question put to us by such Christians, who similarly cannot convince us of their position. When it comes right down to it, whether Jesus is or is not the Christ is purely a matter of faith. We grant Christians the right to believe that he is, and we are careful to treat that ardent faith with respect, even if we do not share it.

2. *Do Christianity and Judaism Agree on Anything? On What Points Do They Differ?*

Christians and Jews share the rich heritage of the Hebrew Bible, with its timeless truths and its unchanging values. We share also the belief in a single all-knowing and ever-merciful God, recognized first by the patriarchs and matriarchs of Genesis. We share a belief in the sanctity of the Ten Commandments, a belief in the ethics of the prophets, and the conviction that all men and women are together a single family with a single destiny, equal before God. Central to both faiths is the firm belief in the Godlike spirit that makes us human. We believe that we were created in God's image, and that we are graced with an imperishable human soul. Both Christian and Jew believe that God has placed us here "not for nothing"; that life has purpose; and that we should leave our mark on the world by acting out of love.

It may seem at times that these shared understandings are trite, even saccharine, so obvious to one and all that they are not worth mentioning. But the history of the twentieth century should convince us that these spiritual convictions are far from universally shared. This century gave us the Holocaust, two world wars, Stalin's gulags, the drowning of boat people, and starvation in Africa, to name but a few events that might be taken as proof that the dream we share as Jews and as Christians is a delusion. It is for that reason worth repeating over and over the spiritual truths that we accept; they are the very core of Jewish and Christian faith, the common ground that allows us to work together.

There are other points of contact too, little things that we take for granted. We both believe that history will end with the coming of a perfect messianic reign of God; in the interim, we both read scripture, keep a Sabbath day, and attend worship services. Christians go to church and Jews attend synagogues; we have similar sacred places where we do similar sacred things for similar sacred reasons.

In the end we are similar, not the same. Jews are passionately in love with the Torah, which we take to be God's eternal word, the place where we may find religious wisdom. Christianity teaches that in the beginning was the word and the word became flesh, whereas for Jews, the word remained the word. Jews believe in a single covenant at Sinai when the Torah was revealed. Christians believe in a second covenant too, the covenant rooted in the death and resurrection of Jesus. Christian scriptures therefore contain the Jewish Bible, but they comprise also the specifically Christian story of the Gospels, the letters of Paul, the account of the early church and such books as the letters of James and Peter, and Revelation. For Jews, the paradigmatic story that we read over and over again is how God brought us out of Egypt, took us to Mount Sinai, gave us the Torah, and led us to the promised land, which is still the sacred center of our universe. Christians replaced that story with a new one: the incarnation, crucifixion, and resurrection of Jesus Christ. Jews cannot accept the doctrine of the incarnation, nor the idea that Jesus died for us, nor that he was resurrected. Like the Rabbis, Jesus remains fully human, but only human, in Jewish consciousness.

Jewish spirituality differs from that of Christians in that the life of a Jew revolves about the study of Torah, whereas Christians have traditionally modeled themselves after Jesus. Jews believe in Israel as a promised land still to this day, and though we are committed to universalist goals, such as world peace and harmony, we identify with, and work though, the Jewish People, which has its own sacred status for us. Our synagogues are holy also, but so are our homes. Much of Jewish religiousness takes place around our tables and in our families: welcoming the Sabbath; a Passover seder; building a sukkah (see pp. 211, 226, 219), and so on.

In a way, our two communities are mirror images of each other. We are recognizable to each other as doing the same thing, but differently. We can each talk about salvation, but we mean different things by that word. Christians emphasize more than Jews the sinfulness of humanity, and speak of being saved from sin. Jews have usually emphasized our potential for doing good, and speak of the world being delivered from injustice and subjugation. Jews have held that we are saved by the good work we do, whereas Christianity has usually taught that people are saved by faith, not works.

We both have a Sabbath, but the Jewish Sabbath is Saturday and recollects creation of the universe and redemption from Egyptian bondage, whereas the Christian Sabbath is Sunday and reminds Christians of Jesus' resurrection. We both have a springtime holy season: Passover for Jews, the anniversary of our founding event, the Exodus; Easter for Christians, the anniversary of their founding event, Jesus' death and rebirth.

Two centuries ago, a German dramatist, Gotthold Ephraim Lessing, caught the essence of this common heritage in a play called *Nathan, the Wise*. One of the most memorable scenes depicts a meeting between a friar and the Jew Nathan. Moved by the beauty of Nathan's character, the friar exclaims, "Nathan! Nathan! You are a Christian!" His friend replies, "We are of one mind, for that which makes me, in your eyes, a Christian, makes you, in my eyes, a Jew!"

3. Does Judaism Accept Converts?

Yes. There was a time when Jews engaged in active missionary work. During Roman rule, many pagan citizens of the Roman Empire were attracted to the teachings of the Rabbis. And in many remote parts of the world today, the existence of devout Jewish tribes, distantly removed from the birthplace of Judaism, gives evidence of earlier Jewish missionary work, so far back in antiquity that its origin cannot be traced. In southeastern Russia, for instance, an entire nation called the Khazars were inducted into Judaism during the Middle Ages, when their monarch was won over to its teachings. The Jews who were saved in 1991 from Ethiopian distress must likewise have found their way to Judaism many centuries ago.

This missionary zeal evaporated, however, particularly after the Christianization of the Western world. Jews were for the most part forbidden to "Judaize," which became a crime punishable by death. On the other hand, Christian missions to the Jews became the norm. At times Jews were forced to attend conversionary sermons in churches in the hope that they would accept baptism. In such an atmosphere, Jews became more intent on preserving their heritage than on adding to their numbers through conversion. Often, in fact, potential candidates for conversion were discouraged by rabbis who warned that the demands of the Jewish religion were great and the burden of being a Jew in an intolerant world was not easy to bear. Nevertheless, throughout our history some conversions to Judaism have continued to take place and today they are more common than ever before.

While we welcome converts to our midst, however, we have not returned to the days when we actively proselytized. First, we know firsthand what it is like to undergo proselytization at the hands of others. There are still Christian missions to the Jews here and there, and Jews resent them. Believing that we have the right to our religious freedom, we are insistent that other faiths have the right to their own. We believe that there are many true religions, an abundance of parallel ways to God. We do not believe that you have to be Jewish to be saved, or that only Jews can do what is right in the eyes of God.

But even if Judaism is not for everyone, it is the right choice for many, and we welcome people who freely elect Judaism. Our tradition makes no distinction between Jews born into Judaism and those who choose Judaism at some later point in their lives. Several of the ancient Rabbis, in fact, including some of those who created the Talmud, traced their ancestry to non-Jews who converted to Judaism as adults.

4. *If Christians Can Pray in Synagogues, Why Can't Jews Pray in Churches?*

There was a time not long ago when Christians and Jews never prayed together; when, moreover, they rarely even spoke except for business transactions and small talk; when Christians had no Jewish friends and vice versa. But the situation has changed dramatically. To be sure, some ultra-Orthodox Jews still choose to live in ghetto-like conditions, just as some highly conservative Christians still seek to talk to Jews primarily to convert them. But for most of us, North America has provided a place where we happily make friends regardless of religious identity.

This openness to others has not been without religious challenge. As we have gotten to know one another, we have had to define more closely the relationship of our two faiths to each other. For Christians particularly, this reassessment has involved the growing awareness that historically speaking, Christianity arose out of Judaism. Jesus was a Jew who kept Shabbat, went to the synagogue, read from the prophets, made pilgrimage to Jerusalem, said Jewish prayers, studied Torah, and celebrated a seder. Whereas once Christian churches ignored what it called the "Old Testament," the trend now has been to reaffirm that testament, and not even to call it *Old* Testament anymore, as if to imply that it has been superseded by the *new* one. Readings from the Hebrew Bible have been inserted into church liturgies, as Christians have claimed their Jewish heritage in addition to the specifically Christian part of their identity.

The Christian accent on reclaiming Jewish roots means that many Christians now feel more comfortable doing Jewish things: going to Jewish services, for instance, or visiting a Jewish Passover seder. By and large, whatever Jews affirm in their prayers, Christians can say also, though they may have their own specifically Christian interpretation of what they are doing. They can affirm the covenant at Sinai, without denying their covenant in Christ; they can read Isaiah publicly just as Jews do and still believe that Isaiah was predicting the coming of Jesus; they can read how God chose the People of Israel for service believing all the while that without Israel's mission, there would be no Christianity. They can and do participate in many Jewish rituals in the hope that their own Christian faith will only strengthen as they rediscover and even relive their Jewish heritage.

Unfortunately, it does not work the other way around. Jews cannot affirm faith in Christianity without at the same time leaving Judaism. By analogy, consider two people who live in the same house and walk a block north on Main Street every day, in order to get to work. Suppose now that the second person decides to quit that job and get another one, still one block north on Main, but an additional block east on Elm Street. That person can still enjoy the walk on Main as part of the route to the new job; but the other person cannot continue past Main Street onto Elm without leaving Main Street behind and arriving at a new job site in the process. Similarly, Jews cannot continue the route through Judaism into Christianity without being untrue to their Judaism, just as Christians cannot join Islam in its affirmation of Mohammed as the last and greatest prophet, whereas Moslems can give credence to Jesus as one of the prophets.

On occasion, Jews do attend church with Christian friends and neighbors, usually for such special ceremonies as weddings, confirmations, funerals, a First Communion, and the like. They go there, however, as visitors, not as participants. To the extent that the services speak of Jesus or express Christian beliefs, Jews will not be able to join in the services; nor will they kneel, cross themselves, or take Communion. To do any of these things would be, in effect, to give up their Jewish integrity. Of course, Jews may join in the reading of psalms, or sing some hymns: songs, for instance, that are neither Christological nor intrinsic to Christian spirituality, but instead are things we have in common, expressing sentiments that Jews and Christians share.

On appropriate occasions, such as American Thanksgiving, most Jews willingly participate in interfaith or community religious services, so long as the prayers, Bible readings, and hymns are acceptable to both Christian and Jew. They will expect, however, that benedictions or invocations not be phrased in trinitarian formulas that would exclude them. They will view the worship in common as a celebration of Jews and Christians standing jointly before God, doing God's work together.

A special case arises frequently when people who have chosen to convert to Judaism are called upon to mourn the deaths of their non-Jewish parents or relatives. In very early times, Judaism made the decision that properly burying the dead—even the non-Jewish dead—is a moral imperative. All the more so is this the case when the deceased in question are our relatives! Jews by choice will therefore want to attend the funeral, even though it is a Christian funeral, and they will want to participate as fully as possible in the burial customs of their family of birth. They will find themselves in a dilemma, however. Many of those customs will be specifically Christian, and as Jews now, they will be unable to say or do certain things without feeling that they are being untrue to themselves. At such times, they will count on their family understanding their situation, and recognizing that were they to participate as a Christian, when they are no longer Christians, they would be compromising both Judaism and Christianity.

In solidarity with their family of origin, they will be present at the funeral ceremony, sharing their grief and participating in the religious rite to the extent that their conscience allows. When they return to their Jewish home, they will want to mourn in a traditionally Jewish way as well.

5. *Can Jews Celebrate Christmas?*

As a religious celebration in commemoration of the birth of Jesus, Christmas has no significance whatsoever for Jews, since the most basic point of difference between Judaism and Christianity lies precisely in the Christian belief in Jesus' divinity, and the Jewish denial of the same thing.

In our modern world, however, Christmas has taken on increasingly secular overtones, which tend to envelop all of society. The elaborate exchange of Christmas gifts, so persistently encouraged by commercial interests; the preponderance of beautifully decorated Christmas trees in public places; and the widespread introduction of Christmas plays, songs, carols, window displays, greeting cards, and other manifestations of the season make it impossible for anyone who leaves the confines of home or who tunes in to radio or television during the month of December not to share in some aspects of the Christmas celebration.

Indeed, the spirit of friendship that abounds at Christmas is one in which everyone can happily join. Jews frequently visit non-Jewish relatives and friends on Christmas day; they give Christmas gifts to Christians they know and love; but they do not keep Christmas themselves since they cannot affirm faith in Jesus as the messiah—which is precisely what Christmas celebrates.

Sometimes Jews are urged to see Christmas as merely a secular event, a time for fun and family warmth, pretty decorations and beautiful music, a Santa Claus for the kids, and gift giving all around. But sensitive Jews are unable to accept the secular definition of Christmas precisely because they respect too much Christianity's religious claims. Jews take Christianity seriously. It may be true that many Americans treat Christmas as just fun and games, but Jews remain aware that religious Christians do not. We therefore respect Christian religious sensitivity, and we refrain from keeping Christmas ourselves, wanting instead to reserve Christmas for Christians, and thereby respect the religious meaning that Christmas has.

Sensitive Jews and Christians alike deplore the growing secularization of Christmas, since it tends to obliterate, for both, the important religious meaning of the holiday. Jews therefore may join Christians and share something of the occasion as visitors, but they cannot observe Christmas themselves without doing both Judaism and Christianity an injustice.

GLOSSARY

Like members of any culture, Jews describe what matters to them using a specialized vocabulary. Throughout this book, I have supplied those words, along with a pronunciation key. Here, I collect all the words in alphabetical order, along with a short definition of each one.

Most Jews do not know all of the following terms. Some of them, however, are used actively in synagogues and Jewish gatherings. The ones that you are apt to hear are marked with an asterisk (*). The others are less common, but should you see or hear them, you can at least look them up here.

Often, there are two or more ways to pronounce a word. Since most of these words are Hebrew, they have Hebrew pronunciations (accent usually on the last syllable). But they have often been "Yiddishized," so that some people use their Yiddish equivalents. Finally, really common terms have even been "Englishized" in that they are pronounced as if they were English words. Common alternatives are given below; I have followed common usage, not grammatical rules.

Some of the keys to pronunciation are:

1. A syllable in capital letters is accented.
2. The most common sound is "a" as in "father," which appears here as "ah."

3. An "e" at the end of a syllable is like the English silent "e," which makes the preceding vowel long.

4. The "kh" is a sound we do not have in English. It is a guttural sound like clearing your throat.

*Alenu [ah-LAY-noo]: a concluding liturgical prayer that affirms God's ultimate reign and the unique destiny of the people Israel.

*Aliyah [ah-lee-YAH or ah-LEE-yah]: literally, "going up"; the term is used for a wave of immigrants "going up" to Israel, or, more commonly, for the person being called to "go up" from the congregation to say the Torah blessings while the Torah is being read. When Jews are called to the Torah, they say they "are getting an aliyah."

*Amidah [ah-mee-DAH or ah-MEE-dah] "the standing prayer," one of the two central prayers in most Jewish services. Another name for the prayer is the **Tefillah**.

Amora'im [ah-moe-rah-EEM]; sing., **Amora** [ah-MOE-rah]: the Rabbis from the third to the seventh centuries who composed the Talmud.

*Ashkenazim [ash-k'nah-ZEEM or ash-k'NAH-zeem]: Jews who trace their ancestry to northern and eastern Europe, as opposed to the Sephardim, whose family history goes back ultimately to Spain and Portugal.

Bal tashchit [BAHL tahsh-KHEET]: "do not destroy"; the Jewish ethical principle banning unnecessary destruction.

*Bar mitzvah [bahr MITS-vah or BAHR meets-VAH] The age at which a boy becomes religiously responsible for his acts; and by extension, the ceremony celebrating his achieving that status, and generally held around his thirteenth birthday.

*Bat mitzvah [baht MITS-vah or BAHT meets-VAH] The age at which a girl becomes religiously responsible for her acts; and by extension, the ceremony celebrating her achieving that status, and generally held around her thirteenth birthday.

*Baruch atah adonai . . . [bah-ROOKH ah-TAH ah-doe-NYE]: the opening phrase of a blessing.

Bedecken [B'DEH-k'n]: the ritual act of veiling the bride before a wedding.

*Bench [bentch]: to "bench" is to say the Grace after Meals, from the Yiddish word *benschen* [BEN-sh'n], to say a blessing; Jews will say, "Let's bench," and then proceed to say the Grace.

*Berachah [B'rah-KHAH or B'ROH-khah]; pl., berachot [b'rah-KHOTE]: a blessing or benediction recited over enjoying something in the universe or upon performing a sacred act commanded by God (a mitzvah).

Bet hakenesset [BAYT hah-K'NES-set]: "a place of gathering," one of three traditional Hebrew terms for "synagogue."

Bet hamidrash [BAYT hah-meed-RAHSH]: "a place of study," one of three traditional Hebrew terms for "synagogue," but also a place where people come to study Torah.

Bet hatefillah [BAYT hah-t'fee-LAH]: "a place of prayer," one of three traditional Hebrew terms for "synagogue."

*Bimah [BEE-mah or bee-MAH]: the dais in the sanctuary from which the Torah is read, and where the leader of the service stands while leading services.

*Birkat Hamazon [beer-KAHT hah-mah-ZONE]: the Grace after Meals, sometimes referred to simply as "the BEER-kaht."

*Brit milah [BREET mee-LAH]: Literally, "covenant of circumcision," this is the ceremony of circumcision, referred to also in the Yiddish short form, B'ris [pronounced as it looks, BRIS].

*Challah [KHAH-lah]: the twisted egg bread used on Sabbath and festival dinners.

*Chanukah [KHAH-nuh-kuh or KHA-noo-kah]: the Feast of Light, usually falling in December, and commemorating the victory of the Maccabees in 167 B.C.E.

*Charoset [khah-ROE-set]: a pasty substance made usually with wine, nuts, and apples, and eaten at the Passover seder in recollection of the mortar made by the Hebrew slaves in Egypt.

*Chasidim [khah-see-DEEM or khah-SEE-dim]; sing., **Chasid** [khah-SEED or KHAH-sid]: ultra-Orthodox Jews who follow an eighteenth-century mystical interpretation of Judaism.

Chavurah [khah-voo-RAH]; pl., **chavurot** [khah-voo-ROTE]: an independent Jewish fellowship group, existing as an alternative to the fully structured synagogue and emphasizing radical egalitarian democracy of all its members, or a semi-independent study or prayer group within a synagogue.

*Chazzan [khah-ZAHN or KHAH-z'n]; pl., **chazzanim** [khah-zah-NEEM]: a cantor.

Cholent [TCHO-lent]: a traditional food; an all-night stew.

Chupah [KHOO-pah]: the canopy under which the Jewish marriage vows are taken.

Daf yomi [DAHF YOH-mee or DAHF yoh-MEE]: the study of a page of Talmud every day.

*Daven [DAH-v'n] The traditional style of Jewish worship, and a work often used instead of the English "pray." Jews say, "It is time to daven," or "I finished davening."

D'var torah [d'VAHR TOE-rah]: a short sermon or homily on the Torah portion of the week.

Erev [EH-rev]: "the eve of" a holy day.

*Erev Shabbat [EH-rev shah-BAHT or EH-rev SHAH-b's]: the day before Shabbat, used frequently, however, just for late Friday, the time when people prepare for Shabbat.

Etrog [ET-roag]: a lemonlike fruit used on Sukkot.

Galut [gah-LOOT]: literally, "exile," a theological term for most of Jewish history when Jews lived outside the Land of Israel.

Gemara [g'MAHR-ah]; another word for Talmud.

Ge'onim [g'oh-NEEM]; sing., **Ga'on** [gah-OAN]: Babylonian rabbinic leaders from roughly the eighth to the twelfth centuries, who initiated the writing of Responsa.

Get [GET]: a Jewish divorce document.

*Haftarah [hahf-tah-RAH or hahf-TOE-rah]: the reading from the prophets at Sabbath and festival services.

*Haggadah [hah-GAH-dah or hah-gah-DAH]: the prayer book for the Passover seder.

hakafah [hah-kah-FAH]: the ritual of walking around the synagogue sanctuary carrying the Torah or (on Sukkot) a lulav and etrog.

*Halachah [hah-lah-KHAH or hah-LAH-khah]: Jewish law.

*Hamotzi [hah-MOE-tsee]: a blessing over bread, and therefore, the name by which Jews refer to the blessing before meals; sometimes referred to as "the Motzi."

*Havdalah [hahv-dah-LAH or hahv-DAH-lah]: the ritual that marks the end of the Sabbath and festivals. Jews say they "make Havdalah."

*Kabbalah [kah-bah-LAH or kah-BAH-lah]: the most influential stream of Jewish mysticism.

*Kaddish [KAH-dish]: the memorial prayer said for a year after the death of an immediate relative, and on the anniversary of that person's death.

Kadosh [kah-DOSH]: the Hebrew word for "holy."

Kashrut [kahsh-ROOT]: the dietary laws (laws of keeping kosher).

Kedushah [k'doo-SHAH or k'DOO-shah]: a familiar prayer declaring God's sanctity with the words of Isaiah, "Holy, holy, holy."

Keriyah [KREE-yah]: literally, "cutting"; the ceremony of cutting a black ribbon affixed to a mourner's clothes, as a sign of mourning.

Ketubah [k'TOO-bah]: the religious marriage document.

Ketuvim [k'too-VEEM]: the third section of the Jewish Bible, literally, the "writings," such as Psalms, Proverbs, and Job.

Kibbutz [kee-BOOTS or ki-BUTS]; pl., **kibbutzim** [kee-boot-SEEM]: collective farms in Israel governed under principles that combine Israeli nationalism with socialism.

***Kiddush** [kee-DOOSH or KID-ish]: the prayer accompanied by wine or grape juice and recited before dinner on the eve of the Sabbath or a festival, to inaugurate the day and proclaim its sanctity; or the food and wine that is customarily served in the synagogue after morning services on the Sabbath or festival.

Kiddushin [kee-doo-SHEEN]: the first part of the Jewish marriage ceremony.

***Kippah** [kee-PAH]; pl., **kippot** [kee-POTE]: ritual headcovering. Also called a **yarmulke** [YAHR-m'l-kuh].

Kohen [koe-HAYN or KOE-hayn]; pl., **Kohanim** [koe-hah-NEEM]: someone of priestly descent.

***Kol Nidre** [kole need-RAY or KOLE NID-ray]: the opening Yom Kippur prayer, sung to a haunting and very famous melody.

***Kosher** [KOE-sh'r]: food that may be eaten, according to the dietary laws; also used to describe someone who keeps those laws, as in "I am kosher," meaning, "I keep the dietary laws."

Kotel [KOE-tel]: The only remaining structure of the ancient Temple in Jerusalem, its western wall; the most holy site for Jews.

Kugel [KUH-g'l]: a festival food; a sort of noodle pudding.

Labriyut [lah-bree-YOOT]: The Hebrew equivalent of "Gesundheit!"—what you say to someone who sneezes.

Ladino [la-DEE-noe]: the folk language of Sephardic Jews, a combination of Hebrew and Spanish.

Lag Ba'omer [lahg bah-OH-mehr]: a minor holiday in the period between Passover and Shavuot.

Lamed vov'nicks [lah-med VOHV-niks]: the mythical thirty-six righteous people who sustain the world.

*****Latkes** [LAHT-kahs]: potato pancakes commonly eaten at Chanukah.

*****L'chayim** [l'KHAH-yim]: "To life," the normal Jewish exclamation before taking a drink of wine or alcohol, or upon making a toast.

Levi [lay-VEE or LAY-vee]: someone who claims to be descended from the Levites.

*****Lulav** [LOO-lahv]: a palm branch waved at the rituals for Sukkot.

Magen David [mah-GAYN dah-VEED]: "shield of David"; the six-pointed Jewish star that appears on the flag of the State of Israel.

*****Matzah** [MAHT-sah]: unleavened bread eaten on Passover.

*****Mazal tov** [MAH-z'l tuff or mah-ZAHL TOVE]: "Congratulations," the usual Jewish exclamation at weddings, or joyful events in general.

Megillah [m'gee-LAH or m'GIL-ah]; pl., **Megillot** [m'gee-LOTE]: "a scroll" used for one of five biblical books that are customarily printed on scrolls and read on specific holidays; especially used for the scroll of Esther that is read on Purim.

*Menorah [m'NOE-rah]: a seven-or eight-branched candelabrum; if the latter, used expressly to hold Chanukah candles.

Mezuzah [m'ZOO-zah]: ritual object affixed to the doorway of Jewish homes.

Midrash [mid-RAHSH or MID-rahsh]: a collection of rabbinical commentary on the Bible.

Mikvah [MIK-vah]: ritual bath used, among other things, for conversion ceremony.

Minhag [min-HAHG or MIN-hahg]; pl., minhagim [min-hah-GEEM]: a custom, as opposed to a law.

Minhag hamakom [min-HAHG hah-mah-KOME]: "the custom of a place," a reference to the fact that when ritual practice differs from place to place, guests follow the practice of their hosts.

*Minyan [MIN-y'n or min-YAHN]: a quorum of ten, traditionally required for public worship.

Mishnah [MISH-nah]: the first comprehensive book of Jewish law, formulated about 200 C.E.

Mitnagdim [mit-nahg-DEEM]: members of the traditional religious establishment in Poland who opposed the philosophy and practices of the Chasidim.

*Mitzvah [MITS-vuh or meets-VAH]; plural: mitzvot [mitz-VOTE or meets-VOTE]: a commandment, or more generally, a good deed.

Mohel [MOE-hayl]; pl., mohalim [moe-hah-LEEM]: a ritual circumcisor.

Navi [nah-VEE]: the Hebrew word for "prophet."

*Ne'illah [n'ee-LAH or n'EE-lah]: the concluding service for Yom Kippur.

Ner tamid [NAYR tah-MEED]: the eternal light that is kept lit over the synagogue ark.

Nevi'im [n'vee-EEM]; sing., **navi** [nah-VEE]: the prophets, either the actual individuals themselves or the biblical books that record their words; if the latter, the second of three sections into which Jews divide their scripture.

Niggun [nee-GOON]; pl., **niggunim** [ncc-goo-NEEM]: a wordless melody, popularized by Chasidic ritual.

*Oneg Shabbat [OH-neg shah-BAHT]: literally, "the joy of Shabbat," the principle that Shabbat should be joyous; but by extension, used also to refer to the collation and socializing following Friday night services, and shortened at times to "the oneg."

Parashah [pah-rah-SHAH]: the weekly reading in the Torah, also referred to as a **sedra**; sometimes referred to more fully as **Parashat Hashavu'ah** [par-rah-SHAHT hah-shah-VOO-ah], literally, "the reading of the week."

*Pesach [PEH-sakh]: the festival of Passover, commemorating the Exodus from Egypt.

Pidyon Haben (pid-YONE hah-BEN or PID-y'n hah-BEN): the traditional ritual of the redemption of the firstborn.

*Purim [POO-rim]: the festival commemorating the victory of the Jews over their would-be murderer, Haman, as described in the biblical Book of Esther.

Rosh Chodesh [rosh KHO-desh]: the new moon, the first day of the new month.

*Rosh Hashanah [ROSH hah-SHAH-nah or ROSH hah-shah-NAH]: the Jewish New Year.

Sandek [SAHN-deck]: The person who holds a baby boy at the time of his ritual circumcision, and thus, traditionally, the Jewish equivalent of one of his godparents.

*Seder [SAY-der]: the evening meal and ritual with which Passover begins.

Sedra [SED-rah]: like **Parashah**, a word for the weekly Torah portion.

Sefer torah [SAY-fer TOE-rah]: a Torah scroll.

Semichah [s'mee-KHAH or SMEE-khah]: rabbinic ordination.

*Sephardim [s'far-DEEM or S'FAR-deem]: As opposed to Ashkenazim, Jews who trace their roots to Spain or Portugal.

Se'udat mitzvah [s'oo-DAHT mits-VAH]: a religiously commanded banquet.

*Shabbat [shah-BAHT]: the Sabbath, often pronounced in its Yiddish form, **Shabbos** [SHAH-b's]; people wish each other **Shabbat shalom** or **Gut Shabbos**.

*Shabbat shalom [shah-BAHT shah-LOME]: "a peaceful Sabbath to you." This is the normal greeting on the Sabbath, or the way you say goodbye on a Thursday or Friday to someone whom you do not expect to see again before the Sabbath arrives. Another Sabbath greeting is the Yiddish **Gut Shabbos** [gut SHAH-b's].

*Shalom [shah-LOME]: peace.

Shanah tovah [shah-NAH toe-VAH]: "a good year"; the traditional greeting for the new year.

*Shavuot [shah-voo-OTE]: the Festival of Weeks, commemorating the giving of Torah on Mount Sinai.

*Shema [sh'MAH]: Perhaps the most famous Jewish prayer, a biblical exclamation affirming the monotheistic principle: "Hear O Israel, the Eternal is our God, the Eternal is One."

Sheva Berachot [SHEH-vah b'rah-KHOTE]: "the Seven Blessings"; the second part of the Jewish marriage ceremony.

*Shiva [SHIH-vah]: literally, "seven," referring to the seven days of mourning following the death of an immediate relative.

Sho'ah [SHOA-ah]: the Holocaust.

*Shofar [sho-FAHR or SHO-fahr]: the ram's horn sounded during worship on the New Year.

Shul [shool]: the Yiddish word for synagogue.

Shulchan Arukh [shool-KHAHN ah-ROOKH or SHOOL-khahn AH-rookh]: the most famous code of Jewish law.

Simchadik [SIM-khah-dik]: "joyous beyond description."

Simchah [SIM-khah]: "a joyous event"; used to refer to a Jewish wedding, a bar mitzvah, or a bat mitzvah.

*Simchat Torah [sim-KHAT toe-RAH or SIM-khs TOE-rah]: the festival following Sukkot, marking the day we conclude one year's cycle of Torah readings and begin another.

Siyyum [see-YOOM]: a party marking the accomplishment of completing the study of a tractate of Talmud.

Sukkah [soo-KAH or SUH-kah]; pl., **sukkot** [soo-KOTE]: the booth made to mark the festival of Sukkot.

*Sukkot [soo-KOTE]: the harvest festival marked by erecting booths and thanking God for the food of the earth.

*Talmud [TAL-m'd]: the most famous collection of Jewish teaching, assembled over the years from the third to the seventh centuries.

*Tallit [tah-LEET]: a prayer shawl.

Tanakh [tah-NAHKH]: the Hebrew name for the Bible.

Tanna'im [tah-nah-EEM]; sing., **Tanna** [TAH-nah]: the Rabbis who lived between the destruction of the Temple and the compilation of the Mishnah, that is, from 70 C.E. to 200 C.E.

Tefillah [t'fee-LAH]: literally, prayer, but used generally for the Amidah prayer. See **Amidah**.

Tefillat Haderech [t'fee-LAHT hah-DEH-rekh]: prayer for a safe journey.

Tefillin [T'FIL-in or t'fee-LEEN]: phylacteries, small black boxes containing citations from Torah, to which leather straps are attached. Using the straps, traditional worshipers affix these to their left arm and forehead while they pray.

*Teshuvah [t'shoo-VAH or TSHOO-vah]: repentance; Jews speak of "doing teshuvah."

*Tikkun olam [tee-KOON oh-LAHM]: literally, the act of "repairing the world," a commonly cited purpose in life that Judaism urges upon Jews.

*Tisha Be'av [tish-AH b'AHV]: the fast marking the destruction of the First and Second temples.

Treyfah [tray-FAH], **treyf** [TRAYF]: not kosher, ritually inedible according to the dietary laws.

*Tsitsit [tsee-TSEET]: the fringes sewn to the four corners of the tallit (the prayer shawl).

Tu Bishvat [too bish-VAHT]: Jewish Arbor Day when trees are planted, especially in Israel.

*Tzedakah [ts'dah-KAH or ts'DAH-kah]: charity.

*Yad [yahd]; the thin pointer shaped at the end like a hand, which a reader of Torah uses so as not to lose the place.

Yad Vashem [YAHD vah-SHEM]: The Holocaust memorial in Israel.

*Yahrtzeit [YAHR-tzite]: the anniversary of the death of an immediate relative.

***Yarmulke** [YAHR-m'l-kuh]: the Yiddish word for a headcovering, otherwise known as a **kippah**.

Yetser hara [YAY-tser hah-RAH]: the "evil inclination," the part of us that tempts us to go astray.

Yetser hatov [YAY-tser hah-TOVE]: the "good inclination," the part of us that leads us to virtue.

***Yiddish** [YID-ish]: the folk language of Ashkenazic Jews, a mixture mainly of Hebrew and German, with some eastern European words added as well.

Yisra'el [yis-rah-AYL]: a traditional way to refer to a Jew who claims no lineage of either biblical priests or Levites; that is to say, just an ordinary member of the people Israel.

***Yizkor** [YIZ-kore]: the memorial prayer recited on certain holidays, particularly Yom Kippur.

Yom Ha'atsma'ut [yome hah-ahts-mah-OOT]: Israel Independence Day.

Yom Hashoah [yome hah-SHOA-ah]: Holocaust Day; Holocaust memorial day.

Yom Hazikaron [yome hah-zee-kah-RONE]: Remembrance Day in Israel, the day on which Israelis remember their fallen soldiers from all their wars.

***Yom Kippur** [yuhm KIP'r or YOME kee-POOR]: the Day of Atonement.

Yom Yerushalayim [yome y'roo-shah-LAH-yeem): Jerusalem Day, a holiday celebrating the reunification of Jerusalem in the 1967 war.

Zohar [ZOE-hahr]: a lengthy set of medieval mystical writings.

INDEX

Aaron, xxiii, 81, 245
Abel, 233
Abortion, 139–41
Abraham, xxiii, xxvii, 50, 51, 114, 179, 181, 233, 244, 265
Adam and Eve, 156, 251
Adoption, 239
Adultery, 147, 148, 149
African-American Jews, 8
African Jews, 8, 9, 188, 280
Agricultural communities, 185–87
Aleichem, Shalom, 97–98
Alenu, 83
Aliyah, 181
American Jewish Committee, 29
American Jews, xxviii, xxix, 10, 12, 14, 16, 18, 25, 27, 97, 125, 145, 178, 181, 189–92, 196, 230, 269; and Israel, 189–92
Amora'im, 20
Amos, xxvi, 30
Animal rights, 158–59
Anti-Defamation League, 29
Aramaic, 98
Arendt, Hannah, 161
Ark, 175–76
Art, Jewish, 161–62, 172
Ashkenazim, 9, 23–25, 97, 103, 183, 244
Assyria, xxvi, 43, 108
Authoritative Jewish organizations, 28–29

Babylonia, xxvi, xxvii, 43, 47, 98, 108, 205, 214
Bal tashchit, 157
Bar mitzvah, 246–49
Bat mitzvah, 246–49
Beliefs, Jewish, 103–27; chosen people, 114–15; coming of the Messiah, 118–20; ethnic identity, 125–27; fate, 121; general beliefs, 107–10; God, 111–13; grace, 124–25; life after death, 117–18; principal tenets, 110–11; prophecy, 122–24; salvation, 124; Satan, 120–21; sin, 115–16; spirituality, 125–27
Benching, 98–99
Ben-Gurion, David, 162
Berachah, 84
Bereshit, 40
Bet hakenesset, 172
Bet hamidrash, 172
Bet hatefillah, 172
Bible, xxvi, 18, 31, 35, 39–47, 52–53, 56–57, 67, 87, 88, 94, 96, 109–10, 114, 117, 126, 141, 146, 152, 154, 170, 177, 179, 184, 211, 220, 233–35, 277, 282; Jewish, 39–47, 56–57; reading the, 56–57. See also specific books
Bimah, 176–77
Birkat Hamazon, 98
Birth control, 131–32, 139–41
B'nai B'rith, 29